Partisan Linkages in Southern Politics

Partisan Linkages
— in —
Southern Politics

Elites, Voters, and Identifiers

Michael A. Maggiotto
Gary D. Wekkin

The University of Tennessee Press / Knoxville

Chapter 2 was written with the assistance of Charles D. Hadley.

The paper used in this book meets the minimum requirements of ANSI/NISO Z39.48-1992 (R 1997) (Permanence of Paper). The binding materials have been chosen for strength and durability.

Library of Congress Cataloging-in-Publication Data

Maggiotto, Michael A.
Partisan linkages in southern politics: elites, voters, and identifiers / Michael A. Maggiotto, Gary D. Wekkin.—1st ed.
          p. cm.
Includes bibliographical references and index.
ISBN 1-57233-088-0 (cl.: alk. paper)
1. Political parties—Southern States. I. Wekkin, Gary D. II. Title.
JK2295.A13 M34   2000
324.2'04'0975—dc21   00-008218

Contents

Tables

Preface

This is the first book from a larger study of partisanship, public opinion, and representation on which we have been collaborating for more than a decade. During that time, we have accumulated a number of very substantial intellectual and personal debts.

The National Science Foundation provided generous funding (grant number SES-9212646) for the broader project, as did the Faculty Research Council of Bowling Green State University and the University Research Council of the University of Central Arkansas. We are also indebted to the late Dr. Robert McLauchlin, graduate dean of the latter institution, for his willingness to support additional funding of the project at every stage. Helpful too was a grant from the Ray Bliss Institute and encouragement from its director, John C. Green.

Charles D. Hadley of the University of New Orleans graciously allowed us the use of some of the data on southern party elites that he and his colleagues in the Southern Grassroots Party Activists Project collected. We are indebted to him as well for the hours he spent to ensure that his data could be successfully merged with ours. Jerry Wicks, Professor Emeritus of Sociology at Bowling Green State University, directed the Population and Society Research Center that conducted all of the mass interviews for this study and the other surveys of the broader project. We are indebted to Jerry and his staff for their care in collecting the survey data and their assistance in transferring it to machine-readable form. We prevailed on Bob Fyfe of Bowling Green's Information Technical Services for advice on how to move data among different platforms at different universities, and on Ron Bise of UCA Computer Services for creative implementation of that task. Lee Stevens of UCA Computer Services and Mary-Sue Passe-Smith of UCA Social Science Microcomputer Laboratory also provided valuable assistance with a variety of technical problems. Their technical wizardry prevented many a mishap.

We owe a very deep debt of gratitude to Professor Malcolm Jewell, who carefully read the manuscript twice and whose suggestions and insights we have tried to incorporate faithfully in the final product. Simply put, *Partisan Linkages in Southern Politics* would be neither as thoughtful nor as accessible to the reader without Mac's careful commentary. As well, we acknowledge the important role the anonymous reviewers of the University of Tennessee Press played in helping us craft a better book. They represent the finest tradition of collaborative scholarship in offering constructive criticism, which, again, we have tried to follow as closely as possible. We also thank Joyce Harrison, Acquisitions Editor at the University of Tennessee Press, for her patience with our schedules and for her encouragement throughout this project.

Our theorizing about the dimensionality of mass partisanship has benefited from presentation at the annual meetings of the American Political Science Association, the Southern Political Science Association, the Midwest Political Science Association, and the Southwestern Social Science Association. We thank our colleagues across the country who have attended the panels at which we have presented papers for their comments and suggestions. We also thank the associations themselves for providing us timely opportunities to work in convivial atmospheres. Some parts of a long-distance collaboration cannot be conducted by phone, fax, or e-mail. They require face-to-face meetings.

Most importantly, however, we thank our families. We appreciate the forbearance of our wives, Ellie and Juli, for accepting our crazy work schedules and late-night phone calls. Their quiet confidence and love have sustained us. We thank our children, Florence, Michael Jr., and Melissa Maggiotto, and Cliff and Erik Wekkin, for allowing us the time and the quiet to work. Theirs was a substantial sacrifice for which we will always be grateful.

While we cheerfully share the credit with those mentioned above for any value the reader may derive from this book, we reserve to ourselves the responsibility for any errors of omission or commission that remain. In that spirit, we lovingly dedicate this book to our wives and children.

Michael A. Maggiotto
Brockport, New York

Gary D. Wekkin
Conway, Arkansas

Introduction

Parties, Linkage, and Southern Politics

This book attempts to answer a straightforward question: Do political parties serve as effective linkage mechanisms in the American South today? This is an important question for several reasons.

First, we believe with E. E. Schattschneider (1942) that "modern democracy is unthinkable save in terms of the parties" (1), and with Giovanni Sartori (1967) that "citizens in Western democracies are represented *through* and *by* parties. This is inevitable" (471). Too often, however, concern with political parties as representative vehicles has concentrated only on those who carry the electoral banner into combat: candidates who stand for election. This is true whether one focuses on democratic politics as a political method of choice (Schumpeter 1942) or as a continuum leading to polyarchy (Dahl 1956, 1971, 1989), whether one views electoral choice retrospectively (Fiorina 1981) or prospectively (Lockerbie 1992). The soldiers of the party organization have been relegated to minor or supporting roles, whose representational aspects have been acknowledged chiefly among convention delegates (see, for example, the literature beginning with McClosky, Hoffman, and O'Hara

1960 and cited in Miller and Jennings 1986). While important in drafting the party platform (the most visible statement of the national party's beliefs) and in validating the will of state primaries, caucuses and conventions, national convention delegates comprise only a small portion of the party's organizational structure. Their roles are well defined and highly circumscribed.

At the other end of the organizational spectrum lie the broader and more pervasive roles of county party chairs and committee members (Maggiotto and Weber 1986). Their activities in recruiting and sustaining candidates, in nurturing and mobilizing rank-and-file adherents, and in maintaining a local presence with which today's more centralized national and state organizations can communicate must be understood if we are to estimate the full impact of parties in democratic linkage (Cotter et al. 1984; Crotty 1986; Mayhew 1986; Shea and Green 1994).

Representation does not stop at the top of the ticket or with the approval of the last platform plank. It is alive among state legislators, county commissioners, school board members—all of the state and local officials in whom we place trust for the management of significant aspects of our civil society. It is alive in our connection with them—in school halls and church halls and union halls, in our living rooms and back yards, at football games on Friday nights, and at Sunday afternoon picnics. It is alive in the party organization that makes many of these connections possible (Breaux, Shaffer, and Cotter 1998).

Therefore, an understanding of party linkage must include not only the supporting cast of the television miniseries *Decision 2000: The (Democratic/Republican) National Convention*—the national convention delegates—but also the activists in our cities and towns and neighborhoods. That is the approach of this book.

The second reason for our inquiry lies in what insights it may provide in determining whether, as Leon Epstein (1967, 8) put it, parties are the captives of their political environments. The causality of political parties versus their environments is an important question, because many authorities on the subject have written off modern parties as irrelevancies or dead letters. Parties, in their view, have been supplanted by interest groups, political action committees, social movements, candidate organizations, and the like. The environment has changed, and parties are ill adapted to survive, much less to succeed.

We disagree with this reasoning and with this reading of contemporary American politics. We think that political parties still have a meaningful role to play in linking government and the governed. Parties, in our view, continue to be active—indeed, to thrive—in an environment designed to be hostile to such organizations. The American system of separated powers and federalism was designed by its founders, and rationalized by Madison, to "cure the mischief of faction"—that is, to frustrate partisan behavior—as well as to limit the power of government. Moreover, institutions and technology have evolved to assume some of the roles that political parties created and headlined on the American political stage. However, to conclude that the people's pulse is weak and thready in parties' hardened arteries belies the reality that we see. In our view, rumors of partisan demise are premature.

The third reason we consider our research question theoretically and practically interesting pertains to the importance we accord the South in contemporary politics. The South has traditionally been considered a unique region, possessing a character that requires separate analysis in explorations of voting behavior and party competition (Campbell et al. 1960). Now there is strong empirical evidence (Erikson, Wright, and McIver 1993) to support that historic and continuing cultural identity, which Elazar (1972) called "traditionalistic."

Moreover, by our political Richter scale, the South is the region that has experienced the most severe and repeated quakes over the last thirty years (Black and Black 1987, 1992; Bullock and Rozell 1998; Lamis 1990). Party ties there have been ripped and resewn, born and born again. This fact is undisputed; it is the meaning of this wrenching change that is in doubt. From the candidacy of Barry Goldwater, which cracked the Deep South for Republicans who crafted a "Southern Strategy" (Phillips 1970), to the impact of the Voting Rights Act and its amendments (Handley and Grofman 1994), amid the rising immigration of nonnative southerners (Rice and Pepper 1997) and the employment surge from the relocation of national and international jobs (Black and Black 1987), change has been one of the few constants in southern politics.

V. O. Key wrote in 1949, "In its grand outlines, the politics of the South revolves around the position of the Negro" (5). Today, more than at any other time in this century, more blacks are registered voters, but so are more whites (Stanley 1987). More blacks hold political office in the South today than at any time in this century (Joint Center for Political Research 1994), and blacks form a larger percentage of core Democratic party identifiers in the South (if not exactly nationwide [Stanley and Niemi 1995]) than at any time in the postwar era. Blacks also play a pivotal role in the electoral coalitions of black and white Democrats (Black 1998), a fact underscored by the electoral results of 1998. But it is still unclear whether the creation of majority-minority districts designed to elect minority candidates (and successfully so; see Lublin 1997a, 1997b) catalyzed increased minority turnout (Brace et al. 1995), thus translating identification into votes, or whether the mobilization of black voters resulted from organizational targeting by the Democratic party.

The implications of racial prejudice, isolation, and stereotyping are never far from the surface in politics nationwide (Gilens 1996; Hurwitz and Peffley 1997; Kinder and Mendelberg 1995; Peffley, Hurwitz, and Sniderman 1997; Vertanin and Huddy 1998) or in the South in particular (Kuklinski, Cobb, and Gilens 1997). They may underlie a secular realignment of the parties, if it has occurred (Carmines and Stimson 1989). However, the evidence does not point to southern white mobilization as the unequivocal result of a "backlash" (Stanley 1987; see also Bullock 1991a; Bullock and Rozell 1998). Nor is the size of the black population in a district a better or more consistent predictor of the election of more liberal Democrats to Congress from the South or their pursuit of a more liberal agenda (Fleischer 1993)—the representative's party and whether a black representative replaced a white one have a clearer policy impact (Bullock 1995a). Indeed, the dilution of minority influence in districts may sum to a decrease in minority influence on legislative outcomes (Cameron, Epstein, and O'Halloran 1996; Overby and Cosgrove 1996), even with the growing presence of minority legislators (Lublin 1997b). Nevertheless, it is true that the New Deal coalition, based in part on the solid Democratic South, is dead. "Democrats can no longer rely on native southern whites; conversely, Republicans can potentially attract them in large numbers" (Stanley and Niemi 1995, 237; see also Black 1998). Needed or not (Brace, Grofman, and Handley 1987), this trend has been abetted, in part, by the creation of "black" districts as a result of challenges under the Voting Rights Act (Hill 1995) and secured by the context of pro-Republican short-term forces (Petrocik and Desposanto 1998).

And Republicans are capitalizing. They are attracting voters. The movement toward the Republican party that began at the presidential level has slowly but inexorably moved down the ballot (Hadley 1993). Delayed by Watergate and the Carter presidential candidacies, the pace of Republican success in Congress and among governors accelerated under the Reagan administration and shows signs of slowly advancing in the smaller, more homogenous districts that elect state legislators and local officials (Bullock 1991b). The results of the post-1990 census and elections through 1996 are explosive reminders that this trend is continuing, though perhaps less dynamically after 1998.

Together, the social, economic, and political changes that have rocked the South make it an important laboratory for understanding if and how political parties have responded adequately. In our view, it is the region where the challenges of, and to, party linkage should be most clearly apparent.

Democracy and Party Linkage

There are innumerable definitions of democracy. At bottom, we believe that each shares two common concerns. First, there must be a correlation between the outputs of the political system and the wishes and values expressed as inputs by the people who live within the system's boundaries. Second, the process by which wishes and values are translated or converted into outputs must be institutionalized and not the product of serendipity or modern noblesse oblige. Put differently, we posit institutionalized responsiveness of the rulers to the ruled as the hallmark of democracy (Pitkin 1967).

Notice we have left open many questions relating to the form or substance of inputs, the type and quality of responses, and, important for our inquiry, the institutions that make the translation or conversion possible. At this point we have only stipulated that there must be a meaningful connection—a linkage—ensuring a realistic expectation that people's demands will be satisfied.

This focus eliminates the equation of participation with representation (Conway 1991). That people register preferences by voting, campaigning, communal and particularized contacting, or protesting (Verba and Nie 1972; Verba, Nie, and Kim 1978;

Dalton 1996) does not mean that those activities translate into outcomes reflective of what animated their participation. Frustration, a common occurrence, sometimes boils over into violence even in seemingly stable democracies (Powell 1982). The fragility of democratic relationships reflects the balance between popular demands and the capacity of a political system to respond (Huntington 1968, 1991), especially if that system's diversity has a tradition of separate expression and reward, as in a consociational system (Lijphart 1977). A political system that is responsive and stable over the long haul must evolve institutions to channel political demands into productive outputs (Pitkin 1967; Wekkin et al. 1993). To endure, that system must be blessed with a culture that prizes moderation over excess (Almond and Verba 1963; Muller and Seligson 1994) but can adjust to the impacts of new agendas spawned by more inclusive participation and the inevitability of socioeconomic and technological change (Inglehart 1990).

Among the institutions that have proven their adaptability to the changing American landscape are political parties, especially in the derivative stage of their development (Chambers and Burnham 1975). To be sure, they are challenged and chastened by interest groups (Berry 1997) and social movements (McGlen and O'Connor 1983); nevertheless, one of the parties' traditional strengths has been to embrace these competitors. Parties are permeable entities that rejuvenate themselves by attracting new activists, new groups, and new interests (Polsby 1983). The result is neither cooptation nor the sterile circulation of elites culminating in a new chiseling of the old oligarchy's death mask. It is more than a stratarchy of mutual deferences (Eldersveld 1964) or the pell-mell pursuit of incentives to satisfy private ambitions (Schlesinger 1966, 1991). It is a conscious renewal of spirit and personnel (Baer and Bositis 1988) born in the recognition that parties perform constant functions in a changing American polity (Epstein 1967, 1986).

To conclude that political parties have been successful at their tasks is far too facile a reading of modern American political history. The tensions created by the "passions and interests" of the people, not just the parties, are too readily apparent, as is the range of conflict over the expectations for party performance (Pomper 1992). It is easy to argue that parties should articulate inchoate interests, aggregate interests to form potent coalitions of mobilized supporters, and communicate the will of the people through partisans in office to create consonant public policy. It is equally easy to argue that such competitive zeal misses the commonweal that binds a diverse people together in a single nation and, thus, jeopardizes the stability of the state and its government. It is more realistic to argue that parties in the United States have managed to muddle through.

Most Americans have found shelter under the umbrellas identified as Democrat and Republican, but not everyone agrees about the shape, size, or color of those umbrellas. Disagreements have led to the formation of third parties (Herrnson and Green 1997; Mazmanian 1974; Rosenstone, Behr, and Lazarus, 1984) and to party factionalization. Fissures defined by issues or leaders as persons have a long tradition in southern politics (Key 1949). The party competition that has arisen in the region over the last thirty years has not fully eclipsed this penchant for faction. One has only to look at Ross Perot's double-digit support in 1992 (Pomper et al. 1993) and the increasing importance of religion as a touchstone for values and issues for confirmation (Baker 1990; Layman and Carmines 1997; Green et al. 1996; Leege and Kellstedt 1993; Rozell and Wilcox 1995; Wald 1987). Yet these tensions may simply be the newest manifestation of precisely those changes to which parties in the derivative stage of development have successfully adapted. Using Hirschman's (1970) terminology, loyalty will be preserved if sufficient mechanisms for voice are provided. Exit from the system will be an option for the few; but exit to another, more congenial party may increasingly be the avenue of choice for the many (Black and Black 1987, 1992; Black 1998).

How should one view such changes in the political landscape? Our concern now is not with the question of partisan realignment but with the parties as linkage mechanisms facilitating the translation of popular inputs into governmental outputs.

As such, movement between the parties does not debilitate the linkage role. Indeed, it highlights the role of choice in a democratic polity. To the degree that parties simplify choice among candidates and policies, they economize decision making. To the degree that such economies are achieved without narrowly delimiting the scope of popular wishes, the range of inputs is embraced and the agenda for decision making approaches completeness. When the major parties fail to simplify economically or fail to appreciate the range of demands abroad in the polity, partisan attachments are splintered or renounced. In the extreme, the competitive system itself is rejected.

As well, we do not limit ourselves to dyadic representation but expand that idea to a regional scope that is explicitly collective in outlook (Weisberg 1978). Dyadic representation is based on geographic districts, which may too narrowly construe party responsiveness, especially to broader social, economic, and international issues. Viewing representation collectively—in this case regionally—embraces the party at the elite and mass levels as diverse units. It enhances the possibility that a more theoretically interesting and politically meaningful foundation for linkage may be discovered within a regional identity and culture. Moreover, the regional focus permits us to elaborate the role of federalism as a qualifier to collective representation, defining issues common to levels of government that transcend district geography. Regional responses to federally differentiated issues highlight the "collective" sinews that bind party organizations in different states and locales within the South to one another and to the rank and file, however dispersed in the region.

We share with Jacobson (1987) the notion that there are a variety of ways in which legislators and other political figures can "represent" constituents. We focus here on descriptive and policy correlations because, although pork-barrel and constituency service activities no doubt respond to constituents' interests (Cain, Ferejohn, and Fiorina 1987), a close association based on descriptive and substantive responsiveness has been central historically to an understanding of agenda building (Kingdon 1984), participation (Verba et al. 1993),

and democracy (Dahl 1989) as outcomes (Swain 1993; Tate 1993). Importantly, however, we treat the success or failure of collective party responsiveness in the region as a question.

Because we acknowledge the outcome of partisan failure as a real possibility, we can describe democracy in terms of party linkage but must treat it as an hypothesis. It is both the beginning point and the ending point of our empirical analysis.

Democratic Linkage and Party Organization in the South

Sullivan and O'Connor (1972) succinctly summarized the elite conditions for popular control of public policy: that elites offer different choices to the electorate and that they follow through on their promises once elected. Because party platforms provide the substance of electoral debate and the agenda for political action (Pomper and Lederman 1971), those party officials most closely associated with their creation and passage—national convention delegates—are easily seen to play a pivotal role in representation. And we agree. In that regard, this work is directly descended from the pioneering study of McClosky, Hoffman, and O'Hara (1960).

But we also wish to focus attention on other levels of the party organization, levels that touch the rank and file more regularly and have continuing, not just quadrennial, responsibilities for the robustness of the local party. From a representational perspective, that part of our work owes its parentage to the efforts of Montjoy, Shaffer, and Weber (1980) to examine county party chairs and their success in representing the policy views of fellow county partisans. Because it is this "lower" level that is less obviously connected to the substance of policy debate and, certainly from a process view of democracy (Ricci 1970), less obviously connected to elite competition for the people's vote (Schumpeter 1942), we must endeavor to "make the case" for its inclusion.

The creation of a viable local organization for whatever purpose is strongly affected by the history and culture of the locale. This conclusion has been a persistent theme in electoral politics, entering the literature via the general heading of "friends and neighbors" effects, with a long tradition in the South (Key 1949), and, more recently, under the general rubric of examinations of local political contexts (Bledsoe et al. 1995; Huckfeldt 1986; Mayhew 1986). Thus it is not surprising that the top-down organizational emphasis of the Republican party, so successful in creating strong state party organizations in the South, was not, as of the early 1980s, equally successful at the county level (Cotter et al. 1984).

This is not to say that local party organizations have been wholly unsuccessful. Our reasoning is inferential. On the one hand, there is a continuing expectation that local party elites will play an important role in the recruitment of candidates, in the conduct of their campaigns, and in the mobilization of voters. We find this true among nonpartisan city council members (Prewitt 1970), state legislators (Seligman et al. 1974), and members of Congress (Fenno 1978). Jewell and Olson (1988) summarize these expectations succinctly: "Candidates expect parties to provide several types of election support: voter registration drives, provision of polling place workers, placement of poll watchers, and get-out-the-vote drives. All four activities are better performed through some collective means than by individual candidates. Voter registration, for example, presumably helps all candidates, not just any single one" (140).

Local parties actually perform many more activities on a regular basis (Cotter et al. 1984, table 3.4) and do so regardless of the organizational incentives that characterized their own recruitment. That is, "amateurs" are not the only local party elites focused on issues and ideology, nor are "professionals" the only local party elites who respond to the infrastructural needs of organization building and maintenance. And both are equally concerned with finding and motivating electable candidates (Maggiotto and Weber 1986). But local parties do not exist in a vacuum. Their success in attracting highly qualified candidates and in mobilizing local voters is not independent of the fortunes of the party in the state, the region, and the nation. Strategic candidates are keenly aware of the tides that wash over constitu-

encies and adjust their rational calculi accordingly (Jacobson and Kernell 1983). Thus we see the fortunes of parties spiraling upward or downward, as good news or bad feeds upon itself.

Despite the focus on candidate-centered campaigns, declining party fortunes, and media hype (Crotty and Jacobson 1984; Wattenberg 1990, 1991), then, local party leaders and the candidates who run under the parties' banners are related symbiotically. For our purposes, two questions remain. First, does our sample of county party chairs and committee members engage actively in local party building and campaign activities, including candidate recruitment? In short, do they contribute meaningfully to providing choice to the electorate, consistent with the assumption of the literature on popular control? And second, what expectations should we entertain about their ability or willingness to reflect the attitudes and values of the local constituency in the conduct of their activities?

We can provide a short empirical answer to the first question in table 0.1, which details the importance our sample of local party elites attach to certain tasks.

Looking at the percentage of our county party chairs and committee members for whom party activities are *important,* the top five activities are, in order, contacting voters, participating in party meetings and organizational business, getting people to register to vote, increasing voters' political information, and campaigning. When asked what was *most important,* the same activities, with one addition, crop up in a slightly different order: getting people to register, contacting voters, increasing voters' political information and getting candidates for local office, campaigning, and participating in party meetings and organizational business. Notice the switch: getting candidates to run for local office (candidate recruitment), ranked tenth in importance, ties for third (with increasing political information for voters) among those who think it most important. Similarly, participating in party meetings and business drops from second to sixth place. Thus activities focused on mobilizing an identifiable rank and file, increas-

TABLE 0.1

IMPORTANCE OF PARTY TASKS TO COUNTY PARTY CHAIRS AND COMMITTEE MEMBERS

Tasks	Percentage for Whom Important	Percentage for Whom Most Important
Contacting voters	76.4	20.4
Participating in party meetings and organizational business	75.9	11.1
Getting people to register	74.8	28.4
Increasing voters' political information	66.8	13.1
Campaigning	66.0	12.7
Contacting new voters	64.3	2.2
Public relations	63.5	7.5
County party organization work	59.0	9.5
Recruiting and organizing workers	58.6	8.4
Getting candidates for local office	55.8	13.1
Policy formulation	48.4	6.8
Raising money	46.8	9.0
Other nominating activities	36.3	1.1

ing the size of that contingent through voter registration drives, and, for those who identify it as important, candidate recruitment are all activities in which our sample engage.

Notice what is least frequently mentioned as *important:* other nominating activities, raising money, and policy formulation. Compare that to what is least frequently identified as being *most important:* other nominating activities, contacting new voters, and policy formulation. Formulating policy and raising money are left to other levels of the party and to candidate organizations. But contacting new voters seems a parallel task to registration. Why is it ranked so low? We might speculate that activation and reinforcement occupy more properly the scarce resources of the party organization. Conversion, the most difficult task, is relegated to a lower priority (Lazarsfeld, Berelson, and Gaudet 1968). Hence increasing the size of the general electorate through registration drives may be equally as effective, if not more so, than targeting new voters.

We might be troubled, too, that involvement in policy activities ranks so low on the priority list of party chairs and committee members, especially since (1) county chairs are certainly not reluctant to hold or express policy opinions (Maggiotto and Weber 1986; Montjoy, Shaffer, and Weber 1980) and (2) on a range of domestic and international issue indexes, county chairs are consistently as close or closer than convention delegates to the modal party identifier of their party and, often, to the modal voter him- or herself (Baer and Bositis, 1988). Following the "McClosky distribution" (Baer and Bositis 1993), this proximity is asymmetrical: Democratic elites are closer to their identifiers and often to Republican identifiers than are Republican elites.

Moreover, how electoral elite activists position themselves ideologically is strongly influenced by the ideological position of party organizational activists (Erikson, Wright, and McIver 1993). Thus, even if party activists at the local level consider their policy views of less importance in the shaping of candidate opinion or less important to their own role in the party structure, those running for office fail to share that view. Those running for office are strongly affected by the ideological position of party organizational activists.

In answer to the second question, the literature suggests that local party activists may reasonably be expected to share the beliefs of their fellow community partisans (Luttbeg 1981). Moreover, those running for office are significantly affected by local beliefs, as they try to structure a winning coalition. Thus activists in local party organizations may find themselves strategically placed to transmit community beliefs, attitudes, and values to candidates and decision-makers (Maggiotto and Weber 1986).

Together, our answers to questions one and two indicate that local party officials, like their brethren at the national party conventions, are intimately involved in the process of representation. To ignore the role they play in reflecting, shaping, filtering, or even expressing policy does injustice to their pivotal roles of communication and mobilization.

The Meanings of Party

Because the linkages that lie at the heart of this book involve political parties, it is important to be specific about what we mean by "party." One way to approach the meaning of party is through party identification. Following Campbell et al. (1960) we define party identification as a long-term, relatively stable, psychological identification with a political party. The adequacy

of this definition is open to challenge. On one level it fails to distinguish between loyalty to the party of one's choice and attitudes toward other parties (Maggiotto and Piereson 1977). As typically measured, it includes independence as the midpoint on a psychometric scale rather than as a separate nonpartisan dimension, as some have deemed correct (Valentine and Van Wingen 1980). The separation of partisans and independents is highlighted more vividly the closer one hews to the understanding of party identification as an affective orientation (Maggiotto and Wekkin 1998b). Thus a cubic representation may be more reflective of our cognitive and affective organizations of the construct (Weisberg 1980, 1983). On another level, the emphasis on length of attachment has both champions among users of the biennial national snapshots (Miller 1991; Miller and Shanks 1996) and challengers among those who see macropartisan fluctuations in quarterly time-series measurements (MacKuen et al. 1989). Are these differences methodological anomalies, or is the underlying causal mechanism so reciprocally entwined with factors and persons in the political environment as to humble efforts at statistical dissection (Marcus and Converse 1979; Page and Jones 1979)? On still another level, viewing partisanship outside of the structural perspective of federalism, as is typically the case, ignores a constitutional feature of the American polity that may affect expectations about the role and purview of government at different levels and thus evaluations about the adequacy of partisan choice in platform and candidates (Maggiotto and Wekkin 1992, 1998a).

Our view of party identification as a measure of party will try to be sensitive to each of these theoretical concerns. First, when identifying partisans we will make no assumptions about their predilections toward the "other" party and will group leaners with partisans as distinct behaviorally (Keith et al. 1992), if not always affectively (Maggiotto and Wekkin 1998b), from pure independents. Second, we will make no assumption about the length of partisan attachment. Indeed, our own research to date (Maggiotto and Wekkin 1992, 1998a; see also Hadley 1985) speaks to both stability and change in partisanship. And third, we will affirm the differences that underlie partisan attachment due to federalism by explicitly incorporating level-based partisan measures into our empirical analyses.

Another way to approach the meaning of party is via its electoral expression. Democracy involves choice, which is an action. Attitudes are not always readily translated into action; nor are attitudes and identifications always the predecessors to activities (Fishbein 1967). Party identification can be itself a function of an electoral decision in context (Franklin and Jackson 1983) or the summation of retrospective decisions on performance (Fiorina 1981), just as one can project on a candidate the issue positions and political values one cherishes (Berelson, Lazarsfeld, and McPhee 1954).

But actions lie at the heart of government. Key (1961) taunts us with the opening lines of his classic *Public Opinion and American Democracy:* "Governments must concern themselves with the opinions of their citizens, if only to provide a basis for repression of disaffection" (3). Having thus hooked us, Key develops his theme, asserting that "public opinion . . . may simply be taken to mean those opinions held by private persons which governments find it prudent to heed" (14). The actions of governments are connected to public opinion most visibly through parties and interest groups, the details of which form the grist of the last section of Key's book, which christens the connection "linkage" politics (1961, 411–531). His last book brings home that connection most vividly, focusing on votes and voters to define the personal and party fortunes of Democrats and Republicans. There he began, "In his reflective moments even the most experienced politician senses a nagging curiosity about why people vote as they do" (1966, 1).

In southern politics, defining partisanship by the manner in which people cast their ballots has special importance. Explanations of split-ticket voting have animated virtually all discussions of the changing or New South. It is one of the principal phenomena to be explained by reference to realignment (Hadley and Howell 1980) or dealignment (Beck 1977), or by segmented partisanship (Maggiotto and Wekkin 1992, 1998a). Thus we feel that how people vote, or which

party typically presents the best candidates, explores another important dimension of partisanship.

Finally, in looking at the elite sample, we choose two focuses: identification and affiliation. Both are relevant to describing elites, and the conflict between them (Hadley 1985) is highly relevant to conceptions of strength and stability. But it is the latter that concerns us when our attention turns to substantive responsiveness. If the party organization is the vehicle for representation, then affiliation with a party organization, regardless of the activist's private identification, is what matters. How well or poorly the organization succeeds may be materially related to the congruence between activist identification and affiliation, but that is not something of which the rank-and-file identifier or rank-and-file voter is aware.

Data

The data for this book come from two sources. The party elite portions were collected in several sections. Between January 15, 1991, and mid-fall 1991, research teams in eleven states of the former Confederacy sent a three-wave, eight-page mailing to Democratic and Republican county chairs and committee members (Hadley and Bowman 1995, 1998; Steed et al. 1998). The response rate ranged from a low of 40 percent, among Louisiana Democrats, to a high of 68 percent, among North Carolina Republicans. Region wide, 10,458 county party committee members returned usable questionnaires for an overall response rate of 53 percent.[1] The 619 Democratic and 611 Republican county chairs in this analysis each represent returns from 55 percent of counties. Among many items, the survey contained fifteen questions on contemporary political issues and one on self-defined political philosophy, all of which are reported below. With sufficient surveys and supplemental funding, a similar three-wave mailing was sent to the national convention delegates from the same states between July 6 and November 12, 1992, the first mailing timed to arrive the week prior to the respective national conventions. The Democratic and Republican delegate response rates were 45 and 43 percent (Ns = 460 and 506), quite respectable for national convention delegate surveys (see Miller and Jennings 1986, 18).[2]

Data for the mass sample come from an omnibus survey of adult U.S. residents in the eleven states of the former Confederacy conducted by the Population and Society Research Center (PSRC) of Bowling Green State University.[3] Portions of the mass survey of the 1992 southern electorate were constructed specifically to dovetail with the Southern Grassroots Party Activists Project. Field operations began with a pretest during the week immediately preceding the 1992 presidential elections. Households were selected using well-established random-number telephone sampling techniques, with the final sample being supplied by Survey Sampling, Inc. Each sampling frame was divided into replicates, with each replicate comprising a microsample. Respondents were also randomly selected within households to improve the representativeness of the sample.

All interviews were conducted at the PSRC's central interviewing facility, where interviewers were under constant supervision, as they used the PSRC's computer-assisted telephone interviewing facilities. The length of the interview averaged thirty-six minutes. Sampled households were phoned a maximum of 6 times over different times of the day and week. Specially supervised attempts to convert refusals were made. A total of 18,043 calls were placed between November 3, 1992, and December 23, 1992. Interviewing was resumed for the day of January 19, 1993, to complete ten additional interviews, when it was determined that the final sample file contained ten cases incorrectly assigned to the study. The final sample contained 802 completions. A total of 375 households refused to participate in the study, yielding a response rate of 68.1 percent.

Plan of Analysis

We will proceed in three steps. In step one, chapter 1 will describe rank-and-file partisans in the South, contrasting them socioeconomically and demographically. It will then establish their ideological orientations and attitudes on issues salient to the region and the nation

in the early 1990s. Each of the descriptions will be distinguished by a separate definition of partisanship: state or national identification, state or national candidate preferences, and 1992 presidential vote. These data form the foundation of *what and who* can be represented by the party organization.

Chapter 2 will present a description of national party elites (convention delegates) and local party elites (county party chairs and committee members), characterizing and contrasting them socioeconomically and demographically. We will then portray their distribution ideologically, as party identifiers, and on the same fifteen issues of national and international significance in the 1990s. This analysis will allow us to evaluate the degree to which southern parties as organizations (1) have offered contrasting political alternatives to a mobilizable electorate (substantive representation) and (2) could represent symbolically the diversity of southern society (descriptive representation), especially in anticipation of changing agendas accompanying the changing complexion of the parties in the South.

Step two of the analysis begins the connection between the party elite and the party mass. Having defined the degree of descriptive representation realized by the party organization, chapter 3 turns to substantive representation of southern mass partisans by Democratic and Republican party organizations in the South. We will compare issue and ideological distributions across elites and mass members of the parties. Guided initially by the McClosky distribution, our conclusions about who is represented will be specific to party and to level of government, as well as to definition of partisan (as identifier or as party voter).

In the third step of our analysis, chapters 4 and 5 contextualize the findings of chapter 3 by placing them in the political and socioeconomic environments within which elite-mass interaction must occur. In the political context, we will be concerned with endogenous variables that are partisan in content, such as the amount of two-party competition in a state, state and local party organizational strength, and the extent of popular partisan identification with one or both parties. We will also look at exogenous variables that may affect elite-mass issue agreement, including socioeconomic variables such as racial composition, religious piety, economic development, urbanization, and education. We employ a multiple analysis of variance (MANOVA) technique to test simultaneously for the direct and interactive effects of these control variables on the representational connection between party elites and mass partisans. This approach also allows us to address the extent to which parties are creators or creatures of their environments.

Finally, chapter 6 will present our conclusions about collective representation through the party organization. Our purpose is to end with a realistic appraisal of the current degree of, and future expectations for, party representation in the changing South.

Chapter 1

Rank-and-File Partisans in the South

This chapter describes the mass sample of 1992 southern electors, looking first at the distribution of socioeconomic and demographic characteristics, then turning to the mass respondents' ideological and issue predispositions. We are concerned with these data because of our definition of democracy and the role of parties as linkage mechanisms within that democracy.

Recall that we conceptualized democracy as the correlation between the outputs of the governing system and the wishes and values of the people in whose name the system, or government, acted. Moreover, we demanded of a democratic political system that the translation of popular demands into government outputs be institutionalized. Parties function as institutions that make the translation possible.

Descriptive Representation

The socioeconomic and demographic characteristics of the sample provide us an interesting window through which to view the parties (Key 1964). The theoretical justification for this approach is amply provided. Group (Bentley 1908) and pluralist (Truman 1971) theorists and early explorations of voting behavior, whether sociologically (Berelson, Lazarsfeld, and McPhee 1954) or social-psychological (Campbell et al. 1960) oriented, concur that the location of individuals in group space helps explain their political choices. Empirical support has been provided by investigations of political behavior (Knoke 1976; Verba and Nie 1972; Nie, Verba, and Petrocik 1976) and elaborated, more recently, by results from social learning theory (Hershey 1984) and social cognition theory (Lodge and McGraw 1995). Patterns of group membership have helped us define and explain partisan realignments (Key 1955, 1959; Ladd and Hadley 1975; Petrocik 1981; Sundquist 1973), the dependencies of parties on constituent elements (Abramson, Aldrich, and Rohde 1994, 1998; Stanley and Niemi 1995), and the resources available for political mobilization (Brady, Verba, and Schlozman 1995). Our socioeconomic and demographic identifications, then, have considerable impact on those who attempt to divine our will, curry our favor, influence our behavior, or justify their actions.

This relationship between measures of social

stratification and politics is not new. The assumption that our position in society helps determine our interests is as old as the Republic itself. Madison told us in *Federalist 10* that

> the diversity in the faculties of men, from which the rights of property originate, is not less an insuperable obstacle to a uniformity of interests. The protection of these faculties is the first object of government. From the protection of different and unequal faculties of acquiring property, the possession of different degrees and kinds of property immediately results; and from the influence of these on the sentiments and views of the respective proprietors, ensues a division of the society into different interests and parties.
>
> The latent causes of faction are thus sown in the nature of man; and we see them everywhere brought into different degrees of activity, according to the different circumstances of civil society (Hamilton, Madison, and Jay 1938, 55).

Madison suggests what later writers verify empirically: ascriptive and achievement characteristics resonate through American politics. Be it gender, race, or ethnicity, bootstrapped economic success or intellectual prowess, each forms an important element of our self-identification—how we think about ourselves and how we present ourselves. It is to these self-identifications that parties appeal through personnel and policy. Balancing the ticket recognizes a symbolic interest often as deeply held as the material or purposive benefits that accrue from a platform plank.

Our socioeconomic and demographic characteristics help explain to which groups we belong or would like to join and from which groups we choose to distance ourselves, even recoil. They help us understand the differential application of selective exposure, perception, and retention—the filters we employ to screen out or focus in on people, policies, candidates, groups, and events. They assist in explaining the agendas with which we empathize or which we advocate ourselves and distinguish them from those which we repudiate or ignore. Whether "one is known by the friends one keeps" or a more abstract notion such as a "comparison level" (Thibaut and Kelley 1959) is operative, the outcome for party linkage is the same.

For parties to aggregate and articulate interests, to succeed in political communication, and to tie people and government more closely together, we must ask for whom they speak. So who are the Democrats and Republicans in the South? Do they differ? By how much? We must answer these questions to learn whose voice has a chance to be heard.

Substantive Representation

Whose voice is heard tells half the story. What is being said tells the other half. To be sure, one can estimate the interests and goals of individuals from their socioeconomic and demographic characteristics. One can identify likely affinities. But one can also ask people directly how they feel, to discover what animates their political selves to expression in the parties. If parties listen as well as look, they will get a clearer, more accurate portrait of those to whom they are accountable. If, as Pitkin tells us, representative institutions must stand in a "constant condition of responsiveness" (1967, 233), then policy expressions must be bedrock foundations for platform planks and campaign promises. This is the grist of substantive representation measured directly.

What are the policy expressions of Democrats and Republicans in the South? Do their voices differ? Within the parties does one find cacophony or harmony? The clarity with which a policy is advocated indicates the coherence of the rank and file behind it. It is easier to represent homogenous partisans than those spread across the policy spectrum. While the latter invites policy latitude by representatives, it also invites policy reprisal by those who disagree. For what, therefore, do the people stand—those who call themselves Democrats and Republicans in the modern South?

Measuring Partisanship in Mass Publics

Before employing our hypothesized measurements of partisanship among the southern electorate—national and state identification, national and state candidate evaluations, and 1992 presidential vote—the

TABLE 1.1

THE RELATIONSHIP AMONG DIFFERENT MEASURES OF PARTISANSHIP USING A PROPORTIONAL
REDUCTION IN ERROR APPROACH

	National Party Identification	State Party Identification	Best Candidate for President	Best Candidate for Governor	Presidential Vote
National party identification	1.00	.60	.38	.39	.37
(N)		(756)	(667)	(632)	(610)
State party identification	.57	1.00	.30	.38	.31
(N)	(756)		(655)	(620)	(599)
Best candidate for president	.49	.42	1.00	.47	.51
(N)	(667)	(655)	(613)	(536)	
Best candidate for governor	.50	.52	.47	1.00	.44
(N)	(632)	(620)	(613)		(516)
Presidential vote	.36	.34	.38	.33	1.00
(N)	(610)	(599)	(536)	(516)	

Note: Coefficients are Goodman and Kruskal's Tau.

first question to ask is whether these measures tap different aspects of partisanship empirically. Clearly, because of the often low correlation between attitude and action, and the imperfect relationship between party identification and candidate evaluation, we enter this investigation expecting to find differences. We do not expect to find replicates of each other among our measures. The question for us is, how big are those differences?

Table 1.1 provides us the answer. Displayed in that table are proportional reduction in error (PRE) coefficients, summarizing the relationship between our various measures of partisanship. We have chosen to consider each measurement at the nominal level in order to avoid the bias introduced by thinking of partisanship as a single continuum from Democrat to Republican with independent identifi-

ers anchoring the center. We also wanted to be able to include independent or "other" candidates, such as Ross Perot, as well as independent identifiers.[1]

PRE measures are easily interpreted as analogous to coefficients of determination that tell us the amount of variance in the dependent variable attributable to the independent variable. Nominal scale PRE measures assess the reduction in the error of predicting the dependent variable from its marginal distribution compared to the prediction provided by knowing the conditional distributions within each category of the independent variable. Since the marginal and conditional distribution of the variables in each pair are probably different, the particular coefficient reported, Goodman and Kruskal's Tau, is an asymmetric measure. Thus while the row headings define the dependent variable and the column headings the independent variable, to express the asymmetry of the relationships, the table is complete above and below the diagonal.

The important point to note in table 1.1 is how low the coefficients are. Although we are dealing with measures of the same underlying concept, clearly we have identified very different aspects or dimensions. The largest coefficient is .6, predicting state partisanship from national partisanship. The reciprocal relationship yields a closely corresponding coefficient of .57. Thus in both instances about 60 percent of state or national party identification is explained by the other, leaving 40 percent unexplained.

Of the twenty off-diagonal coefficients in the table, fifteen are below .5. That is, three-quarters of the coefficients indicate that less than half of the variance in the dependent variable is explained by the independent variable. And three of the remaining five are nestled together at .50, .51, and .52. To reason by analogy again, this is a long way from collinearity.

However, in the tables that follow, we do not present the data in the form that is assessed in table 1.1. We reduce the data to Democrats and Republicans in every case, thus eliminating independent identifiers and independent or "other" candidates. As a consequence, we reduce the variance to be explained and increase the probability of higher PRE coefficients.[2] We incur that cost because we are satisfied that our underlying measures tap different dimensions, and because we wish only to contrast Democrats and Republicans. It is southern Democrats and southern Republicans who are "represented" by the party organization. While each organization may and probably does reach out to the southern Independent, it must do so from a secure base (Maggiotto and Wekkin 1993).

The Socioeconomic and Demographic Character of Southern Partisans

Tables 1.2, 1.3, and 1.4 present data on the socioeconomic and demographic character of the 1992 southern electorate. The first thing to note in these tables is the difference in the number of cases in each column

as one moves among definitions. For example, in table 1.2, the number of Democratic identifiers at the national and state levels remains roughly constant, but the number of Republican identifiers drops an average of 20 percent from national to state identification. In table 1.3, the numerical differences are even more pronounced. The number of southerners who think the Democrats "usually" offer the better candidate for governor is nearly one-third larger, on average, than the number of those who think the Democrats usually offer the better presidential candidate. We find exactly the reverse trend among Republicans. Nearly one-third fewer southerners think the Republicans usually offer the better gubernatorial candidates than opt for Republicans as usually having the better presidential candidates. No comparison can be made with actual presidential vote, since there is only one time point, 1992. But it is instructive to compare the number of cases in the partisan definition by "usually offering the best presidential candidate" with those who are defined by having cast a partisan ballot. The Democrats got their full measure of support in 1992—and possibly more. The Republicans failed to fully capitalize on the reservoir of "usual" support. Though we offer no direct data at this point, it is fair to conclude that in the South, Ross Perot hurt Republicans more than Democrats.

There are marked differences in gender that reach statistical significance in three of the five partisan definitions. In four of the five definitions, at least 60 percent of Democrats were women. Only in the definition by usual gubernatorial preference did that fail, and there the percentage, 58.9, was meagerly different. Among Republican identifiers, men edged out women at both the national and state levels. Women reversed that to approximately a 3.5 percent difference in their favor among usual preferences and expanded that to more than a 7 percent difference in the presidential vote of 1992. Thus, defined by their 1992 presidential vote, there were more women than men in both parties.

Predictably, the Republican party was overwhelmingly white (between 93 and 96 percent), regardless of partisan definition. Democrats, by contrast, were 70–75 percent white. Twenty to 25 percent of Democrats were African Americans, whereas they never comprised more than 4.4 percent of Republicans, regardless of definition. The racial distributions were significantly different in every partisan definition.

The partisan educational distributions were significantly different in four of five definitions, a fact not surprising, especially looking at partisanship from a national perspective. More Democrats were concentrated at the grade school and high school levels. Republicans began to pull away among those with some college or a college degree. The gap narrows considerably at the graduate school/degree level, but does not close. National Republicans, however defined, are clearly better educated than national Democrats. The tendency remains at the state level, but, significantly, is moderated. In fact, a higher proportion of Democrats than Republicans have the highest level of education measured among those whom we defined by their usual gubernatorial preferences. The educational distribution of state-level Democrats and Republicans seems more similar than the educational distribution of their national-level counterparts. And it is in the definition of party by usual gubernatorial preference that significant difference is not achieved.

Southern Republicans are not exactly plutocrats, even compared to their Democratic brethren, but they are on average richer, and the difference is statistically significant across all partisan definitions. Approximately 30 percent of Republican identifiers, 27 percent of southerners who usually prefer Republican presidential or gubernatorial candidates, and fully 35 percent of Bush voters came from families with an income of at least sixty thousand dollars per year. The comparison for Democrats is just over 10 percent for identifiers, 8.8 percent for those usually preferring Democrats for president, and 12.5 percent for both those usually preferring Democrats for governor and those voting for Clinton. At the other extreme, 29 percent of Democratic identifiers, 32 percent of usual Democratic presidential supporters, 27 percent of usual Democratic gubernatorial supporters, and 29 percent of Clinton voters came from families with annual incomes of less than twenty thousand dollars. The comparable figures for Republicans were, 14, 15, 15, and 12 percent. While the midranges of the income distributions for each party

are relatively similar, the extremes of these distributions are skewed in the opposite directions.

The contrasts are not so stark among the age distributions. Indeed, the partisan differences reach statistical significance only in the definition of usual presidential preferences and in the 1992 presidential vote. The tendency, however, is for Republican identifiers to be younger, especially overpopulating the thirty- to forty-year-old decade and to a lesser degree the forty- to fifty-year-old group at the national level. There are more older Democrats, especially among the oldest cohorts of identifiers at both levels of government. Presidential preferences clearly mark the ascendancy of Republicans among Generation X, the youngest cohort, and among the youngest of the baby boomers. Those over fifty usually preferred Democratic aspirants. Interestingly, these differences all but disappear when preferences for governors become the defining characteristic of partisanship. The largest difference is among fifty to sixty year olds who lean more heavily toward the Democrats. Clinton's candidacy seemed to have a more positive impact on Generation Xers than did Bush's, but that was not repeated among baby boomers, who made up larger proportions of Republicans than Democrats. Democrats weighed in the fifty-to-sixty crowd, Republicans concentrated more heavily among those ages sixty to seventy; but the oldest cohort remained more important to the Democratic than the Republican distribution. Age is not monotonically, nor typically statistically, related to southern partisanship by these definitions.

Looking at the distributions of religious preferences paints a similarly complex portrait. The overall structure of both distributions is similar, reflecting the marginal distribution of religion in the region as being overwhelmingly Protestant, of one type or another, with Roman Catholics coming in a distant second and nonbelievers trailing an even more distant third. The remaining religious groups are scattered. For example, while there are more Jewish Democrats than Jewish Republicans, and Roman Catholics form a weightier segment of the Democratic distribution than the Republican distribution, the differences are small. "General" Protestants are somewhat more important for the

TABLE 1.2

SOCIODEMOGRAPHIC AND IDEOLOGICAL CHARACTERISTICS OF DEMOCRATS AND
REPUBLICANS DEFINED BY THEIR PARTY IDENTIFICATIONS

| | NATIONAL PARTISANSHIP | | STATE PARTISANSHIP | |
Characteristic	Democrats (%)	Republicans (%)	Democrats (%)	Republicans (%)
Ideology				
Liberal	24.8	6.5*	23.6	6.3*
Moderate	45.5	26.1	46.6	25.0
Conservative	29.7	67.3	29.8	68.7
(*N* of cases)	(303)	(306)	(309)	(252)
Gender				
Male	36.0	50.3*	39.0	50.6*
Female	64.0	49.7	61.0	49.4
(*N* of cases)	(339)	(320)	(341)	(263)
Race/ethnicity				
White	73.5	94.7*	73.9	95.1*
Black	24.2	1.9	22.9	1.5
Asian American	.3	1.3	.6	1.1
Native American	.9	.9	.9	1.1
Other	1.2	1.3	1.8	1.1
(*N* of Cases)	(339)	(318)	(341)	(263)
Education				
Grade school	18.5	9.1*	18.5	10.3*
High school	35.4	28.4	32.6	28.4
Some college	25.6	29.3	24.4	29.9
College graduate	11.0	20.5	13.5	19.9
Graduate school/degree	9.5	12.6	10.9	11.5
(*N* of cases)	(336)	(317)	(340)	(261)
Family income ($)				
<10,000	10.2	3.6*	9.1	3.2*
10,000–<20,000	19.0	10.9	19.7	10.8
20,000–<30,000	24.1	17.5	21.9	17.2
30,000–<40,000	14.6	13.2	14.4	13.2
40,000–<50,000	15.6	17.2	16.3	17.6

TABLE 1.2 (CONTINUED)

Characteristic	NATIONAL PARTISANSHIP		STATE PARTISANSHIP	
	Democrats (%)	Republicans (%)	Democrats (%)	Republicans (%)
50,000–<60,000	6.0	8.3	6.6	7.2
60,000–<70,000	4.4	13.2	5.9	13.2
70,000+	6.0	16.2	6.3	17.2
(*N* of cases)	(315)	(303)	(320)	(250)
Age (years)				
<30	18.0	18.4	18.2	18.6
30–39	18.6	23.4	17.0	24.7
40–49	17.7	20.3	19.9	19.4
50–59	16.2	12.8	16.1	13.3
60–69	15.0	14.7	14.7	13.3
70+	14.5	10.3	14.1	10.6
(*N* of cases)	(339)	(320)	(341)	(263)
Religion				
General Protestant	5.4	5.7	5.1	6.6
Mainline Protestant	6.6	10.2	5.7	10.0
Pietistic Protestant	27.6	27.1	27.2	28.2
Fundamentalist	31.2	28.3	32.3	27.8
Nontraditional	.6	.6	.9	.4
Roman Catholic	17.7	16.6	18.0	16.6
Jewish	1.5	.3	1.5	.4
Other	1.2	.6	1.8	.4
Nonbeliever	8.1	10.5	7.5	9.7
(*N* of cases)	(333)	(314)	(334)	(259)
Length of residence (years)				
<10	34.0	37.9*	30.6	37.4*
10–19	18.0	27.0	19.1	30.2
20–29	17.5	14.7	17.9	12.6
30+	30.5	20.4	32.4	19.8
(*N* of cases)	(338)	(319)	(340)	(262)

*Statistically significant at *p* ≤ .05.

TABLE 1.3

SOCIODEMOGRAPHIC AND IDEOLOGICAL CHARACTERISTICS OF DEMOCRATS AND REPUBLICANS DEFINED BY THEIR USUAL PREFERENCES FOR PARTY CANDIDATES

Characteristic	BEST CANDIDATE FOR PRESIDENT		BEST CANDIDATE FOR GOVERNOR	
	Democrats (%)	Republicans (%)	Democrats (%)	Republicans (%)
Ideology				
Liberal	25.3	8.9*	22.8	7.9*
Moderate	46.1	29.8	47.1	23.4
Conservative	28.6	61.2	30.2	68.7
(*N* of cases)	(245)	(369)	(325)	(265)
Gender				
Male	38.8	47.9*	41.1	48.2*
Female	61.2	52.1	58.9	51.8
(*N* of cases)	(273)	(390)	(353)	(278)
Race/ethnicity				
White	71.8	93.3*	75.6	96.4*
Black	24.9	4.4	20.7	2.9
Asian American	.4	1.0	.9	0.0
Native American	1.1	.8	.9	.7
Other	1.8	.5	2.0	0.0
(*N* of cases)	(273)	(388)	(352)	(278)
Education				
Grade school	20.9	10.1*	15.8	11.6
High school	37.7	28.9	33.9	30.8
Some college	21.3	28.4	25.6	27.2
College graduate	11.2	20.1	13.2	20.3
Graduate school/degree	9.0	12.6	11.5	10.1
(*N* of cases)	(268)	(388)	(348)	(276)
Family income ($)				
<10,000	11.2	3.5*	8.5	3.0*
10,000–<20,000	21.1	12.1	18.5	12.4
20,000–<30,000	22.3	20.4	21.9	21.1
30,000–<40,000	15.1	13.1	13.1	13.5
40,000–<50,000	15.9	16.6	17.9	16.5

TABLE 1.3 CONTINUED

| Characteristic | BEST CANDIDATE FOR PRESIDENT | | BEST CANDIDATE FOR GOVERNOR | |
	Democrats (%)	Republicans (%)	Democrats (%)	Republicans (%)
50,000–<60,000	5.6	7.2	7.6	6.0
60,000–<70,000	4.8	11.5	5.2	12.8
70,000+	4.0	15.5	7.3	14.7
(*N* of cases)	(251)	(373)	(329)	(266)
Age (years)				
<30	16.5	20.3*	18.1	18.7
30–39	16.1	24.6	19.5	21.6
40–49	19.8	20.0	19.3	20.9
50–59	18.7	12.3	16.7	12.6
60–69	15.8	12.6	14.2	13.3
70+	13.2	10.3	12.2	12.9
(*N* of cases)	(273)	(390)	(353)	(278)
Religion				
General Protestant	4.9	5.2	5.2	5.8
Mainline Protestant	6.0	9.1	5.7	11.3
Pietistic Protestant	26.9	27.0	25.6	28.1
Fundamentalist	32.1	33.0	33.3	31.0
Nontraditional	.7	.5	.6	.4
Roman Catholic	16.0	15.6	17.5	15.3
Jewish	2.2	.3	1.7	.4
Other	1.1	.3	.6	0.0
Nonbeliever	10.1	9.1	9.8	7.7
(*N* of cases)	(268)	(385)	(348)	(274)
Length of residence (years)				
<10	32.7	38.0*	31.8	39.7*
10–19	19.9	25.4	20.5	25.6
20–29	17.3	15.4	17.6	13.7
30+	30.1	21.1	30.1	20.9
(*N* of cases)	(272)	(389)	(352)	(277)

*Statistically significant at $p \le .05$.

TABLE 1.4
SOCIODEMOGRAPHIC AND IDEOLOGICAL CHARACTERISTICS OF DEMOCRATS AND
REPUBLICANS DEFINED BY THEIR 1992 MAJOR PARTY PRESIDENTIAL VOTE

| | PRESIDENTIAL VOTE | |
Characteristic	Democrats	Republicans
Ideology		
Liberal	25.9	3.3
Moderate	51.4	26.2
Conservative	22.7	70.5
(*N* of cases)	(255)	(244)
Gender		
Male	38.9	46.3
Female	61.1	53.7
(*N* of cases)	(280)	(255)
Race/ethnicity		
White	74.3	96.4*
Black	22.1	2.0
Asian American	.7	.4
Native American	1.1	.4
Other	1.8	.8
(*N* of cases)	(280)	(253)
Education		
Grade school	15.5	8.3*
High school	31.4	27.7
Some college	27.4	28.1
College graduate	13.4	22.9
Graduate school/degree	12.3	13.0
(*N* of cases)	(277)	(253)
Family income ($)		
<10,000	8.7	2.9*
10,000–<20,000	20.2	9.5
20,000–<30,000	22.8	16.5
30,000–<40,000	12.5	14.0
40,000–<50,000	18.3	15.7
50,000–<60,000	4.9	7.0

TABLE 1.4 (CONTINUED)

Characteristic	PRESIDENTIAL VOTE	
	Democrats	Republicans
60,000–<70,000	4.9	15.3
70,000+	7.6	19.8
(*N* of cases)	(263)	(242)
Age (years)		
<30	16.4	12.2*
30–39	13.9	22.4
40–49	20.4	22.7
50–59	18.2	13.3
60–69	15.4	18.8
70+	15.7	10.6
(*N* of cases)	(280)	(255)
Religion		
General Protestant	5.1	5.6*
Mainline Protestant	7.6	10.8
Pietistic Protestant	24.6	28.5
Fundamentalist	28.6	32.5
Nontraditional	.7	.8
Roman Catholic	18.5	16.5
Jewish	2.2	0.0
Other	1.1	.4
Nonbeliever	11.6	4.8
(*N* of cases)	(276)	(249)
Length of residence (years)		
<10	32.3	31.5
10–19	20.1	26.0
20–29	19.0	14.6
30+	28.7	28.0
(*N* of cases)	(279)	(254)

*Statistically significant at $p \leq .05$.

Republican distribution than the Democratic distribution. Mainline Protestants are nearly twice as well represented among Republicans as Democrats. Pietistic Protestants are nearly equivalently distributed among party definitions by national and state identifiers, and usual presidential preferences, but weighted toward Republicans in gubernatorial preferences and in the 1992 presidential vote. Fundamentalists reverse the trend, more heavily weighted among Democratic than Republican identifiers at each level, nearly equivalent but tending toward Republicans among usual presidential preferences, yet falling back toward Democrats among usual gubernatorial preferences. Fundamentalists formed a larger core of Republican than of Democratic partisans, defined by presidential votes cast in 1992. Similarly, more nonbelievers show up proportionately in the Republican than in the Democratic identifiers column. But when it comes to usual preferences, they populate the Democrats more heavily than the Republicans and are clearly more represented among Democrats than Republicans when partisanship is defined according to 1992 presidential vote. Religious differences are statistically significant only when partisanship is defined according to 1992 presidential vote.

Finally, looking at length of residence, we see confirmation of the power of migration on two of the three definitions of partisanship, where it is a statistically significant discriminator between the parties. Among identifiers and usual preferrers, Republicans come most often from those who have lived in the region or at their current address for the fewest years, Democrats dominating longtime residency. Using presidential vote as the operative definition, however, mitigates this distinction. The differences are small at the extremes and flip-flop in the midranges. Cutting the distribution in half, it is still true that Republicans tend to occupy a heavier proportion of the newer arrivals than Democrats.

In general, then, what can we say about the socioeconomic and demographic distributions of the parties as variously defined? Compared to Republicans, Democrats tend to be much more often female or African American, more likely to be less well educated and poorer, possibly older (but able to attract Generation X) and longer-term residents, and more likely to be fundamentalist or pietistic Protestants than general or mainline Protestants, and somewhat more likely to be Catholics or Jews. Republicans, by contrast, showed a gender split much more reflective of the population as a whole, were overwhelmingly white, more likely to have extended their education beyond high school, more likely to be financially secure than marginal, were younger, and were newer to their communities. Republicans, like Democrats, held more pietistic and fundamentalist Protestants than general and mainline Protestants, but, compared to Democrats, were denominationally weighted more heavily among the latter group.

These differences are hardly surprising. They conform broadly to the general stereotypes that one holds of the parties and reflect, in religion, for example, the gross outlines of the whole population of the southern electorate. Moreover, despite the important distinctions between the distributions in gender, race, income, education, and length of residence, it is not the case that the distributions are diametric opposites (there being no poor Republicans or no well-educated Democrats, for instance). There is a distribution on each variable. The issue that has been addressed by the data above refers to the concentrations of the distributions. These may tell us where the coalitional bases of the parties are most likely to be found. And where those clusters are visible enough to be distinguished, does that imply that interests thought to inhere in social stratification are articulated or stimulated or anticipated by the parties? That implication is addressed in the next chapter. But its foundation is completed in the next sections of this chapter, which deal with the ideological orientations and issue positions of southern Democrats and southern Republicans.

Ideology and Southern Partisanship

There are several caricatures of the South that affect any discussion of ideology. First, it is a bastion of conservatism. The congressional alliance between Republicans and southern Democrats was called the "conservative coalition." The boll weevils could be counted upon to frustrate the liberal advocacy of northern Democrats in the names of race and states' rights. But counterpoised to that image, second, is the long and boisterous tradition of southern populism that condemned large institutions as exploitive, vilified the rich as rapacious, and looked to government to unyoke the downtrodden from their oppression. And third, there is the bourbon culture of cultivated detachment. It is a culture of manners and etiquette that softens the bruises of economic competition and social isolation and papers over the plaster cracks in the wall of regional coexistence. The ideology panels of tables 1.2, 1.3, and 1.4 provide us some data with which to evaluate the adequacy of these images.

First, the image of the southern Democrat as unswervingly conservative is false. By 1992 the Democratic party had evolved a unimodal and nearly symmetric distribution, centering on moderates and winged with liberals and a slightly heavier concentration of conservatives, except when defined by presidential balloting. It is the southern Republican who emerges as the modal conservative, quite in line with the ideological portrait of the national Republican party given as early as the 1970s (Nie, Verba, and Petrocik 1976). Few liberals, a modest number of moderates, and a two-thirds majority of conservatives describes the ideological distribution of Republicans.

Second, the liberalism and conservatism that we define in the South, as elsewhere in the nation, comes in many guises, at least two of which are important for a fuller appreciation of this discussion: social conservatives and economic conservatives. The agenda of the social conservative concerns our daily interactions and the values expressed in the communities in which we live. The ability to pray in school, the condemnation of abortion as murder, the control of public education by local citizens rather than by a federal department and a bevy of national unions, the right to carry even concealed weapons—even this abbreviation of the litany is familiar. The economic conservative can eschew all of the above and concentrate on the evils of deficit spending, the need for fiscal restraint to contain the national debt, the wisdom or the fallacy of protectionism, the need

for tax cuts to stimulate economic growth—again a familiar litany, even in this short rendition.

Cannot these tenets of "conservatism" be reconciled, in part, with the populist plea of freedom? Rhetorically, at least, Ronald Reagan discovered that government was the problem, because it created the loopholes through which large institutions and the absentee rich manipulated the lives of working men and women. Getting government off our backs meant declawing the oppressors. But is that not a typical objective of "liberalism," especially when coupled with continued attention to the "social safety net"? We forget that the early New Deal depended upon the southern congressional contingent to support Franklin Roosevelt's proposals for social and economic reform. We forget too that it was a son of the South, Lyndon Johnson, who completed Roosevelt's work with the Great Society, among whose continuing legacies we can number the Civil Rights Act of 1964, the Voting Rights Act of 1965, and Medicare.

Whatever manners prevail in the South today, the paper has been peeled back from the walls. The cracks are visible. And with that visibility has come the emergence of two-party competition to replace one-party factionalism. The commentators we cited in the introduction would call that an improvement.

Thus the caricature of the South ideologically, like all caricatures, is both exaggerated and facile. Perhaps it was never true to the extent that it was believed. What is true is that two parties exist in the South today—of uneven strength, with pockets of support, but competing nonetheless—that have the opportunity to express the complex culture of southern politics in a way not thought of, perhaps unthinkable, as recently as thirty years ago. Southern Democrats number nearly as many liberals as conservatives today, although modally they are moderates. Southern Republicans are overwhelmingly conservative. But conservatism, just as liberalism, is a term bandied about without a full appreciation of its complexity (Maggiotto 1983, 1984a, 1984b). That is especially important when ideology is to be understood regionally, and when we know conceptually (Elazar 1972) and empirically (Erikson, Wright, and McIver,

1993) the importance of a regional impact on attitude objects.

Issues and Southern Partisanship

Our sample of the southern electorate was asked a battery of questions tapping issues salient during the 1992 election cycle. We present their responses in tables 1.5 to 1.9. The presentation in each of those tables is parallel. The mode, or most frequent response, is provided as a measure of central tendency. The percentage of respondents who answered in the direction of the mode—either A, "agree," or D, "disagree," with the issue statement—is then given. For example, assuming that for an arbitrarily chosen question the mode was "agree," then the percentage answering in the direction of the mode would be the sum of the agree and strongly agree responses divided by the total number of responses to the question. The party difference column registers the result of the subtraction of the modal Republican percentage from the modal Democratic percentage. A positive value indicates a higher fraction of Democrats than Republicans adopted the same modal direction.

The asterisks indicate the statistical significance of the relationship between the issue distribution and partisanship, as measured by chi-squared. When an asterisk appears, we know that the hypothesis that the issue distributions among Democrats and Republicans came from the same distribution can be rejected at the .05 level. Thus the test of significance is not simply the significance of the difference of proportions; however, in all cases, the two approaches agree. When the modal tendencies differed between the parties (or when the modal majorities differed in direction), the hypothesis that the partisan distributions originated from the same distribution could be rejected substantively, and is so noted in the tables.

The first thing to note about these tables is that both parties are usually consistent in their modal responses to each question. Question ten on the federal government's obligation to ensure that everyone has a job is an exception on each table. Additionally, question two, abortion should be a personal choice,

and question nine, the federal government should improve the economic condition of blacks, are exceptions in the definition of partisanship by 1992 presidential vote. Thus we are typically talking about differences in degree of cohesiveness around choices about which the parties share a modal preference. This is a critically important observation for understanding the potential for party competition in the region and for establishing expectations for representation by the party organizations.

The next thing to note about these tables is the degree of cohesiveness expressed by the Democrats and Republicans. As there is no generally accepted standard of cohesiveness, let us, for argument's sake, take the lowest level of agreement on a single issue for national Democrats in table 1.5 as the minimum standard. That threshold is 70 percent. For all definitions of national Democratic partisanship, Democrats passed that threshold on every issue. For both definitions of state Democratic partisanship, Democrats passed that threshold on fourteen of fifteen issues. Among Republicans, the threshold was reached on nine of fifteen issues in four definitions of partisanship, and fell to eight of fifteen when the definition of Republican rested on 1992 presidential ballot preference.

These figures tell us that reading the preferences of the southern partisan is generally not difficult on at least a majority of issues. Those who choose to represent as "delegates" (Wahlke et al. 1962) in the party organization should be able to do so. Moreover, these figures tell us that Democrats are more homogenous on our fifteen issues, despite their ideological diversity, than Republicans, who appear more ideologically homogenous, confirming our speculation that the terms "liberal" and "conservative" may embrace a variety of meanings. So it should be easier to represent Democrats than Republicans on the issues, if not on the labels liberal and conservative.

These figures also tell us that there are differences between the parties on their preference distributions that are not attributable to chance, even when they share high levels of cohesion. The tables indicate that differences in modal direction or significant differences of degree occur on at least thirteen of fifteen issues in each

TABLE 1.5

ISSUE DIFFERENCES BETWEEN DEMOCRATS AND REPUBLICANS WHEN PARTY DEFINED BY
NATIONAL IDENTIFICATION

| Issues | DEMOCRATS | | REPUBLICANS | | |
	Mode	Percentage in Mode	Mode	Percentage in mode	Party Difference
Feds should improve economic condition of women	A	94.5 (330)	A	81.4 (311)	13.1*
By law, abortion should be a personal choice	A	74.8 (317)	A	56.2 (306)	18.6*
Increase defense spending	D	76.2 (311)	D	69.3 (300)	6.9
Feds should provide fewer services to reduce spending	D	79.6 (324)	D	55.3 (302)	24.3*
Prayer should be allowed in public schools	A	84.0 (326)	A	90.7 (312)	-6.7*
Increase government spending to protect environment	A	83.5 (316)	A	64.4 (298)	19.1*
Pass constitutional amendment to balance budget	A	79.9 (303)	A	87.5 (304)	-7.6*
In financial crisis, state legislatures should raise taxes	D	72.5 (316)	D	88.1 (303)	-15.6*
Feds should improve economic condition of blacks	A	76.1 (339)	A	52.8 (320)	23.3*
Feds should ensure everyone has a job	A	70.7 (317)	D	57.0 (305)	**
Women should have equal role in running business	A	94.6 (331)	A	87.8 (311)	6.8*
Pay more attention to problems at home	A	88.5 (321)	A	71.8 (298)	16.7*
Continue to cooperate with Russia	A	88.0 (301)	A	92.7 (302)	-4.7
Give blacks preference in hiring and promotion	D	73.9 (318)	D	91.7 (315)	-17.8*
Government should help lower cost of doctors and hospital care	A	95.5 (330)	A	78.9 (303)	16.6*

Note: A = agree; D = disagree.
*Statistically significant at $p \leq .05$.
**Significant difference: different modal direction.

TABLE 1.6

ISSUE DIFFERENCES BETWEEN DEMOCRATS AND REPUBLICANS WHEN PARTY DEFINED BY STATE IDENTIFICATION

| Issues | DEMOCRATS | | REPUBLICANS | | Party Difference |
	Mode	Percentage in Mode	Mode	Percentage in mode	
Feds should improve economic condition of women	A	94.3 (333)	A	81.6 (256)	12.7*
By law, abortion should be a personal choice	A	73.5 (317)	A	52.0 (252)	21.5*
Increase defense spending	D	76.4 (318)	D	68.0 (250)	8.4*
Feds should provide fewer services to reduce spending	D	77.4 (328)	D	56.2 (249)	21.2*
Prayer should be allowed in public schools	A	83.9 (329)	A	92.2 (257)	-8.3*
Increase government spending to protect environment	A	81.8 (319)	A	65.4 (246)	16.4*
Pass constitutional amendment to balance budget	A	81.0 (305)	A	86.9 (252)	-5.9
In financial crisis, state legislatures should raise taxes	D	72.8 (320)	D	89.3 (252)	-16.5*
Feds should improve economic condition of blacks	A	76.0 (341)	A	52.9 (263)	23.1*
Feds should ensure everyone has a job	A	67.4 (322)	D	54.4 (250)	**
Women should have equal role in running business	A	93.7 (333)	A	88.3 (257)	5.4*
Pay more attention to problems at home	A	86.6 (321)	A	71.9 (249)	14.7*
Continue to cooperate with Russia	A	88.2 (304)	A	93.2 (251)	-5.0*
Give blacks preference in hiring and promotion	D	73.8 (321)	D	92.3 (259)	-18.5*
Government should help lower cost of doctors and hospital care	94.8 A	(330)	78.3 A	(253)	16.5*

Note: A = agree; D = disagree.
*Statistically significant at $p \leq .05$.
**Significant difference: different modal direction.

TABLE 1.7

ISSUE DIFFERENCES BETWEEN DEMOCRATS AND REPUBLICANS WHEN PARTY DEFINED BY ONE USUALLY OFFERING THE BEST CANDIDATE FOR PRESIDENT

Issues	DEMOCRATS		REPUBLICANS		Party Difference
	Mode	Percentage in Mode	Mode	Percentage in mode	
Feds should improve economic condition of women	A	93.3 (268)	A	83.3 (377)	10.0*
By law, abortion should be a personal choice	A	78.3 (258)	A	57.0 (374)	21.3*
Increase defense spending	D	77.7 (251)	D	67.8 (366)	9.9*
Feds should provide fewer services to reduce spending	D	81.0 (263)	D	61.2 (371)	19.8*
Prayer should be allowed in public schools	A	81.6 (266)	A	90.2 (379)	-8.6*
Increase government spending to protect environment	A	83.1 (254)	A	66.4 (366)	16.7*
Pass constitutional amendment to balance budget	A	81.7 (251)	A	85.8 (367)	-4.1
In financial crisis, state legislatures should raise taxes	D	74.2 (252)	D	85.6 (376)	-11.4*
Feds should improve economic conditions of blacks	A	77.7 (273)	A	55.1 (390)	22.6*
Feds should ensure everyone has a job	A	74.0 (258)	D	53.1 (373)	**
Women should have equal role in running business	A	92.9 (267)	A	90.8 (382)	2.1*
Pay more attention to problems at home	A	89.6 (259)	A	73.1 (372)	16.5*
Continue to cooperate with Russia	A	85.8 (246)	A	92.9 (366)	-7.1*
Give blacks preference in hiring and promotion	D	71.0 (252)	D	90.3 (381)	-19.3*
Government should help lower cost of doctors and hospital care	A	95.8 (265)	A	81.2 (373)	14.6*

Note: A = agree; D = disagree.
*Statistically significant at $p \leq .05$.
**Significant difference: different modal direction.

TABLE 1.8

ISSUE DIFFERENCES BETWEEN DEMOCRATS AND REPUBLICANS WHEN PARTY DEFINED BY ONE USUALLY OFFERING THE BEST CANDIDATE FOR GOVERNOR

Issues	DEMOCRATS		REPUBLICANS		Party Difference
	Mode	Percentage in Mode	Mode	Percentage in mode	
Feds should improve economic condition of women	A	93.9 (343)	A	82.6 (270)	11.3*
By law, abortion should be a personal choice	A	73.0 (333)	A	55.6 (266)	17.4*
Increase defense spending	D	76.9 (333)	D	66.0 (259)	10.9*
Feds should provide fewer services to reduce spending	D	76.4 (339)	D	59.0 (266)	17.4*
Prayer should be allowed in public schools	A	82.7 (342)	A	92.3 (272)	-9.6*
Increase government spending to protect environment	A	82.6 (333)	A	64.1 (259)	18.5*
Pass constitutional amendment to balance budget	A	81.1 (322)	A	86.6 (268)	-5.5
In financial crisis, state legislatures should raise taxes	D	73.6 (330)	D	89.2 (269)	-15.6*
Feds should improve economic conditions of blacks	A	72.8 (353)	A	52.5 (278)	20.3*
Feds should ensure everyone has a job	A	69.5 (331)	D	53.4 (268)	**
Women should have equal role in running business	A	93.6 (346)	A	89.3 (271)	4.3*
Pay more attention to problems at home	A	86.9 (337)	A	73.6 (265)	13.3*
Continue to cooperate with Russia	A	87.8 (320)	A	92.0 (262)	-4.2*
Give blacks preference in hiring and promotion	D	74.3 (335)	D	90.7 (270)	-16.4*
Government should help lower cost of doctors and hospital care	A	94.2 (342)	A	79.2 (269)	15.0*

Note: A = agree; D = disagree.
*Statistically significant at $p \leq 05$.
**Significant difference: different modal direction.

TABLE 1.9

ISSUE DIFFERENCES BETWEEN DEMOCRATS AND REPUBLICANS WHEN PARTY DEFINED BY 1992 MAJOR PARTY PRESIDENTIAL VOTE

Issues	DEMOCRATS		REPUBLICANS		Party Difference
	Mode	Percentage in Mode	Mode	Percentage in mode	
Feds should improve economic condition of women	A	95.6 (272)	A	78.7 (249)	16.9*
By law, abortion should be a personal choice	A	82.1 (262)	A	47.5 (242)	***
Increase defense spending	D	81.9 (259)	D	69.0 (232)	12.9*
Feds should provide fewer services to reduce spending	D	81.9 (270)	D	53.8 (240)	28.1*
Prayer should be allowed in public schools	A	80.1 (272)	A	93.2 (250)	-13.1*
Increase government spending to protect environment	A	82.6 (265)	A	61.6 (237)	21.0*
Pass constitutional amendment to balance budget	A	78.3 (253)	A	86.1 (237)	-7.8*
In financial crisis, state legislatures should raise taxes	D	71.3 (258)	D	87.6 (241)	-16.3*
Feds should improve economic conditions of blacks	A	78.6 (280)	D	50.2 (255)	**
Feds should ensure everyone has a job	A	70.8 (260)	D	65.7 (242)	**
Women should have equal role in running business	A	95.3 (276)	A	88.4 (250)	6.9*
Pay more attention to problems at home	A	87.1 (264)	A	67.9 (237)	19.2*
Continue to cooperate with Russia	A	89.2 (251)	A	93.6 (236)	-4.4*
Give blacks preference in hiring and promotion	D	75.9 (261)	D	92.8 (249)	-16.9*
Government should help lower cost of doctors and hospital care	A	97.4 (273)	A	75.6 (242)	21.8*

Note: A = agree; D = disagree.

*Statistically significant at $p \leq 05$.

**Significant difference: different modal direction.

***Significant difference: The modal category for Republicans (A) did not reflect the direction of the party majority; therefore, a majority of Republicans disagreed (D) with the statement.

table. And the signs of the party difference coefficients point to the recognizable patterns of issue cleavages between the parties. For example, in four of five definitions of Republicans, these partisans were more likely than Democrats to agree that prayer should be allowed in the public schools, to pass a constitutional amendment to balance the budget, to continue cooperation with Russia, and to disagree with higher state taxes in a financial crisis and with giving blacks preferences in hiring and promotion. To these we add that, in four of five definitions of Republicans, they disagreed that the federal government should ensure that everyone has a job, whereas Democrats agreed. When it came to defining Republicans by their behavior, the list expanded. Instead of marginally agreeing that abortion was a personal choice by law, now Republicans disagreed. The same flip occurred on the issue of whether the federal government should improve economic conditions for blacks.

Southern Democrats generally prefer a greater degree of governmental activism than southern Republicans, especially in support of social welfare and of gender and minority equity issues. Democrats generally are more likely to want government to improve the economic condition of women, to treat abortion as a personal choice, to increase environmental spending, to improve the economic condition of blacks, to ensure that everyone has a job, to believe that women should play an equal role in running business, to pay more attention to problems at home, and to help lower the cost of doctors and hospital care. They are similarly more likely to disagree that defense spending should be increased and to disagree that the federal government should provide fewer services to reduce spending. With the exception of defense spending among national identifiers, and the place of women in the business world among both presidential and gubernatorial preferrers, all of these differences are statistically significant.

Appraising the Southern Mass Sample

We began this chapter by focusing on the need to establish to what the parties as organizations would be held accountable to respond. We indicated that the socioeconomic and demographic characteristics of the southern electorate would provide us a window on their potential interests, agendas, and group loyalties, things to which any party organization should attend if it wishes to succeed. We noted that our perspective was not new, but shared by our Founding Fathers, as well as by a long scholarly literature.

That the parties differed was not a surprise. Neither were the fault lines of their differences. They reflected images of Democrats and Republicans widely shared in the popular consciousness, indeed, reminiscent of class lectures delivered by each of the authors and, no doubt, by many of this book's readers. Affirming that portrait is, nevertheless, an important task, and it lays the foundation for descriptive representation by party organizations.

The partisan ideological distributions may have raised some eyebrows. Democrats are more symmetric around a modal moderate orientation than the Dixiecrat portrait of the pre–Voting Rights Act era. Republicans, on the other hand, are now both numerous and modally conservative. Yet we must strike an important note of caution and alert the reader that we are not at all confident that the meanings of liberal and conservative are transcendently shared, especially when overlaid on the history of southern populism.

The legacy of the Reagan revolution against the expanded liberal agenda of New Deal/Great Society Democrats is fresh in the issue portraits of the two parties. The national partisan divide has punched through the Mason-Dixon line and grabbed the South, suggesting that the years of southern isolation and unique politics may be waning, if not over. To be sure, we do not disagree with Tip O'Neill's aphorism "All politics is local." We simply have observed that local politics in the South is being played against a national, not only a regional, landscape. This leads us to expect that collective representation is possible at all levels of the party organization, unless southern occasional activists, especially among convention delegates (Nexon 1971), eschew their local origins.

Chapter 2

Southern Party Elites

We have a portrait now of the southern rank-and-file party member from a number of different definitional perspectives. This chapter provides us the same type of portrait for southern party leaders. However, we will focus on only one definition of party for the leadership cadre, their formal membership, because our ultimate concern lies in assessing the effectiveness of party organizational representation.

Party Membership and Party Identification

To be sure, the literature provides examples of conflict between formal party membership and party identification even for elites. Hadley's (1985) findings of conflict between party membership and party identification for significant percentages of southern party elites were and are startling. Because the psychological tensions leaders experience as individuals

---

This chapter was written with the assistance of Charles D. Hadley.

may affect how well or how diligently they represent rank-and-file partisans, it is important for us to provide a rough measurement of the party member–party identifier divergence. Table 2.1 shows the distribution of party identification for national and state partisanship by formal party membership for county party chairs, committee members, and convention delegates. Independent leaners have been classified as Democrats or Republicans, leaving only pure independents in the central category (Keith et al. 1992).

The greatest divergence occurs between formal membership and national party identification among southern Democratic elites. Nearly 10 percent of Democratic county committee members and 6 percent of Democratic county party chairs did not identify with the Democratic party nationally. Their state identifications were more consistent with formal membership, county committee members lagging somewhat behind county chairs and convention delegates. Little variation occurs among southern Republican elites. A small percentage diverge, but nothing that approaches the cleavage among local Democratic party elites and national

TABLE 2.1

PERCENTAGE OF SOUTHERN DEMOCRATIC AND REPUBLICAN PARTY LEADERS IDENTIFYING
THEMSELVES AS NATIONAL AND STATE DEMOCRATS, INDEPENDENTS, AND REPUBLICANS

Party Identification	DEMOCRATS			REPUBLICANS		
	Party Chairs	Committee Members	Convention Delegates	Party Chairs	Committee Members	Convention Delegates
National						
Democrat	94.0	90.7	98.4	0.5	0.5	0.2
Independent	2.7	3.4	0.8	0.7	1.1	0.4
Republican	3.3	5.9	0.8	98.8	98.4	99.4
(N)	583	4,399	493	603	4,197	499
State						
Democrat	98.5	96.3	99.6	0.7	1.0	0.6
Independent	0.8	1.8	0.4	0.5	1.4	0.4
Republican	0.7	2.0	0.0	98.8	97.7	99.0
(N)	602	4,563	495	604	4,193	499

party identification. Reinforcing this observation is the voting behavior of southern party elites in 1988. Among Republicans, southern county chairs, committee members, and convention delegates supported the Bush/Quayle ticket by percentages of 98.0, 97.9, and 98.6, respectively. Southern Democrats were less loyal to the top of the ticket. While 94.2 percent of southern Democratic convention delegates balloted for Dukakis/Bentsen, 84 percent of county chairs and only 77.7 percent of county committee members followed suit. Assuming that partisanship summarizes an approach to politics, especially when it is confirmed by voting behavior, these findings suggest that we should be prepared for the possibility of two outcomes. First, we may see greater disagreement among southern Democratic elites than Republican elites on issues that have a national, as opposed to a local, orientation. Second, we may observe greater variation in Democrats' ability to represent their rank and file than Republicans display in representing theirs.

Political Ideology

While it is true that "ideology" is a term used loosely in American politics, even among elites, it is also generally accepted that those for whom politics is a greater preoccupation should have a better developed belief system. Hence, southern party elites should feel less discomfited by liberal, moderate, or conservative labels and should be more able than the rank and file, on average, to use those terms to characterize themselves. But what should our expectations be about homogeneity within the southern parties? At least since the middle 1970s, observers of mass political behavior have noted that Republicans were becoming more homogeneously conservative, while the Democratic party retained identifiable liberal and conservative wings (Nie, Verba, and Petrocik 1976). At the same time, the migration of northerners into the South and the gradual emergence of the Republican party as a realistic alternative to Democrats, at least for federal and statewide offices, occurred (Black and Black 1987). Would this migration moderate the conservative tendencies of traditionalistic southern politics (Elazar 1972)? Similarly, would the mobilization of African Americans since the Voting Rights Act (Stanley 1987) and their persistent loyalty to the Democratic party (Stanley and Niemi 1995) have a similar effect on the conservatism of southern Democrats? And how would these trends, whose legacy we observed in chapter 1's mass sample analysis, emerge in our sample of elites, if at all? Table 2.2 addresses these concerns.

The ideological distributions of southern party elites could not be more different. Republicans are well skewed toward the conservative camp: 90.5 percent of county party chairs, 84.5 percent of county committee members, and 90.9 percent of national convention delegates called themselves conservative. Nothing even close to that can be found among Democrats. The greatest ideological concentration is liberals among Democratic convention delegates, and that totals a meager 57.8 percent. Southern Democratic chairs and committee members are almost equivalently distributed in nearly equal thirds among liberals, moderates, and conservatives. Only 5.1 percent of southern Democratic convention delegates in our sample identified themselves as conservative, however. Heavily moderate, reflecting their fellow southern party leaders, delegates

were leavened with many more liberals. The "wings" of the Democratic rank and file are reproduced among the local elite, but *not* among the delegates. Recall that Dukakis/Bentsen received their most solid support from among convention delegates in our sample. Republicans, by contrast, almost caricature the rank-and-file distribution presented in the literature and depicted in the last chapter, so overwhelming is their conservatism.

How do these findings contribute to our expectations for representation? Again, to the degree that liberalism and conservatism possess some consensual meaning in American politics—a point of some dispute (Maggiotto 1983, 1984a, 1984b)—we might infer that a greater consensus on policy preferences will exist among Republican than among Democratic party elites. Representationally, however, to the degree that Republican party elites fall farther to the right than the Republican rank and file, policy agreement across levels should break down. It may be, therefore, that the diversity of the Democratic party's ideological image in the South may be more reflective of the party's rank-and-file turmoil, thus contributing to the Democratic party organization's ability to better represent its mass partisans. We shall see to what degree this speculation contributes to explaining party linkage in chapter 3.

TABLE 2.2

PERCENTAGE OF SOUTHERN DEMOCRATIC AND REPUBLICAN PARTY LEADERS IDENTIFYING THEMSELVES AS LIBERALS, MODERATES, OR CONSERVATIVES

| Ideology | DEMOCRATS | | | REPUBLICANS | | |
	Party Chairs	Committee Members	Convention Delegates	Party Chairs	Committee Members	Convention Delegates
Liberal	35.2	37.3	57.8	1.2	2.6	0.4
Moderate	35.4	34.7	37.1	8.3	13.0	8.6
Conservative	29.3	28.0	5.1	90.5	84.5	90.9
(N)	604	4794	493	603	4,193	487

The Sociodemography of Southern Party Elites

As was the case in chapter 1, we delve into the socio-demographic makeup of southern party elites because we recognize the importance of social groups as the catalyst for, and the manifestation of, interests. We trace the value of descriptive representation to the belief-sharing model presented by Luttbeg (1981). Common experiences rooted in social location affect the wishes and values that become the political demands and supports of the body politic. It is easier for the party organization to understand the language of the rank and file if it can empathize with its fellow partisans. Merely recognizing a problem may fail to reveal its intensity. Absent a visceral connection, an agenda item may be overlooked or misperceived. If the sociodemographic distribution of the party elite maps accurately the same distributions of the rank-and-file partisans, at least that portion of representation that owes to empathy born of social location will be part of the party organization's repertoire. The data describing salient characteristics of southern party elites are contained in the panels of table 2.3.

Gender

For both political parties, the role of county party chair was dominated by men in the early 1990s. From nearly three-quarters male among chairs, male dominance among party committee members drops to just over 60 percent in our sample. Greater parity between the sexes is achieved among convention delegates. National party delegate selection rules contribute to this phenomenon, but not equivalently so (Polsby 1983; Shafer 1983; Kirkpatrick 1978). Democrats and Republicans are mirror opposites in the sample proportion of men and women who represented the South in the party conventions of 1992: 56.6 percent of southern Democratic delegates were female; 55.1 percent of southern Republican delegates were men. Recall that, by comparison, over 60 percent of Democratic national and state party identifiers in our sample were female, whereas Republicans were nearly evenly split.

Race/Ethnicity

As would be expected from the voting strength of African Americans in the South and their loyalty to the Democratic party, a larger percentage of Democratic county chairs, committee members, and convention delegates are African American. Although the numbers are small, a greater proportion of Democratic, as opposed to Republican, party leadership positions are staffed in the South by Hispanic Americans. This is true, as well, of Native Americans at the local level, but not among convention delegates. Republicans are considerably more racially and ethnically homogeneous than Democrats, as measured here. Over 90 percent of each Republican leadership element in our southern sample is white, figures that approach the racial composition of the southern Republican rank and file.

Education

Democrats have traditionally attracted more adherents from the lower rungs of the socioeconomic ladder than have Republicans. We might expect Democratic party leaders, therefore, to be somewhat less well educated than Republicans. At the same time, Democrats have traditionally attracted members of the academic and artistic elite, which should skew the educational distribution upwards. Perhaps again, the "wing" metaphor is most appropriate. Republicans should bulk in the middle and upper reaches of educational achievement. Neither party's leadership cadre should include substantial numbers from the lowest educational levels. The image of the machine party hack burlesques the characteristics of local party leaders (Maggiotto and Weber 1986), and even more so those of convention delegates (Miller and Jennings 1986). Thus we expect to see a higher level of education in both parties than in the mass public, but among leaders we expect to see a "winged" structure among Democrats and an upward skewness among Republicans.

The data conform to these expectations. Virtually none of the leaders of either party terminated their education at the grade school level. But at this point it is worth distinguishing convention delegates from county-based leaders. Convention delegates in both parties are highly educated. The differences within party levels are most apparent among Democrats, as almost 48 percent of Democratic convention delegates held graduate degrees or pursued some postgraduate education. County-level Democrats were more likely to be high school graduates or to have had only some college experience. The drop-off in college graduates is counterbalanced by the heavy weighting of leaders in the postgraduate cells of the table. Loosely, this corresponds to a wing depiction among local Democrats which is not repeated among Republicans. With some variation, especially among county committee members, the Republican distribution mounds at higher educational levels, although its peak in the postgraduate cells is lower than among Democrats.

Income

The party expectations for income should parallel those for education, because each is a component of the usual measures of socioeconomic status and each is typically positively correlated with the other. In fact, the same broad outlines appear in the data.

Few leaders from either party earned less than ten thousand dollars per year in our samples. More Democrats than Republicans and, for each party, more committee members than county chairs or convention delegates earned less than thirty thousand dollars per year. The income distribution for local leaders is not substantially dissimilar between thirty thousand and seventy thousand dollars, although Republicans are somewhat advantaged. The highest measurement category is populated by a few more Democrat than Republican county party chairs, but substantially more Republican than Democratic committee members. The Republican edge continues among convention delegates, with just shy of 50 percent falling in the category of seventy thousand dollars or more per year. Indeed, for all but Democratic county committee members, the modal income category is seventy thousand or more. Compared to the rank and file, the party leadership cadres of both parties are a well-heeled lot.

Age

The well-known relationship between age and political activism suggests that party activity should not loom large in any cohort until it enters early middle age (Verba and Nie 1972). While we recognize that protest movements are well populated by the young and affected by the sociopolitical context within which the young find themselves (Barnes and Kaase 1979; Jennings and Niemi 1981), party organizational involvement in the United States throughout the period in question is much more mundane an activity than even the social movements from which modern parties routinely draw their more innovative, if older, leaders (Baer and Bositis 1988). Thus we should expect the leadership cadres of both parties to be older than their rank-and-file identifiers. This difference should be particularly apparent in the youngest category.

Indeed that is the case. Only small numbers of those less than thirty years old appear in our samples of either party. They were most numerous among delegates to national conventions, where parties consciously seek to showcase young faces for television audiences. For both parties, local organizational involvement is the province of middle-aged activists, typically between ages forty and seventy. After seventy the drop-off is substantial, again, as would be expected from a disengagement hypothesis, unless one assumed that this older cohort participated with less frequency in the party organization throughout its lifetime. While it is true that the opportunities for Republican party activism were dramatically fewer in earlier decades, there was no dearth of opportunities for Democratic party activity, especially for white males and increasingly for a more representative cross-section of the population in the last twenty to twenty-five years.

Religion

If we take our cues from the responses of the mass samples, Democratic leaders should be concentrated among the pietistic and fundamentalist Protestant denominations and among Roman Catholics. To

TABLE 2.3

SOCIODEMOGRAPHIC PORTRAIT OF SOUTHERN DEMOCRATIC AND REPUBLICAN PARTY
ORGANIZATION LEADERS

	DEMOCRATS			REPUBLICANS		
	Party Chairs	Committee Members	Convention Delegates	Party Chairs	Committee Members	Convention Delegates
Characteristics	(%)	(%)	(%)	(%)	(%)	(%)
Gender						
Male	77.7	61.6	43.4	74.1	62.3	55.1
Female	22.3	38.4	56.6	25.9	37.7	44.9
(N)	611	4,844	505	603	4,199	505
Race						
White	86.9	78.8	75.9	96.0	91.3	92.3
Black	6.0	14.3	16.0	0.8	2.0	2.5
Hispanic American	2.7	1.3	4.9	0.3	0.6	1.9
Asian American	0.0	0.1	0.4	0.0	0.1	0.0
Native American	1.2	1.0	0.6	0.3	0.6	0.9
Other	3.3	4.4	2.2	2.5	5.4	2.0
(N)	602	4,787	493	598	4,171	483
Education						
Grade school	0.3	3.8	0.2	0.5	1.0	0.4
High school	14.4	22.4	5.0	8.7	12.6	5.8
Some college	26.1	28.3	23.9	27.3	31.8	26.9
College	20.6	17.2	23.1	32.5	29.8	34.1
Graduate school	38.7	28.3	47.8	31.0	24.7	32.9
(N)	613	4,895	502	607	4,214	502
Income ($)						
<10K	1.8	4.8	1.8	1.0	1.8	0.8
10–<20K	5.3	11.8	2.6	4.2	7.2	1.3
20–<30K	10.1	16.2	5.5	8.5	13.0	5.7
30–<40K	14.1	16.9	12.6	15.1	16.0	9.5
40–<50K	13.8	14.8	11.6	17.1	14.6	15.0
50–<60K	14.0	11.3	12.8	13.7	13.2	10.4
60–<70K	8.0	7.4	11.0	11.3	8.8	8.0
>70K	32.9	16.8	42.2	29.1	25.3	49.3
(N)	602	4,728	493	591	4,057	473

TABLE 2.3 (CONTINUED)

Characteristics	DEMOCRATS			REPUBLICANS		
	Party Chairs (%)	Committee Members (%)	Convention Delegates (%)	Party Chairs (%)	Committee Members (%)	Convention Delegates (%)
Age (years)						
<30	1.7	2.3	5.4	2.3	4.1	5.6
30–<40	14.0	12.3	19.4	16.4	15.3	14.8
40–<50	26.3	22.1	30.1	22.6	21.4	24.6
50–<60	23.3	21.1	25.4	25.5	22.1	27.9
60–<70	25.0	25.0	15.3	23.6	23.8	20.0
>70	9.8	17.3	4.5	9.5	13.5	7.1
(*N*)	605	4,778	485	597	4,159	480
Religion						
General						
Protestant	7.3	5.5	5.6	10.6	9.8	8.4
Mainline Protestant	12.2	13.5	18.5	20.7	22.3	29.1
Pietistic Protestant	45.3	46.5	34.5	38.9	34.3	29.3
Fundamentalist	21.0	19.0	6.5	21.2	20.6	16.1
Nontraditional	0.7	1.6	3.4	0.8	1.1	1.4
Roman Catholic	10.9	9.0	18.8	6.3	9.3	13.7
Jewish	0.8	2.0	7.3	0.3	0.7	1.2
Other	0.7	0.6	0.6	0.2	0.3	0.2
Nonbeliever	1.1	2.4	4.8	1.0	1.5	0.6
(*N*)	614	4,874	496	604	4,193	502
Length of residence (years)						
<10	1.0	2.9	7.4	5.5	7.5	6.8
10–<20	4.6	8.0	9.7	8.7	15.8	13.1
20–<30	5.8	8.6	14.7	11.4	15.2	20.1
>30	88.6	80.5	68.2	74.5	61.5	60.0
(*N*)	603	4,790	484	597	4,154	482

that, Republican leaders would add mainline Protestant denominations and a somewhat larger number of nonbelievers.

The broad outlines of these distributions are consistent with our expectations, although the specifics vary, especially among convention delegates. Leaders of both parties were less likely to be members of fundamentalist denominations and more likely to be members of pietistic and mainline Protestant denominations than rank-and-file partisans. There is also a smaller representation of Roman Catholics among leaders than among mass partisans of either party. The mass-elite Protestant denominational differences are most apparent among convention delegates, yet there are more Roman Catholics among delegates than among local party elites, and delegates more nearly map the proportions of Catholics among mass partisans than do local party elites.

To the degree that fundamentalism and Roman Catholicism are correlated with politically expressed values, there may be some divergence in the Democratic party's ability to respond in line with the demands of its rank-and-file partisans.

Length of Residence

Length of residence is a measure of one's community embeddedness, which, we know, is correlated positively with political participation (Verba, Schlozman, and Brady 1995). Moreover, because of the local focus of local party activity, those particularly well enmeshed in the locale might be expected to be most involved in the organizational dynamics of the party. Issue activism that transcends parochial boundaries should be less affected by length of residence. Similarly, national activism should be less affected by residence conceptually. That should be reflected in the residential longevity distribution of delegates, whose loyalties of late are more reflective of candidate commitment than of party organizational loyalty (Bartels 1988). Practically, however, residential longevity should continue to have some impact, for status as a delegate remains partly a reward for party service (Crotty and Jackson 1985).

Moreover, even primary campaigning often enlists state and local organization elites, especially if they are tied to popular statewide or local officeholders (Norrander 1992; Trish 1994).

Our results clearly document the impact of community embeddedness as indexed by length of residence. The overwhelming majority of leaders resided in their communities for more than thirty years. County chairs show the highest percentages of long-time residents, and delegates the least, although among Democrats the difference between committee members and delegates is very small.

Party leaders differ from rank-and-file partisans in important ways. To the degree that their sociodemographic characteristics are fertile ground for political and life experiences to germinate, we might anticipate some divergence between leaders and rank-and-file partisans in political agendas, issue positions, or the intensity of commitment. We begin that exploration by portraying the position of party elites on fifteen core issues of the 1992 electoral cycle.

Issue Positions of Southern Party Elites

Symbolic representation without an alliance structure that produces winning coalitions will ultimately fail to satisfy substantive demands (Browning, Marshall, and Tabb 1984). Thus cracking the race or gender or age or income barrier is not enough. For organizations to represent their members, organizational leaders must reflect the views of the rank and file. To be sure, to get something on the agenda for discussion and legitimation (Kingdon 1984), the distribution of elite attitudes is less important than the presence of the attitude, but for an agenda item to become important, to have a chance at becoming policy, it must have a coalitional basis for success (Kingdon 1981). These congressional analogies are important for the party organization, insofar as we seek to measure the party organization's capacity for transmitting popular views to the actionable arenas of legislatures, courts, and executive offices. Let us turn to that now by examining first the Democratic, then the Republican, leaders in our southern sample.

Democratic Party Leaders

Table 2.4 presents two bits of data: the modal response given by each element of the party leadership cadre in our sample of Democrats for each issue and the percentage of respondents in that modal category. These data will allow us to assess attitudinal consistency across and cohesion within leader categories.

The southern Democratic leadership group presents a consistent policy image on twelve of the fifteen issues in table 2.4. On the three issues where disagreement exists, it is convention delegates who are out of step with local leaders. County party chairs and committee members agree that prayer should be allowed in the public schools and that a constitutional amendment balancing the budget should be passed. Convention delegates disagree with both initiatives. Delegates agree that the federal government should ensure that everyone has a job, a guarantee with which county party chairs and committee members disagree. Recalling the answers given by the mass sample to these three questions, for every definition of partisan, the rank-and-file Democrats agreed with all three of these policies: allowing prayer in the public schools, balancing the budget through a constitutional amendment, and ensuring full employment even through federal government action.

The cohesion expressed by each leadership cadre differs. Generally, convention delegates appear more united in their commitment than county chairs or committee members. On average, 82.9 percent of delegates, 77.3 percent of chairs, and 76.5 percent of members adhered to the modal response. Moreover, on eight issues, Democratic convention delegates registered over 90 percent agreement with the modal alternative. By contrast, county chairs evidenced that degree of unanimity only once, when asked whether the United States should continue to cooperate with Russia. Committee members exceeded 90 percent support of the modal response on two issues, cooperation with Russia and government help to lower the cost of doctor and hospital care.

Let us look more closely at the issues on which there was strong agreement in at least one leadership cohort. Three issues elicited high support across the board: women having an equal role in running businesses, continuing cooperation with Russia, and government assistance in controlling health-care costs. While chairs dipped below 90 percent support on two issues and members on one, chairs and members supported the consistent agree mode at least 88 percent of the time. Less agreement existed among the other five issues. Increasing government spending to protect the environment was greeted with somewhat less enthusiasm at the local level than among convention delegates.

More substantial disagreements existed on "wedge" issues, likely to separate people ideologically. Economic gender equity and prochoice abortion were greeted with much less enthusiasm among local elites than among convention delegates. Local elites were also much less likely to disagree with increases in defense spending. And less than 70 percent of both chairs and members agreed that the federal government should work to improve the economic condition of African Americans. Not only are these issues laden with ideological baggage, but they are identified with the *national* agenda of the Democratic party. That disagreement on elements of the national agenda is most clearly evident between local leaders and convention delegates may help explain some of the gap between organizational affiliation and party identification. Local Democratic leaders simply disagree more often with their party's national issue positions. Convention delegates, being more close tied to the creation of the party platform, may feel a greater degree of ownership of the national agenda and, therefore, may feel fewer conflicts that would manifest themselves in a divergence between organizational partisanship and party identification.

Representationally, we can suggest several conclusions. First, southern Democratic party leaders generally appear to present a united front on issues. On the three issues on which the leaders disagreed, there were generally lower levels of coherence among each leadership cohort, suggesting a real internal debate within all levels of leadership. Second, Democrats appeared relatively cohesive about their policy preferences, averaging above 75 percent support for

TABLE 2.4
ISSUES DIFFERENCES AMONG DEMOCRATIC PARTY LEADERS

Issue	PARTY CHAIRS		COMMITTEE MEMBERS		CONVENTION DELEGATES	
	Mode	Percentage in Mode	Mode	Percentage in Mode	Mode	Percentage in Mode
Feds improve economic condition women	A	86.4 (591)	A	80.8 (4,638)	A	95.9 (487)
By law, abortion should be a personal choice	A	80.1 (588)	A	72.9 (4,668)	A	96.3 (484)
Increase defense spending	D	73.3 (586)	D	70.7 (4,557)	D	96.5 (484)
Feds provide fewer services to reduce spending	D	71.6 (595)	D	73.6 (4,701)	D	85.5 (482)
Prayer should be allowed in public schools	A	67.1 (590)	A	72.1 (4,624)	D	56.2 (475)
Increase government spending to protect environment	A	83.9 (601)	A	84.3 (4,663)	A	90.9 (483)
Pass constitutional amendment to balance budget	A	63.4 (585)	A	69.7 (4,575)	D	61.1 (465)
In financial crisis state legislatures should raise taxes	D	67.4 (583)	D	71.5 (4,671)	D	62.6 (468)
Feds should improve economic conditions of blacks	A	69.6 (585)	A	68.1 (4,629)	A	90.3 (483)
Feds should ensure everyone has a job	D	61.0 (593)	D	53 (4,651)	D	68.8 (474)
Women should have equal role in running business	S	88.4 (587)	A	88.7 (4,679)	A	97.9 (486)
Pay more attention to problems at home	A	81.8 (600)	A	82.1 (4,723)	A	85.2 (479)
Continue to cooperate with Russia	A	95.3 (588)	A	90.6 (4,595)	A	97.9 (475)
Give blacks preference in hiring and promotion	D	81.4 (592)	D	78.3 (4,679)	D	63.7 (474)
Government should help lower costs of doctors and hospital care	A	88.5 (597)	A	90.7 (4,705)	A	94.8 (482)

Note: A = agree; D = disagree.

the modal choice for each cohort. There was dispersion around the cohort means, with delegates more likely to cluster above the 90 percent threshold than local elites. But chairs and delegates cohered at more than 70 percent on ten issues, members on twelve. Third, while the Democratic alternative was clear on most, if not all, issues, on at least one leadership level, sufficient diversity of opinion existed to suggest that multiple agendas were being voiced within the party.

Republican Party Leaders

The same information presented in table 2.4 is repeated for Republican party leaders in table 2.5. Thus we will be able to identify Republican issue consistency and cohesion.

Republicans were consistent on ten of fifteen issues, two fewer than Democrats. But there was no issue overlap between the two parties. In fact, on the issues on which Democratic leadership cohorts disagreed, Republicans showed relatively solid cohesion. They favored school prayer and a balanced budget amendment and opposed federal employment guarantees. Republicans disagreed among themselves on economic gender equity, increasing defense spending, increasing spending to protect the environment, focusing more attention at home, and government assistance in controlling health-care costs. However, unlike Democrats, there is no readily identifiable local-national split separating Republicans on the issues that divided them. On three issues—gender equity, attention to home problems, and health-care cost containment—county committee members were out of step with chairs and delegates, who opposed the initiatives. On two issues—increasing defense spending and increasing spending for environmental protection—convention delegates marched to a different drummer, opposing what local party officials supported.

Broadly, Republicans displayed the same pattern of cohesion as Democrats, but at a slightly lower level: 78.4 percent of delegates, 74.9 percent of chairs, and 73.1 percent of members supported cohort modal alternatives on average. Delegates supported the mode at the 90 percent level six times, chairs four and members twice. The contrast in levels of cohesion between

delegates and chairs was less stark among Republicans than among Democrats. At the 70 percent support threshold, delegates and chairs held firm on nine issues, members on only eight—a substantial drop from the twelve issues on which Democratic committee members crossed the 70 percent line.

More revealing, perhaps, is the degree of marginal issue support. Summing the number of instances in which at least one leadership cohort failed to support the modal response by at least 70 percent provides an interesting contrast between the two parties. Democrats fell below the bar thirteen times, Republicans nineteen. But of the thirteen instances, Democratic support fell below 60 percent only twice. On fully thirteen of nineteen instances among Republicans, modal support was between 50 and 60 percent.

Let us look at the issues where at least one cohort expressed 90 percent cohesion around its modal response. On two issues, all three Republican leadership cohorts registered their opposition by at least 90 percent: allowing state legislatures to raise taxes in cases of financial crisis and giving blacks preference in hiring and promotions. The support of committee members is just shy of the 90 percent threshold, which would have pushed agreement with the enactment of a school prayer amendment into the first and highest category of cohesion. Both chairs and delegates dissented from governmental guarantees of employment at the 90 percent level; committee members dissented at the high 80 percent level. Again, strong agreement existed across cohorts, although only convention delegates passed the 90 percent threshold, in favoring passage of a balanced budget amendment. These high levels of agreement broke down somewhat when Republicans were asked about continued cooperation with Russia. Over 93 percent of delegates, but only about 80 percent of chairs and members, agreed with this policy.

Let us repeat this exercise at the other end of the spectrum, looking at the thirteen instances where at least one Republican cohort's modal position lay between 50 and 60 percent. On two issues, economic gender equity and the amount of attention paid to problems at home, all three cohorts registered low

TABLE 2.5

ISSUES DIFFERENCES AMONG REPUBLICAN PARTY LEADERS

| Issue | PARTY CHAIRS | | COMMITTEE MEMBERS | | CONVENTION DELEGATES | |
	Mode	Percentage in Mode	Mode	Percentage in Mode	Mode	Percentage in Mode
Feds improve economic condition women	D	55.5 (585)	A	52.5 (4,047)	D	52.2 (475)
By law, abortion should be a personal choice	D	58.4 (586)	D	57.3 (4,110)	D	65.3 (475)
Increase defense spending	A	57.8 (584)	A	59.3 (4045)	D	75.8 (475)
Feds provide fewer services to reduce spending	A	84.9 (593)	A	73.3 (4,093)	A	82.9 (484)
Prayer should be allowed in public schools	A	94.0 (596)	A	89.6 (4,090)	A	91.3 (474)
Increase government spending to protect environment	A	55.3 (586)	A	64.7 (4,079)	D	62.3 (482)
Pass constitutional amendment to balance budget	A	88.9 (596)	A	87.7 (4,072)	A	91.5 (480)
In financial crisis, state legislatures should raise taxes	D	95.8 (597)	D	92.5 (4,130)	D	98.4 (484)
Feds should improve economic conditions of blacks	D	73.8 (588)	D	67.5 (4,051)	D	66.7 (474)
Feds should ensure everyone has a job	D	91.1 (595)	D	87.4 (4,095)	D	92.9 (483)
Women should have equal role in running business	A	80.0 (590)	A	80.4 (4,059)	A	84.8 (467)
Pay more attention to problems at home	D	50.9 (582)	A	55.2 (4,085)	D	56.6 (472)
Continue to cooperate with Russia	A	81.7 (579)	A	79.9 (4,020)	A	93.7 (478)
Give blacks preference in hiring and promotion	D	97.8 (593)	D	96.6 (4,143)	D	96.9 (485)
Government should help lower costs of doctors and hospital care	D	56.8 (586)	A	52.3 (4,047)	A	64.7 (478)

Note: A = agree; D = disagree.

levels of support. Note that these issues are among the five on which the party showed strains of inconsistency. Two more issues, from among the five inconsistent issues, produced at least two Republican cohorts with low cohesion levels: increasing defense spending and government involvement in health-care cost control. The last of the five inconsistent issues, increasing government spending to protect the environment, is supported by only 55 percent of chairs but more than 60 percent of committee members, while more than 60 percent of convention delegates opposed the policy. Interestingly, the only other issue to produce instances of modal support in the lowest cohesion category was abortion. Prochoice opposition, though somewhat more pronounced among delegates, remained below 60 percent for both local party cohorts.

In sum, southern Republicans in our leadership sample proved to be both less consistent and less cohesive in their issue positions than their Democratic counterparts. Whether we counted the number of issue-cohort discrepancies or assessed the degree of modal support, Republican leaders showed less coherence than Democrats. This is certainly not what one would have hypothesized from the party leaders' ideological self-identifications or from the parties' sociodemographic portraits. Democratic leaders were more divided ideologically, consistent with the "wing" metaphor, than Republicans, whose distribution was skewed in the direction of conservatism. Moreover, Democrat leaders were more racially diverse and appeared to be more inclusive of those with differing economic resources and educational backgrounds. In short, Democratic leaders seemed more heterogeneous than Republicans. But that comparative heterogeneity did not manifest itself in greater issue-cohort dissensus: quite the contrary.

Representation and Party Elites

Democratic and Republican organizational leaders in the South are not clones of one another. Comparing the data presented in this chapter with those in chapter 1, we can conclude that each party "describes" its own sociodemographic and ideological coalition somewhat better than the other. To the degree that agenda items originate in group experiences, both parties in the South present a leadership capable of appreciating the value of their partisan coalition's experiences on a visceral as well as a cognitive level.

Representation is also assisted by the clarity of the parties' positions. We can evaluate this most readily, within our samples of elites, where party elites take consistent positions that can be contrasted with those of the other party. On seven of the fifteen issues, both parties took internally consistent positions: prochoice, reducing federal spending by reducing government services, whether state and local taxes should be raised to avert fiscal crisis, improving the economic condition of blacks, ensuring that women have an equal role in running businesses, cooperating with Russia, and preferences for blacks in hiring and promotions. On three, the parties took opposite positions. Democrats agreed with prochoice and federal assistance to improve the economic condition of blacks; Republicans disagreed. Democrats dissented from cutting services to balance the federal budget; Republicans cheered. On two more, Democrats and Republicans both disagreed with the policy: raising state and local taxes to avert a fiscal crisis and providing blacks workplace preferences. But Republicans were more united than Democrats in their opposition. On the remaining two issues, while both parties agreed with the policies, Democrats were somewhat more favorably disposed to women having an equal role in running business and to cooperation with Russia. Thus, southern party organizational leaders do represent alternative futures to the rank and file.

If one examines party issue positions at each level of leadership, one gets a somewhat different picture. Democratic and Republican county committee members disagreed with each other's policy choices four times, county party chairs seven times, and convention delegates ten times. The greatest partisan differentiation is found among those nominally responsible for selecting the national executive candidates, approving the national platform and crystallizing the national partisan agenda for the next four years. Those whose responsibility is more circumscribed by local affairs differed less from one another. And among local organizational elites, those least organizationally visible, committee members, were least distinguishable by partisan-issue orientation.

Recall from the data in chapter 1 that rank-and-file partisans of each party, however measured, differed not so much in their modal policy choices but in their cohesiveness around that choice. Thus the greater the partisan differentiation on issues, the less reflective the parties would be of the potential southern electorate.

The historic candidate-centered context of southern politics seems to invite parties to differ in degree, not kind. It may be rational organizationally for parties to submerge their differences (Downs 1957). From these data, then, we might anticipate a representational gradient that may owe its principal connection to the belief sharing model of representation (Luttbeg 1981). We might expect that the least visible and most locally rooted organizational elites, county committee members, would most closely reflect mass policy attitudes and values, followed by county party chairs and convention delegates.

Chapter 3

Collective Representation by Southern Party Organizations

This chapter begins our assessment of collective representation (Weisberg 1978) of the southern party rank and file by political party organizations. Do the parties respond substantively to the wishes and values, the attitudes and opinions, and the general orientations of southern partisans? Can we report what Pitkin (1967) hoped to find: institutionalized substantive responsiveness? We are guided in this exploration by several expectations.

First, we approach the topic from the perspective of collective, not dyadic, representation because our focus is on a regional phenomenon. Thus, whether a Virginia Democrat is better represented by a Democrat from Georgia or Mississippi or by a fellow Virginian is less important than the fact that his or her voice is heard and expressed somewhere by the southern party. Moreover, we calibrate the accuracy of collective representation by comparing the central tendency of the distribution of rank-and-file expressions to the central tendency of the distribution of party elite expressions. To evaluate the statistical significance of these differences, we must account for the dispersion around the distributional means as well.[1] This is a measure of cohesion that chapters 1 and 2 showed varied by party, organizational role, and status as rank-and-file partisan or organization leader. In chapters 1 and 2 we were principally interested in determining a *modal* tendency in the data that would allow us to make preliminary statements about the level of general agreement or disagreement on issues and ideology. Here, we consider both central tendency (*mean*) and dispersion through the analysis of variance and paired comparisons tests, described below. This permits a much more sensitive analysis of the *relative* agreement/disagreement levels between party elites and mass partisans.

Second, we are guided empirically by the results of previous chapters. That is, we expect that the Republican rank and file, while easier to represent ideologically because its distribution is skewed sharply toward the conservative end of the spectrum, gives less coherent issue guidance to its party leaders. Democrats, by contrast, should be harder to represent ideologically, precisely because they are spread across the ideological spectrum. On the other hand, Democrats should be easier to represent on the majority of issues, because they are more homogenous than Republicans. This, of course, again emphasizes the imprecision that accompanies musings about ideology in the American political system. What do the words "liberal" and "conservative" mean? How are they translated into policy? Clearly, our findings in previous chapters underscore the complexity of these relationships in general, and we anticipate their effect on the relationship we will explore in this chapter.

Third, we take a hypothetical cue from the literature that reports an asymmetry in the ability of the parties to represent. Following the pioneering work of Herbert McClosky, Paul J. Hoffman, and Rosemary O'Hara (1960), others have shown that the Republican party elites are "out of step" not only with Democratic elites and rank-and-file Democrats but also with their own Republican rank and file (Baer and Bositis 1988; Jackson et al. 1982; Miller and Jennings 1986; Montjoy, Shaffer, and Weber 1980). The McClosky distribution, which these authors affirm, describes a situation in which greater extremism and higher levels of attitude consistency, even "constraint," are found among the elite cohorts than the mass partisans. This tendency only exacerbates the situation in which a party elite—in the case of our expectations, members of the Republican party—is already expected to diverge. Thus we hypothesize that the Democratic party will better reflect, generally, not only their own partisans, but the Republican rank and file as well.

Fourth, by dividing partisans into national and state partisans and selecting organizational elites who have a primary responsibility for a set of national outcomes—convention delegates—as opposed to county chairs and county committee members whose portfolio is arguably more locally focused, we hope to shed additional light on the relationship between federalism and representation in the South. At its most simplistic level, we expect county officials to be generally closer to the rank and file, but especially in definitions of partisanship that reflect state concerns.

We cannot take this fourth expectation too far

for several reasons. The culture of the South is a shared experience for partisans of both parties, as we saw in the common modal directionality of their issue responses. Moreover, while the Democratic party is undoubtedly undergoing massive changes in composition and strength, the Republican party is only beginning to make inroads at the state legislative and local levels. Its organizational efforts have had a top-down, not bottom-up, quality. This focus is quickly apparent from a comparison of the web sites maintained by each party's national committee.[2] In addition to providing information on policies, programs, organizations, and membership, the Republican site delves into the hows and whys of becoming a local activist and invites activists to consider "Nuts and Bolts" seminars on how to become a candidate. Democrats are not so well focused on mobilization. They invite visitors to register to vote and to contact the state party organization.

Moreover, the sociodemographic differences revealed in the last chapter are reflected in residential patterns which affect constituencies that are defined geographically in the South as elsewhere. We are likely to find a patchwork of party dominant districts rather than two parties pervasively competing in a host of districts marginal to each.

Thus, there are effects that both strengthen and weaken the power of federalism as an interaction effect on representation.

Methodology

The tables that follow permit a visualization of the representational differences within and between parties that are discussed in the text. The textual presentation is based on 320 analyses of variance (ANOVA) tables: 15 issues + ideology × 5 definitions of partisanship × 4 partisan analyses (within each of the two parties and across the two parties). Each ANOVA run compared the three categories of party elite with a definition of partisanship. In addition to calculating whether party elites and mass partisans differed over-

TABLE 3.1
MATRIX–SUBMATRIX FORMAT (PARTY ELITES)

Mass Party Definitions	DEMOCRATS			REPUBLICANS		
	Convention Delegates	Party Chairs	Committee Members	Convention Delegates	Party Chairs	Committee Members
Democrats						
National identification						
State identification						
Best president		$R(1,1)$			$R(1,2)$	
Best governor						
Vote president						
Republicans						
National identification						
State identification						
Best president		$R(2,1)$			$R(2,2)$	
Best governor						
Best governor						
Vote president						

all in each of the 320 ANOVAs, by requesting an analysis of paired comparisons using the Scheffe test, we are able to discuss what comparisons "drive" significant variation in each analysis. The results of the paired comparison tests are what allow us to determine the degree of representation in the tables reported below. Where elite representation exists, an *A* is reported to depict elite-mass *agreement*. Where representation fails—that is, where statistically significant differences in the mean scores of party elites and mass partisans occur at or below the .05 level—we provide an indication of the ideological direction of elite disagreement with mass partisans. Are party elites more *liberal* (L) or more *conservative* (C) than the respective mass partisans?

Each table is divided into four blocks. For convenience, let us think of each table as a large matrix, *R*, for "representation." Each of the blocks can be considered

submatrixes of the larger *R* matrix. The matrix/submatrix format in table 3.1 looks like a large 2 × 2 table, where *R* (1,1) corresponds to Democratic elites representing Democratic partisans, and *R* (2,1) shows the cross-party representation that Democratic elites provide of Republicans partisans. Similarly, *R* (2,2) depicts Republican elites' success in representing fellow Republicans, and *R* (1,2) reflects the ability of Republican elites to represent Democratic partisans.

Elite Representation

In the context of collective representation, we hypothesized that Republican elites would be closer ideologically to their fellow partisans than would Democratic elites to Democratic partisans. Table 3.2 tests this expectation. The data consist of responses to a self-anchoring question that uses the cue words "liberal"

TABLE 3.2
PARTY ELITE REPRESENTATION OF MASS IDEOLOGICAL PREFERENCES

Mass Party Definitions	DEMOCRATS			REPUBLICANS		
	Convention Delegates	Party Chairs	Committee Members	Convention Delegates	Party Chairs	Committee Members
Democrats						
National identification	L	A	L	C	C	C
State identification	L	A	L	C	C	C
Best president	L	A	L	C	C	C
Best governor	L	A	L	C	C	C
Vote president	L	A	A	C	C	C
Republicans						
National identification	L	L	L	A	A	A
State identification	L	L	L	A	A	A
Best president	L	L	L	C	C	C
Best government	L	L	L	A	A	A
Vote president	L	L	L	A	A	C

Note: A = elite-mass agreement; L = party elites more liberal than mass partisans; C = party elites more conservative than mass partisans.

and "conservative" without any attempt to provide content.[3] Thus table 3.2 evaluates how solidly the parties commit themselves to ideological symbols as much as anything else.

Looking at $R(1,1)$ and $R(2,2)$, we see that Democratic party elites are less successful than their fellow Republican elites in reflecting the ideological predispositions of their partisan followers. Only Democratic county party chairs show a somewhat consistent pattern of agreement with different definitions of mass Democratic partisans. Generally, Democratic convention delegates and county party committee members are significantly more liberal, statistically, than southern Democratic mass partisans. Republican party elites in the South are uniformly more reflective of the more conservative trend among southern Republican mass partisans. Republican elites are significantly more conservative across the board only with partisans who are defined as Republicans because of their assessment of which party typically puts forward the best presidential candidates. And, unlike Democratic county party members, Republican county party members differ ideologically from mass partisans defined by their 1992 vote choice.

The off-diagonal blocks allow us to compare cross-party representation. At least with respect to ideological symbols, neither party's elites successfully reflect mass partisans of the opposite party. Democrats are uniformly more liberal, and Republicans are uniformly more conservative.

We also hypothesized that whatever symbolic agreement existed that advantaged representation of mass partisans by Republican elites would be tempered by their more dogmatic and consistent adherence to conservative tenets in specific policy than would be true of mass partisans. Thus, in general, we would expect that, following the McClosky distribution, Democrats would be more successful in representing Democrats than Republicans would be in representing Republicans, once we turned to specific issues. Recall that the literature supporting this expectation derives mainly, but not exclusively, from examinations of convention delegates.

Table 3.3 summarizes the percentage of agreement of party elites with various definitions of mass partisans within and between parties across 15 issues. Looking first at the main diagonal blocks (submatrixes R (1,1) and R (2,2)), we note several interesting patterns. The first column in each block shows the agreement of convention delegates with variously defined fellow partisans. Republican elites are ever so modestly more reflective of Republican partisans than Democratic elites are of fellow Democrats. But when we turn to local elite comparisons, Democratic county party chairs and members are overwhelmingly more representative

of fellow Democrats than are local Republican elites of fellow Republicans. And among Democrats, county party chairs are slightly more representative than are county committee members, regardless of the definition of party among mass partisans.

The cross-party comparisons in submatrixes R (2,1) and R (1,2) are equally instructive. Following the second part of the McClosky distribution, we would hypothesize that Democratic elites would be more representative of *both* Democratic and Republican partisans. Again, let us begin with convention delegates. Comparing the first columns of each submatrix we see that Republican delegates are more successful than Democratic delegates in representing the policy interests of members of the opposite party, contrary to the McClosky thesis. Yet the advantage shifts when we focus on local party elites. Here, Democratic county chairs and committee members are more representative of Republican mass partisans than are local Republican

TABLE 3.3

SUMMARY OF PARTY ELITE AGREEMENT WITH MASS ISSUE PREFERENCES

Mass Party Definitions	DEMOCRATS			REPUBLICANS		
	Convention Delegates (%)	Party Chairs (%)	Committee Members (%)	Convention Delegates (%)	Party Chairs (%)	Committee Members (%)
Democrats						
National identification	20.0	73.3	66.7	13.3	6.7	0.0
State identification	20.0	73.3	66.7	13.3	6.7	0.0
Best president	20.0	73.3	60.0	13.3	6.7	6.7
Best governor	20.0	73.3	66.7	13.3	6.7	0.0
Vote president	26.7	80.0	73.3	20.0	6.7	0.0
Republicans						
National identification	0.0	20.0	20.0	20.0	13.3	13.3
State identification	0.0	20.0	20.0	26.7	13.3	13.3
Best president	0.0	20.0	20.0	20.0	6.7	6.7
Best governor	0.0	20.0	26.7	26.7	13.3	13.3
Vote president	0.0	20.0	26.7	26.7	13.3	33.3

elites of Democratic mass partisans. Admittedly, the absolute level of responsiveness is low. But the absolute level of responsiveness of local Republican elites to Republican partisans is also low. Indeed, looking at the local elites of both parties, Democratic county chairs and committee members better represent the issue positions of mass Republicans than local Republicans in all definitions of Republican partisanship save one. Republican committee members are somewhat more reflective of their fellow partisans, identified as Republicans by their 1992 vote, than are Democratic committee members.

When parties err, in what direction do they err? Based on our portraits of party elites in chapter 2, we would hypothesize that Democrats err on the liberal side and Republicans err on the conservative side. Indeed, that is what table 3.4 shows us.

Comparing the convention delegate columns of each party with one another, the portrait of liberal Democratic elites confronting conservative Republican elites is affirmed. The pattern is even sharper when Democratic convention delegates are compared to local Republican elites. Not surprisingly, the cross-party deviations reflect these trends too. Republican elites are significantly more conservative than Democratic partisans, and this trend is accentuated as one descends from higher to lower levels of elites. The opposite is true of Democratic elites. While overwhelmingly more liberal than Republican partisans, it is Democratic convention delegates who are furthest from the average Republican partisan.

The exceptions to these party tendencies allow us to glimpse important divisions within the parties. On two issues, local Democratic party elites erred by being

TABLE 3.4
SUMMARY OF THE IDEOLOGICAL DIRECTION OF PARTY ELITE–MASS ISSUE DIVERGENCE

Mass Party Definitions	LIBERAL DEVIATION AMONG DEMOCRATIC PARTY ELITE			CONSERVATIVE DEVIATION AMONG REPUBLICAN PARTY ELITE		
	Convention Delegates (%)	Party Chairs (%)	Committee Members (%)	Convention Delegates (%)	Party Chairs (%)	Committee Members (%)
Democrats						
National identification	80.0	13.3	20.0	73.3	86.7	93.3
State identification	80.0	13.3	20.0	73.3	86.7	93.3
Best president	80.0	13.3	26.7	73.3	86.7	86.7
Best governor	80.0	13.3	20.0	73.3	86.7	93.3
Vote president	73.3	6.7	20.0	73.3	86.7	93.3
Republicans						
National identification	93.3	73.3	73.3	73.3	80.0	80.0
State identification	93.3	73.3	73.3	66.7	80.0	80.0
Best president	93.3	73.3	73.3	73.3	86.7	86.7
Best governor	93.3	73.3	66.7	66.7	80.0	80.0
Vote president	93.3	73.3	66.7	66.7	73.3	66.7

more *conservative* than Democratic partisans. Local Democratic elites were significantly less likely than rank-and-file Democrats, however defined, to support affirmative action.[4] Democratic convention delegates, by contrast, agreed with all definitions of Democratic partisans on this issue. Both sets of local elites were also significantly more opposed to government guaranteeing job and living standards than Democratic partisans. Again, Democratic convention delegates agreed with all definitions of partisans on this issue.

The deviation of local elites from the rank and file on these two issues, especially in the face of national convention delegate responsiveness, highlights a potentially important schism within the Democratic party. Affirmative action and job/living standard guarantees have been staples of the Democratic platform and sacred to the liberal wing of the party. That both have been attacked by referendums and court action in the ensuing years and compromised by the reformation of welfare policy has not changed the commitment of liberal Democrats to more pristine statements of governmental social responsibility than desired by conservative Democrats. The question is, have moderate and conservative Democratic partisans migrated to the local elite position or out of the party entirely, leaving a more homogeneously liberal, if smaller, group of partisans behind? And in the process, have local party elites switched parties as well, following the slow but steady erosion of the ranks of Democratic elected officials in the South?

Interestingly, Republican elites were more *liberal* than their rank and file on one issue: internationalism. Republican elites were more likely than the average southern Republican to disagree that government should pay more attention to problems at home than to other parts of the world.[5] Democratic elites agreed with their fellow partisans and were more conservative across the board than rank-and-file southern Republicans. That is, Democrats in the party organization and neighborhoods across the South were more domestically focused than Republican party elites or their Republican mass neighbors.

In this section, we have seen qualified support for the hypotheses with which we began this inquiry into the collective representation of southern party elites. We observed a closer ideological correspondence between Republican party elites and mass Republicans than between Democratic party elites and mass Democrats. But this symbolic connection did not carry over to issues. Democratic local elites, not convention delegates, were overwhelmingly more successful in representing fellow Democrats than were Republican elites in representing Republican partisans. Cross-party representation marginally favored Democratic elites at the local level. When party elites failed to reflect the issue positions of the rank and file, generally, Democratic elites were more liberal, and Republican elites were more conservative. We also noted some important exceptions to the ideological direction of representational errors. These will be discussed in greater detail below.

Now, let us look behind these trends to specific issue representation on each of the fifteen issues in our data set.

Women and Minorities

Among our issues, we identified two groups—women and minorities—who have been the focus of substantial political and legal attention of late. Economic and legal statistics have affirmed the impact of all manner of discrimination and harassment on both groups. We wanted to know not only what our mass and elite samples felt about policies to rectify this situation, but, equally important, how well southern party elites reflected attitudes among mass partisans.

Tables 3.5 and 3.6 present representational data pertaining to improving the economic condition of women and improving the social and economic condition of blacks and other minorities. For both of these tables, the representational pattern is the same. Democratic national convention delegates are more liberal than all definitions of Democratic partisans. By contrast, Democratic county party chairs and committee members represented accurately the Democratic rank and file. Republican party elites were consistently less supportive of these improvements in the condition of

TABLE 3.5

PARTY ELITE REPRESENTATION OF MASS ISSUE PREFERENCES AND IDEOLOGICAL DIRECTION OF ELITE-MASS DIVERGENCE ON IMPROVING THE ECONOMIC CONDITION OF WOMEN

Mass Party Definitions	DEMOCRATS			REPUBLICANS		
	Convention Delegates	Party Chairs	Committee Members	Convention Delegates	Party Chairs	Committee Members
Democrats						
National identification	L	A	A	C	C	C
State identification	L	A	A	C	C	C
Best president	L	A	A	C	C	C
Best governor	L	A	A	C	C	C
Vote president	L	A	A	C	C	C
Republicans						
National identification	L	L	L	C	C	C
State identification	L	L	L	C	C	C
Best president	L	L	L	C	C	C
Best governor	L	L	L	C	C	C
Vote president	L	L	L	C	C	C

Note: A = elite-mass agreement; L = party elites more liberal than mass partisans; C = party elites more conservative than mass partisans.

women, black and other minorities than was the Republican rank and file, however defined. Both party elites did an equally bad job of cross-party representation, Democrats erring on the liberal side and Republicans erring on the conservative side.

The referent changes in table 3.7. Respondents were asked their opinions on providing women an "equal role" in economics and government. We expected the cue word "equal" to generate greater consensus, tapping as it does a core American political value. Republican party elites do a good job of representing their partisans—better, in fact, than Democratic elites, among whom convention delegates are consistently more liberal. Interestingly, local misrepresentation occurs in the same place in both parties: between committee members and partisanship defined by the party typically offering the best presi-

dential candidates. Democratic members are more liberal and Republican members are more conservative than their fellow partisans.

There is a measurable degree of cross-party representation as well. Republican convention delegates are not significantly different from Democratic partisans, however defined. Democratic county party chairs fairly represented three of five definitions of Republican partisans, including both state-level definitions.

Table 3.8 presents the data on affirmative action to which we alluded above. Notice that only Democratic convention delegates agree with Democrats across all mass partisan definitions, and Democratic county committee members agree with Clinton voters. Cross-party representation is the province of local Democrats, especially Democratic county party

TABLE 3.6

PARTY ELITE REPRESENTATION OF MASS ISSUE PREFERENCES AND IDEOLOGICAL DIRECTION OF ELITE-MASS DIVERGENCE ON IMPROVING THE SOCIAL AND ECONOMIC POSITION OF BLACKS AND OTHER MINORITIES

Mass Party Definitions	DEMOCRATS			REPUBLICANS		
	Convention Delegates	Party Chairs	Committee Members	Convention Delegates	Party Chairs	Committee Members
Democrats						
National identification	L	A	A	C	C	C
State identification	L	A	A	C	C	C
Best president	L	A	A	C	C	C
Best governor	L	A	A	C	C	C
Vote president	L	A	A	C	C	C
Republicans						
National identification	L	L	L	C	C	C
State identification	L	L	L	C	C	C
Best president	L	L	L	C	C	C
Best governor	L	L	L	C	C	C
Vote president	L	L	L	C	C	C

Note: A = elite-mass agreement; L = party elites more liberal than mass partisans; C = party elites more conservative than mass partisans.

chairs, who were more conservative than all definitions of mass Democratic partisans. Democratic county committee members agree with Republican masses as defined by measures of state partisanship and Bush voters. Republican elites were uniformly more conservative than all definitions of fellow Republicans and the Democratic rank and file.

Thus the pattern of party elite representation on issues affecting women and minorities is affected by the political action suggested in the question. It is not simply the target group referent to which respondents react. On one level this complicates the problem of representation for elites, for they cannot simply observe the likely beneficiary of the policy and adduce an appropriate response. On another level it opens up new opportunities for representation, de-

pending on how the issues are conceptualized. Persuasive elite rhetoric might channel mass sentiment along dimensions more easily represented, as long as we construe the process of representation as a dynamic interaction among elites and mass partisans.

Domestic Policy

In this section we group an eclectic set of issues that have dominated the domestic agenda of both parties. The first issue, abortion, is clearly one of the litmus tests of party politics. While there are prolife and prochoice forces in each political party, Republicans are commonly seen as the party most visibly and, possibly, more cohesively associated with the prolife position. That is due in part to the connection

TABLE 3.7
PARTY ELITE REPRESENTATION OF MASS ISSUE PREFERENCES AND IDEOLOGICAL DIRECTION
OF ELITE-MASS DIVERGENCE ON THE EQUAL ROLE OF WOMEN IN RUNNING BUSINESS,
INDUSTRY, AND GOVERNMENT

Mass Party Definitions	DEMOCRATS			REPUBLICANS		
	Convention Delegates	Party Chairs	Committee Members	Convention Delegates	Party Chairs	Committee Members
Democrats						
National identification	L	A	A	A	C	C
State identification	L	A	A	A	C	C
Best president	L	A	L	A	C	C
Best governor	L	A	A	A	C	C
Vote president	L	A	A	A	C	C
Republicans						
National identification	L	L	L	A	A	A
State identification	L	A	L	A	A	A
Best president	L	A	L	A	A	C
Best governor	L	A	L	A	A	A
Vote president	L	L	L	A	A	A

Note: A = elite-mass agreement; L = party elites more liberal than mass partisans; C = party elites more conservative than mass partisans.

between the Christian Coalition and the Republican party and the success of many Coalition members or sympathizers in gaining local election and Republican party office. Based on these facts, we would expect there to be a closer correspondence between the positions of Republican party elites and the Republican rank and file than we would observe among Democrats on abortion. Table 3.9 tests this expectation.

Contrary to our expectation, what little party elite responsiveness exists appears among Democratic county committee members (and among Democratic county chairs when Clinton voters are added). Among Republicans only the rank and file defined by a vote for George Bush are reflected by the local Republican organization. Elsewhere, among all categories of partisans, Democratic party elites are more liberal and Republican party elites are more conservative than either party's average member, however defined. That is, Democratic elites are more willing, and Republican elites are less willing, than either party's partisans to make abortion a matter of personal choice.

Like abortion, school prayer is a "hot-button" issue that has long been part of the social agenda of American conservatism. Again, while both parties contain supporters and opponents, the Republican party is more clearly perceived as supporting school prayer. Yet, at least in the South, table 3.10 shows that it is the Democratic local party that best reflects the positions of Democratic partisans, however defined. Only Democratic convention delegates deviate from the rank and file significantly: delegates were significantly less likely to support school prayer.

TABLE 3.8

PARTY ELITE REPRESENTATION OF MASS ISSUE PREFERENCES AND IDEOLOGICAL DIRECTION OF ELITE-MASS DIVERGENCE IN GIVING BLACKS PREFERENCE IN HIRING AND PROMOTION BECAUSE OF PAST DISCRIMINATION

Mass Party Definitions	DEMOCRATS			REPUBLICANS		
	Convention Delegates	Party Chairs	Committee Members	Convention Delegates	Party Chairs	Committee Members
Democrats						
National identification	A	C	C	C	C	C
State identification	A	C	C	C	C	C
Best president	A	C	C	C	C	C
Best governor	A	C	C	C	C	C
Vote president	A	C	A	C	C	C
Republicans						
National identification	L	A	L	C	C	C
State identification	L	A	A	C	C	C
Bestpresident	L	A	L	C	C	C
Best governor	L	A	A	C	C	C
Vote president	L	A	A	C	C	C

Note: A = elite-mass agreement; L = party elites more liberal than mass partisans; C = party elites more conservative than mass partisans.

Republicans show a spotty record of representation on this issue, despite rhetorical support from the Reagan and Bush administrations and the introduction of bills and constitutional amendments supporting school prayer in Congress. Local Republicans are more supportive (i.e., conservative) of school prayer than the rank and file, with the exception of county committee members paired with Bush voters. Republican convention delegates reflected the views of Republican partisans as defined by both state measures and their 1992 presidential vote, but not by national identification or best presidential candidate historically.

This pattern, like the pattern we observed on abortion, suggests that Republicans may lack a coherent vision of, as well as cohesion about, conservatism, as it pertains to the social agenda. In the re-

gion that is often thought to be the seedbed of American conservatism and the home of the Christian Coalition, the Republican party has a more difficult time reflecting the policy desires of its ostensibly more conservative and, on this issue at least, more cohesive party members.

Government support for low-cost doctor and hospital care is not a new agenda item. Some form of national health care has been a feature of the Democratic party platform at least since the Truman administration. Medicare for the elderly became national policy as part of Lyndon Johnson's Great Society program, and Medicaid is a growing presence in state budgets, serving the needy across the country. But health care became a prominent feature of the Clinton administration. He referred to it on the 1992 campaign trail and, through the First Lady,

TABLE 3.9

PARTY ELITE REPRESENTATION OF MASS ISSUE PREFERENCES AND IDEOLOGICAL DIRECTION OF ELITE-MASS DIVERGENCE ON LAW MAKING ABORTION A MATTER OF PERSONAL CHOICE

Mass Party Definitions	DEMOCRATS			REPUBLICANS		
	Convention Delegates	Party Chairs	Committee Members	Convention Delegates	Party Chairs	Committee Members
Democrats						
National identification	L	L	A	C	C	C
State identification	L	L	A	C	C	C
Best president	L	L	A	C	C	C
Best governor	L	L	A	C	C	C
Vote president	L	A	A	C	C	C
Republicans						
National identification	L	L	L	C	C	C
State identification	L	L	L	C	C	C
Best president	L	L	L	C	C	C
Best governor	L	L	L	C	C	C
Vote president	L	L	L	C	A	A

Note: A = elite-mass agreement; L = party elites more liberal than mass partisans; C = party elites more conservative than mass partisans.

championed a massive overhaul of America's delivery system once elected. While Clinton's specific program was unknown at election time, he had reopened that national conversation. Our question is how reflective were southern parties of the position of southern party members, variously defined, on this longstanding domestic issue rekindled by Clinton. Table 3.11 provides the answer.

Given the phrasing of the question (see Appendix A), and its historic position on the agenda, we expected more consensus than table 3.11 shows. Only Democratic county chairs represent Democratic mass partisans' views. Democratic delegates and county committee members are significantly more liberal than Democratic partisans. Republican party elites are uniformly more conservative—that is, less supportive of government help—than the Republican

rank and file. And there is no effective cross-party representation.

Environmental spending evinces quite a different pattern. Table 3.12 shows that local Republican elites reflect more accurately their fellow partisans than do Democrats. Only Democratic county party chairs are not consistently more liberal than rank-and-file Democrats.

The more traditional issue of government guarantees for job and living standards produces no partisan consensus within the Democratic party, which has been so closely associated with this issue for so long. Table 3.13 shows that local party elites of both parties are more conservative than their respective partisans. Only Democratic party convention delegates share a common perspective with the Democratic rank and file. Interestingly, Democratic county

TABLE 3.10

PARTY ELITE REPRESENTATION OF MASS ISSUE PREFERENCES AND IDEOLOGICAL DIRECTION OF ELITE-MASS DIVERGENCE ON ALLOWING PRAYER IN THE PUBLIC SCHOOLS

Mass Party Definitions	DEMOCRATS			REPUBLICANS		
	Convention Delegates	Party Chairs	Committee Members	Convention Delegates	Party Chairs	Committee Members
Democrats						
National identification	L	A	A	C	C	C
State identification	L	A	A	C	C	C
Best president	L	A	A	C	C	C
Best governor	L	A	A	C	C	C
Vote president	L	A	A	C	C	C
Republicans						
National identification	L	L	L	C	C	C
State identification	L	L	L	A	C	C
Best president	L	L	L	C	C	C
Best governor	L	L	L	A	C	C
Vote president	L	L	L	A	C	A

Note: A = elite-mass agreement; L = party elites more liberal than mass partisans; C = party elites more conservative than mass partisans.

party chairs do a better job of representing Republicans than they do of their own partisans and better too than any category of Republican party elite. The same is true for county committee members with three of the five definitions of mass Republican partisanship: national party identification, best presidential candidates historically, and best gubernatorial candidates historically.

Juxtaposing the representational patterns for environmental spending and government job and standard of living guarantees prompts us to speculate about how these issues are conceived by elites and masses. The liberal wing of the Democratic party, which is clearly not strong in the South, has championed the cause of environmental regulation, especially against the depredations of big business and public utilities. However, the South, while benefiting from the Tennessee Valley Authority (TVA) and other rural electrification and conservation projects, has been loathe to oppose economic development projects. And this is historically fertile territory for Republicans. Yet President Bush prided himself on his support for conservation projects and the Environmental Protection Agency.

Similarly, while liberal Democrats have led the way for government job and living standard guarantees, more "conservative" rank-and-file southern Democrats do not appear to have lagged behind national trends that support benefits and opportunities for the poor. Perhaps this reflects a surfacing of southern populism, which has strong roots and a venerable tradition in oratory and action. Thus it seems that on each issue both parties are conflicted. One would not predict stable success for either party elite in representing their rank

TABLE 3.11

PARTY ELITE REPRESENTATION OF MASS ISSUE PREFERENCES AND IDEOLOGICAL DIRECTION OF ELITE-MASS DIVERGENCE ON GOVERNMENT HELP IN GETTING LOW-COST DOCTOR AND HOSPITAL CARE

Mass Party Definitions	DEMOCRATS			REPUBLICANS		
	Convention Delegates	Party Chairs	Committee Members	Convention Delegates	Party Chairs	Committee Members
Democrats						
National identification	L	A	L	C	C	C
State identification	L	A	L	C	C	C
Best president	L	A	L	C	C	C
Best governor	L	A	L	C	C	C
Vote president	L	A	L	C	C	C
Republicans						
National identification	L	L	L	C	C	C
State identification	L	L	L	C	C	C
Best president	L	L	L	C	C	C
Best governor	L	L	L	C	C	C
Vote president	L	L	L	C	C	C

Note: A = elite-mass agreement; L = party elites more liberal than mass partisans; C = party elites more conservative than mass partisans.

and file until a common perspective from which to view issues such as these is established. Our data suggest that such a perspective is absent.

Fiscal Management

Each of the three issues we have grouped under fiscal management pose the contrast between taxing and spending in a different way. On each, the Democratic party has been portrayed, historically, as the party of increased taxes and increased spending. Republicans have been cast, traditionally, as more fiscally prudent, advocating reduced spending and incentive-based tax cuts. More radically, in calling government the problem, not the solution, the Reagan administration demonized government as undermining the strength,

even the health, of the American economy. President Bush initially followed this path with his memorable campaign pledge in 1988, "Read my lips. No new taxes!" Two years later he was forced to renege on his promise: he acquiesced to a tax increase as part of the budget reconciliation compromise that promised to reduce the deficit by five hundred billion dollars.

Also blurring the line separating Democrats and Republicans, especially for southerners, was the moderation preached by Democratic Leadership Conference moderates such as Arkansas Governor and 1992 presidential candidate, Bill Clinton. Gone from the 1992 campaign was the passionate rhetoric of Hubert Humphrey. In a lunge for the center, Clinton eschewed the big spender image and dodged successfully the liberal tag that stuck so easily to 1988

TABLE 3.12

PARTY ELITE REPRESENTATION OF MASS ISSUE PREFERENCES AND IDEOLOGICAL DIRECTION OF
ELITE-MASS DIVERGENCE ON INCREASING GOVERNMENT SPENDING FOR THE ENVIRONMENT

Mass Party Definitions	DEMOCRATS			REPUBLICANS		
	Convention Delegates	Party Chairs	Committee Members	Convention Delegates	Party Chairs	Committee Members
Democrats						
National identification	L	A	L	C	C	C
State identification	L	A	L	C	C	C
Best president	L	A	L	C	C	C
Best governor	L	A	L	C	C	C
Vote president	L	A	L	C	C	C
Republicans						
National identification	L	L	L	C	A	A
State identification	L	L	L	C	A	A
Best president	L	L	L	C	C	A
Best governor	L	L	L	C	A	A
Vote president	L	L	L	C	A	A

Note: A = elite-mass agreement; L = party elites more liberal than mass partisans; C = party elites more conservative than mass partisans.

Democratic nominee Michael Dukakis, governor of Massachusetts.

With this confused family portrait of Democrats and Republicans in 1992 before us and remembering the conceptual difficulties occasioned by the comparison of environmental spending and government economic guarantees, we are reluctant to hypothesize strong representational patterns within either party.

Our caution is rewarded in looking at Republican linkages in tables 3.14, 3.15, and 3.16. Republican party elites are uniformly more conservative than rank-and-file Republicans, however defined, on each issue: reductions in federal services to reduce spending, support of a balanced budget amendment, and preferring service reductions to tax increases as a remedy during state financial crises. Democratic convention delegates are significantly more liberal than southern mass Democrats on all issues and partisan definitions with the exception of Clinton voters on the choice between tax increases and spending cuts to remedy state financial crises. But local Democrats are attuned to their fellow partisans across the board.

National Defense and International Issues

We have grouped three issues under this rubric: defense spending (table 3.17), isolationism/internationalism (table 3.18), and cooperation with Russia (table 3.19). We identify holding the line on defense spending, internationalism, and the desire for continued cooperation with Russia as the "liberal" alternatives, although we recognize that this interpretation suggests a level of interrelatedness between

TABLE 3.13

PARTY ELITE REPRESENTATION OF MASS ISSUE PREFERENCES AND IDEOLOGICAL DIRECTION OF ELITE-MASS DIVERGENCE ON GOVERNMENT JOB AND LIVING-STANDARD GUARANTEES

Mass Party Definitions	DEMOCRATS			REPUBLICANS		
	Convention Delegates	Party Chairs	Committee Members	Convention Delegates	Party Chairs	Committee Members
Democrats						
National identification	A	C	C	C	C	C
State identification	A	C	C	C	C	C
Best president	A	C	C	C	C	C
Best governor	A	C	C	C	C	C
Vote president	A	C	C	C	C	C
Republicans						
National identification	L	A	A	C	C	C
State identification	L	A	L	C	C	C
Best president	L	A	A	C	C	C
Best governor	L	A	A	C	C	C
Vote president	L	A	L	C	C	C

Note: A = elite-mass agreement; L = party elites more liberal than mass partisans; C = party elites more conservative than mass partisans.

domestic and foreign affairs that may be misleading. We are not suggesting that a constrained, unidimensional perspective defines the issue space of most Americans. But we adopt a convention here—hopefully, clearly qualified with this caveat—to facilitate interpretation of our major point: the degree of elite representation and the relative direction of elite deviation from mass opinion.

With that in mind, table 3.17 again shows that local Democratic elites are more successful in reflecting the issue positions of Democratic partisans than are local Republicans of Republican partisans. Indeed, Democratic county committee members are more successful than their Republican counterparts in representing rank-and-file Republicans. This cross-party success is also achieved by Democratic county chairs and Republicans defined by national identification and 1992 ballots for Bush. However, at the convention delegate level, it is Republicans who better reflect the issue posi-

tions of their own partisans *and* of Democrats. Democratic delegates and local Republican elites find themselves consistently out of step with the rank and file of both parties: Democrats being significantly less willing, and Republicans significantly more willing, to spend on national defense.

The same pattern does not evince itself in table 3.18. Democratic elites are uniformly aligned with all definitions of Democratic party membership. Republican party elites (save county committee members and Bush voters) are more internationalist (i.e., liberal, in our vocabulary) than rank-and-file Republicans. Predictably, there is no cross-party representation. Republican elites are more internationalist than Democratic partisans, and Democratic elites are more isolationist than Republican partisans.

Yet another representational pattern is displayed in table 3.19, which deals with cooperation with Russia. Republican convention delegates best represent

TABLE 3.14

PARTY ELITE REPRESENTATION OF MASS ISSUE PREFERENCES AND IDEOLOGICAL DIRECTION
OF ELITE-MASS DIVERGENCE ON FEDERAL SERVICE REDUCTION TO REDUCE SPENDING

Mass Party Definitions	DEMOCRATS			REPUBLICANS		
	Convention Delegates	Party Chairs	Committee Members	Convention Delegates	Party Chairs	Committee Members
Democrats						
National identification	L	A	A	C	C	C
State identification	L	A	A	C	C	C
Best president	L	A	A	C	C	C
Best governor	L	A	A	C	C	C
Vote president	L	A	A	C	C	C
Republicans						
National identification	L	L	L	C	C	C
State identification	L	L	L	C	C	C
Best president	L	L	L	C	C	C
Best governor	L	L	L	C	C	C
Vote president	L	L	L	C	C	C

Note: A = elite-mass agreement; L = party elites more liberal than mass partisans; C = party elites more conservative than mass partisans.

rank-and-file southern Republicans. Local Republican elites seem less willing to cooperate with the remnants of the "evil empire." Democratic elites of all stripes display more cooperative (i.e., liberal) sentiments than rank-and-file Democrats of all definitions. Yet there is observable cross-party representation. Democratic committee members reflect Republican sentiment, and Republican county chairs reflect Democratic sentiment. To the latter, we add Republican delegates and Clinton voters and Republican committee members and Democrats defined by their traditional presidential preferences.

Spending

Perhaps some of the confusion in the patterns above may be erased by reconceptualizing some of the issues as spending issues. The common political party caricature poses Republicans as fiscal conservatives

protecting the public purse from the ravages of Democratic party splurges on domestic entitlements and other programs. By contrast, Republicans are portrayed as more willing to spend for national defense, if not for foreign aid. We realigned five issues into a spending theme: defense spending, cutting federal services to cut federal spending, environmental spending, the balanced budget amendment, and raising taxes rather than lowering spending to avert state fiscal distress.

Across all five issues, Democratic county chairs accurately reflected Democratic partisan positions. They are joined in all but environmental spending by county committee members. Democratic convention delegates, however, are consistently more liberal—that is, more willing to spend—on all issues than all categories of partisans except Clinton voters on the tax-spend tradeoff to avert state financial crises.

On three issues all Republican party elites were

TABLE 3.15
PARTY ELITE REPRESENTATION OF MASS ISSUE PREFERENCES AND IDEOLOGICAL DIRECTION OF
ELITE-MASS DIVERGENCE ON A BALANCED BUDGET AMENDMENT

Mass Party Definitions	DEMOCRATS			REPUBLICANS		
	Convention Delegates	Party Chairs	Committee Members	Convention Delegates	Party Chairs	Committee Members
Democrats						
National identification	L	A	A	C	C	C
State identification	L	A	A	C	C	C
Best president	L	A	A	C	C	C
Best governor	L	A	A	C	C	C
Vote president	L	A	A	C	C	C
Republicans						
National identification	L	L	L	C	C	C
State identification	L	L	L	C	C	C
Best president	L	L	L	C	C	C
Best governor	L	L	L	C	C	C
Vote president	L	L	A	C	C	C

Note: A = elite-mass agreement; L = party elites more liberal than mass partisans; C = party elites more conservative than mass partisans.

more conservative than the southern Republican rank and file. Republican elites were more willing than their partisans to cut federal services to cut spending, to support the balanced budget amendment, and to prefer service reductions over tax increases to avert a state fiscal crisis. Republican delegates reflected partisan views on defense spending. Local Republican elites better reflected partisan attitudes on environmental spending.

Grouping issues by their relationship to spending as an appropriate governmental activity highlights the success of local Democrats in representing the rank-and-file southern Democrat.

This chapter presented data that allowed us to assess the amount of symbolic and issue representation provided by each party's organization for five definitions of mass partisanship. We conclude that while Republican elites are better able to reflect the symbolic commitment of their party to "conservatism," their ability to represent issue content falters. Local Democratic party elites—county party chairs and county committee members—best represent the issue position of their fellow partisans. By comparison, Democratic delegates tend to be more liberal and Republican elites tend to be more conservative than their respective mass partisans. The McClosky distribution, evaluated across parties, favors Democrats only when local Democratic elites are incorporated. Otherwise, Republicans convention delegates are slightly more able to reflect Democrats than Democratic delegates are to reflect Republicans.

Our speculation about the broader impact of different definitions of partisanship as anchors for local versus national elites was swamped by the abil-

TABLE 3.16
PARTY ELITE REPRESENTATION OF MASS ISSUE PREFERENCES AND IDEOLOGICAL DIRECTION
OF ELITE-MASS DIVERGENCE ON PREFERRING STATE TAX INCREASE TO SERVICE
REDUCTIONS IN STATE FINANCIAL CRISES

Mass Party Definitions	DEMOCRATS			REPUBLICANS		
	Convention Delegates	Party Chairs	Committee Members	Convention Delegates	Party Chairs	Committee Members
Democrats						
National identification	L	A	A	C	C	C
State identification	L	A	A	C	C	C
Best president	L	A	A	C	C	C
Best governor	L	A	A	C	C	C
Vote president	A	A	A	C	C	C
Republicans						
National identification	L	L	L	C	C	C
State identification	L	L	L	C	C	C
Best president	L	L	L	C	C	C
Best governor	L	L	L	C	C	C
Vote president	L	L	L	C	C	C

Note: A = elite-mass agreement; L = party elites more liberal than mass partisans; C = party elites more conservative than mass partisans.

ity of local Democrats to represent. Among Republicans, the impact of different partisan definitions appeared more idiosyncratic than patterned.

Looking at specific issues, local Democrats were best able to represent more traditional aspects of the Democratic party platform. On all three issues of fiscal management, defense spending, internationalism/isolationism, improving the economic (and, in the case of blacks and other minorities, the social) condition of women and minorities, affirmative action and school prayer, local Democrats were not significantly different from mass Democratic partisans. The connection broke down on abortion and cooperating with Russia. Only Democratic county chairs agreed with Democratic partisans on health care. And local Democratic elites were more conservative on the traditional liberal support for job and living standard guarantees.

Qualifying the Statistical Analysis

It can be and should be asked: are we making a mountain out of a molehill? To be sure, the ANOVA tables and Scheffe paired comparisons which informed the discussion of tables in this chapter support a conclusion that, statistically, Democratic convention delegates and sometimes Democratic local officials and nearly all Republican party functionaries are usually unreflective of the attitudes of their party's rank and file. But how does that square with the words that lie behind the numbers, the words that showed in chapter 1 that southern Republicans

TABLE 3.17

PARTY ELITE REPRESENTATION OF MASS ISSUE PREFERENCES AND IDEOLOGICAL DIRECTION
OF ELITE-MASS DIVERGENCE ON INCREASING DEFENSE SPENDING

Mass Party Definitions	DEMOCRATS			REPUBLICANS		
	Convention Delegates	Party Chairs	Committee Members	Convention Delegates	Party Chairs	Committee Members
Democrats						
National identification	L	A	A	A	C	C
State identification	L	A	A	A	C	C
Best president	L	A	A	A	C	C
Best governor	L	A	A	A	C	C
Vote president	L	A	A	A	C	C
Republicans						
National identification	L	A	A	A	C	C
State identification	L	L	A	A	C	C
Best president	L	L	A	A	C	C
Best governor	L	L	A	A	C	C
Vote president	L	A	A	A	C	C

Note: A = elite-mass agreement; L = party elites more liberal than mass partisans; C = party elites more conservative than mass partisans.

and southern Democrats were modally similar to one another on nearly all the issues?

Go back to tables 1.5 to 1.9 and compare them to tables 2.4 and 2.5. There you will find that an answer is suggested by the *modal* tendencies in the data. What one sees is a Democratic organizational elite whose convictions are more settled and whose divergences among themselves are more extreme than those found among rank-and-file Democrats. But the tendency for such divergence is *more pronounced* among Republicans at all levels. Despite their conservative protestations, Republicans seem more conflicted on policy, especially when compared to their Democratic neighbors. Perhaps because the Republican party is undergoing such an influx of new members—some, undoubtedly former Democrats who bring with them different values and agendas—

the table metaphorically set by rank-and-file southern Republicans boasts a main course that looks less like a country club prime rib au jus than a Kiwanis Club Brunswick stew. Statistical comparisons that employ a combination of measures of central tendency *and* measures of dispersion to diagnose statistical significance, as in this chapter, take these discrepancies more fully and more accurately into account. And so should the analyst looking for a substantive interpretation.

Such a conclusion would comport well with many of our initial expectations about collective representation in the region. The McClosky distribution appears to hold: Democratic and Republican organizational elites do differ from each other more widely than rank-and-file partisans, however defined.[6] But the asymmetry that usually accompa-

TABLE 3.18

PARTY ELITE REPRESENTATION OF MASS ISSUE PREFERENCES AND IDEOLOGICAL DIRECTION
OF ELITE-MASS DIVERGENCE ON PAYING MORE ATTENTION TO PROBLEMS AT HOME
COMPARED TO OTHER PARTS OF THE WORLD

Mass Party Definitions	DEMOCRATS			REPUBLICANS		
	Convention Delegates	Party Chairs	Committee Members	Convention Delegates	Party Chairs	Committee Members
Democrats						
National identification	A	A	A	L	L	L
State identification	A	A	A	L	L	L
Best president	A	A	A	L	L	L
Best governor	A	A	A	L	L	L
Vote president	A	A	A	L	L	L
Republicans						
National identification	C	C	C	L	L	L
State identification	C	C	C	L	L	L
Best president	C	C	C	L	L	L
Best governor	C	C	C	L	L	L
Vote president	C	C	C	L	L	A

Note: A = elite-mass agreement; L = party elites more liberal than mass partisans; C = party elites more conservative than mass partisans.

nies that finding as the second part of that distribution appears undermined by our findings. Democrats are better represented by Democrats, the convention delegates' more extreme views notwithstanding. But Democrats do not *in reality* give truer voice to the changing Republican rank and file than do Republican party elites. The southern Republican rank and file remains apart from both organizations on many issues precisely because of its diversity, compared to either party's organizational elite. The rhetorical confluence of Republicans around the word and symbol "conservative" may be something on which the party can build, as long as it shuns issue specificity. Certainly the election results of 1994 and 1996 suggest that possibility. Indeed, so do the results of 1998. Imbuing "conservative" with a moral tone in response

to President Clinton's escapades did not yield substantial benefits in the South.

Similarly, the difference between local and national representatives and state and national measures of partisanship open our eyes to the ability of the parties to represent on different levels. County party chairs and committee members represent fellow Democrats better than do national convention delegates. This reflects the continued strength of the Democratic party as a local organization not only in the South, but of the South. That the Republican party could not boast of the same connection probably owes to two factors at a minimum. First, local Republican organizations are new and certainly not as pervasive across the South. Second, the organizational dynamic of the Republican party has been from the top down, as indicated

TABLE 3.19
PARTY ELITE REPRESENTATION OF MASS ISSUE PREFERENCES AND IDEOLOGICAL DIRECTION
OF ELITE-MASS DIVERGENCE ON CONTINUING COOPERATION WITH RUSSIA

Mass Party Definitions	DEMOCRATS			REPUBLICANS		
	Convention Delegates	Party Chairs	Committee Members	Convention Delegates	Party Chairs	Committee Members
Democrats						
National identification	L	L	L	L	A	C
State identification	L	L	L	L	A	C
Best president	L	L	L	L	A	C
Best governor	L	L	L	L	A	C
Vote president	L	L	L	A	A	C
Republicans						
National identification	L	L	A	A	C	C
State identification	L	L	A	A	C	C
Best president	L	L	A	A	C	C
Best governor	L	L	A	A	C	C
Vote president	L	L	A	A	C	C

Note: A = elite-mass agreement; L = party elites more liberal than mass partisans; C = party elites more conservative than mass partisans.

previously. It is only as Republican successes at the national level enlivened interest in the party that the party has moved organizationally into lower federal, statewide, and state legislative arenas. Its future lies at the local level, as the religious Right is demonstrating (Hosansky 1996; Leege and Kellstedt 1993; Rozell and Wilcox 1995, 1996). But the Republican party of the South remains an evolving organization from rank and file to convention delegate, groping for a common identity that will form a representational base (Bullock and Rozell 1998).

Democrats are not standing still. Some might argue that they are withering, especially given the number of senators and representatives who have retired in the last decade rather than face reelection. Whether Democrats will regain the majority in Congress is an open question, despite their recent inroads into for-

merly Republican suburbia (Cook 1997) and the impressive mobilization of blacks and union members in the 1998 midterm election. Minority status in Congress deprives the party organization of some of its most cherished inducements, the highly visible prospect of policy fulfillment. While the local party organization might not be involved in policy formulation itself, it can use purposive incentives to mobilize—an activity that is, as the introduction showed, of major concern to organizational activists.

Some might argue, too, that Democrats have been victimized by their own quest for diversity—fashioning districts that made the election of minorities more likely but in so doing making Republican majorities easier to achieve in neighboring districts (Barone and Ujifusa 1993; Bullock 1995c; Cameron, Epstein, and O'Halloran 1996; Overby and Cosgrove

1996; Lublin 1997a, 1997b). One need only look at the profound changes in the delegations representing the South in Washington over the last thirty years and particularly since the 1990 census, or look at Democratic party representation in southern state legislatures. One can see this trend reflected in the parties' competition for statewide constitutional offices, especially governorships (see, for example, Bullock 1995b), although Deep South gubernatorial victories in 1998 may suggest an easing of the rate of decline.

The solid Democratic South is gone. But what remains of the Democratic party, despite its demonstrable changes in complexion and diversity, is still more unified and easier to represent collectively than what appears among Republicans. How long that will remain true is an open question. The racial differences in the composition of the two parties, revealed in chapter 1 for example, may be widened if the integrationist foundations of Rev. Martin Luther King's message and 1963 march are eclipsed or supplanted by the separatist message of some contemporary black leaders. What will be the long-run effect of the "Million Man March"? Of the Rodney King and O. J. Simpson trials? Of efforts to eliminate affirmative action programs in the states? What does the future hold for race, class, and party in districting schemes on which federal courts must rule? As relevant as these questions are for southern politics and partisan representation in the South, especially if society's divisions deepen and cleave parties more sharply from one another, they are, unfortunately, beyond the capacity of this book to answer.

This chapter has focused on zero-order relationships. A fuller treatment of the nature of southern party representation requires us to contextualize the relationships we have uncovered. In the following chapters, we introduce several covariates to condition the relationships discussed above. Our goal is to see whether controlling for third variables important to southern politics improves the abilities of the parties to represent their respective partisans.

Chapter 4

Political Context and Intraparty Cohesion

Typically, a study of this nature hopes to find that not only does the expected theoretical relationship hold true, but the relationship holds up regardless of the sociopolitical context in which the respondents find themselves. That is not fully the case as far as this study is concerned. On the one hand, if the understanding of elite-mass issue integration informing this research is correct, exogenous considerations such as institutional, politocultural, and demographic differences among the states should not induce significant variation in the results. Elite-mass opinion differences and similarities that withstand changes of political environment permit stronger theoretical generalizations. On the other hand, should the distribution of elite-mass opinions show some responsiveness to institutional and politocultural variables that are comparatively endogenous to intraparty issue cohesion, such as party organizational vitality, the presence in public office of sufficient numbers of elected elites from both parties to mediate mass awareness of party positions, and the prevailing partisan predisposition of the voting masses in each state, we happily would have evidence of the causal influence of the parties themselves, rather than that of their environments. The existence of such causal influence would be theoretically as important as the degree of intraparty cohesion itself, because prevailing wisdom holds that the political parties are creatures, not creators, of their environments.

In the professional literature on political parties, the causal contributions of contextual variables has received prominent attention. For example, the recent rise of the Republican party to competitive status in the once "solid South" has been attributed by some to demographic factors, such as the in-migration of job seekers and retirees with affective ties to the Republican party (Bass and DeVries 1976), or a theorized "white flight" from the Democratic party precipitated by the color change wrought in southern Democratic parties when the Voting Rights Act of 1965 added 3.2 million new African American voters to the rolls in those states (Davison and Krassa 1991a). Black and Black (1987, 1992) argue that demographic differences between the peripheral South and Deep South states are critical in the two regions' respective rates of electoral change. Bullock, among others, attributes down-ticket Republican gains in the South to institutional factors such as (1) the greater availability of Republican candidates to contest seats (Bullock 1991b), and (2) post-1990 racial gerrymandering, which concentrated Democratic voting strength into a few "majority-minority" districts at the expense of Democratic competitiveness in a number of southern congressional districts (Bullock 1995c; see generally Bullock and Rozell 1998).

Another case in point is the increase in congressional party unity voting that has taken place since the 1970s, which some attribute to demographic and attendant ideological changes wrought in the electoral base of the southern Democratic parties by the 1965 Voting Rights Act (Whitby and Gilliam 1989, 1991). Other students of congressional partisanship stress the causality of institutional innovations, such as the floor leadership's increased use of extended whip systems and policy task forces (Sinclair 1981, 1989; Garand 1988a, 1988b).

In short, much of the literature on political parties and related topics appears to confirm Leon Epstein's (1967) statement that political parties are less what they make of themselves than what their political environment makes of them. In the face of such a body of evidence and such an authoritative assessment, few if any political party specialists working today accept, rather than dispute, Schattschneider's (1942) claim that democracy is unthinkable save in terms of political parties.

In this chapter we shall specify contextual variables of three types—institutional, politocultural, and demographic, respectively—which also can be typed according to whether they are by nature endogenous or exogenous to party elites and masses. The latter distinction is important, for it is our expectation that variables in some way endogenous to these partisan affiliates would be more likely than exogenous variables to interact with, as well as covary with, the distributions of opinions for such partisan groups. The recent literature on southern party and electoral politics (e.g., Black and Black 1987, 1992) is very much preoccupied with the influence of undeniably important demographic variables such as race, religious

fundamentalism, and urbanization and other socio-economic indicators of development and modernization. However, it is our contention that while such exogenous environmental influences may prove useful covariates (control variables) in tests of group means, they lack any compelling theoretical rationale for dynamic interaction with either party elites or masses. By contrast, we would expect endogenous variables, such as (1) party organizational strength and (2) the overall ideological tendencies of party identifiers in each state to be not only useful controls, but also to interact in some significant fashion with the elite/mass pairings (factors) for whom issue agreement is in question.

Our working assumption is that environment conditions political attitudes and orientations by more than just its mere presence. Elite-mass agreement may be less responsive to environmental influence for certain issues than it is for others. It may be affected more by certain types of environmental variables than by others. It may be affected within one party more than the other for certain kinds of issues. Or it may be affected by every environmental variable for certain pairings of elites and masses, and by few or none for other elite/mass dyads.

Our approach here draws inspiration from Leon Epstein's 1958 work on Wisconsin politics, in which he presented an early formulation of his now-famous 1967 argument that environments shape parties, not vice versa: "Certain institutional features of Wisconsin politics are so firmly established by constitution or custom that they provide part of the environmental setting for political behavior in a way that is at least analogous to the influence of social and economic characteristics" (1958, 11). For example, "the institution of the open primary in Wisconsin dates from 1906, and by now the political habits associated with it are deeply fixed. To many Wisconsin citizens, it would seem undemocratic to be asked to identify publicly with a party as a prerequisite for primary voting" (1958, 25). The accuracy of this linkage of behavior to institutional environment was later validated in Wekkin's (1984) study of how Democratic party elites and voters reacted much more vehemently in Wisconsin than in any other state to the Democratic National Committee's delegate selection rule restricting voting in Democratic presidential primaries to registered Democrats only.

The inference drawn here is that not only may a given contextual variable covary from one state to the next, thus necessitating controlling for it across the data set, but other variables may vary from state to state as well, creating a total context unique to each state. Within that total context, a given environmental covariate may affect indigenous partisan elites and masses, and thereby their political attitudes, differently than it does those of any other state. This is why, in this chapter on the influence of state context upon intraparty issue cohesion, we control not only for the cross-state variance of numerous contextual covariates but also for any interaction of the covariates with the partisan elites and masses of the respective states.

Which brings us to the *crux* of the contextual analysis performed in this chapter: Do environmental differences across the eleven southern states significantly influence the elite-mass issue cohesion described in the preceding chapters? We focus our analysis here on the central question of whether and how the mean distributions of responses for paired groups of elites and masses are affected by environmental control variables, as well as by potential interaction effects between these environmental covariates and such group factors. This analysis speaks directly to the theoretical concerns just outlined, which are specified in greater detail in the next section.

It should be noted here, however, that the various hypotheses about the impact that certain variables may have upon elite-mass issue cohesion are specified below with the sole intent of justifying theoretically the contextual analysis that follows. They were not created as propositions to be tested within the confines of this treatment. The microtheoretical analysis needed to deal with each proposition would blind us to the larger issues of party responsiveness to, and interaction with, the surrounding political environment which more properly concern us now. Moreover, neither the type of data from which the

dependent variables are constructed nor the testing techniques used here permit inferences about the direction of the relationships between issue distributions and environmental variables. We can only test whether the latter significantly alter the former. Consequently, complementary reports focusing on some of the specific hypotheses mentioned below await future dissemination.

The Potential Influence of State Political Context

Institutional Variables

Institutions, usually treated as dependent variables, may nonetheless influence affects and behavior, and may even help to create political culture. As Epstein noted, the open-primary format employed today in Wisconsin is a prime illustration of how an institution may alter political culture. Known for clean elections and government since the adoption of this and other reforms during the Progressive era, Wisconsin's elections and politics were as corrupt as any state's during the preceding decades referred to as the "Gilded Age" (Nesbit 1973; see especially La Follette 1911). Other scholars, such as Haeberle (1985), have followed Epstein's lead by assaying the question of whether type of nomination primary format can account for various other partisan behaviors (e.g., roll-call partisanship).

Following such lines of inquiry, we shall undertake to explore whether institutional variables of direct or indirect relevance to partisan electoral politics have any influence upon elite-mass linkage. In particular, we shall look at the degree of interparty competition for public office and at the strength of state and local party organizations, respectively, as endogenous variables that may be more closely linked to issue cohesion between party elites and masses.[1]

Interparty competition. When both the Democratic and the Republican parties are organizationally strong at state and local levels, the usual product is healthy party competition for electoral offices. Such competition is important in a democracy not only because it helps to assure the accountability of governors to the governed, but also in the sense of helping to assure each party a sufficient supply of high-profile spokespersons to mediate the issue perspectives of party organization elites to the party's mass following, and vice versa. Austin Ranney (1965) and many others since (e.g., Bibby et al. 1990; Fleury 1992) have provided well-known and frequently used indexes of the extent of two-party competition present in the various states. Although at one time not too long ago the variance in two-party competition could have been dismissed as non-existent in any study of southern politics, during the decade of the 1980s the southern states ranged from one-party control by the traditionally dominant Democrats in Louisiana (Democratic index = .93), Mississippi (.92), and Georgia (.92), through modified one-party control in Virginia (.81), Arkansas (.78), South Carolina (.77), Alabama (.76), and Florida (.74), to the almost two-party competitive states of Tennessee (.65), Texas (.67), and North Carolina (.68) (Fleury 1992, 262–63). Where there is two-party competition, the competition to attract the support of the median voter should have the effect of drawing the politics of party organization elites toward the median, with attendant positive consequences for elite-mass issue cohesion. Where there is one-party dominance, on the other hand, both the absence of significant partisan opposition and the tendency for political cleavage to occur within the dominant party along regional, charismatic, or other factional lines usually should have the effect of divorcing the concerns of many if not most party elites from those of the voting mass. As the updated Ranney index figures above suggest, even in the modern South, the latter is to be expected much more than the former: electoral coalitions typically still will center on the candidates themselves, and campaigns will be essentially devoid of issue content. However, since the variable we are interested in here is the extent to which the southern states are electorally competitive rather than the degree to which they are Democratic, it is Fleury's folded index of interparty competition that is used below as a control variable (1992, 262–63).

Party organizational strength. Traditionally, state and local party organizations have been weak in the South, perhaps because the prevailing political culture so favored the Democrats (see next section) that it was uneconomical for either party to make organizational efforts. The Democrats had little need of organization, and their badly outnumbered Republican opponents had insufficient prospects and resources to make such organization-building rational. However, national Republican tickets began to make headway with conservative southern voters in the 1960s, 1970s, and, especially, the 1980s by appealing to their concerns about methods of achieving racial integration, expansive national government power, abortion rights, and the separation of church and state. As such success at the top of the ticket slowly spread, the national Republican party (in particular, the Republican National Committee and the National Republican Senate Committee) and southern Republicans alike began to hold out hope for a payoff from party organization building in targeted southern venues. Confronted by such Republican efforts, southern Democrats in some locales responded in kind by attempting to build their own party organizationally (Wekkin, Davis, and Maggiotto 1988).

Data gathered by Cotter et al. (1984) during the Party Transformation Study (PTS) of the late 1970s and early 1980s enable us to test (with appropriate caveats regarding the lifespan of such data) whether the organizational vitality of state and local party organizations is of consequence for party elite-mass linkage. In brief, these data reveal that state Democratic organizations are at best of weak-to-moderate strength, tend to be noticeably weaker than state Republican organizations, and also tend to be weaker in the Deep South than in the rim South.[2] In contrast, neither party comes even close to having strong local party organizations, in either the rim South or the Deep South.

When party organizations are thus weak, as in the case of the state and local southern Democratic parties, there is little reason to expect significant elite-mass issue integration to exist. Absent effective party organization, who mediates the respective issue perspectives of party elites and masses, and how? The same is perhaps true where strong state party organizations exist without local units of similar strength (a scenario that almost describes southern Republican organizations): such state organizations would epitomize the cadre-type party, in which one does not find a strong mass following. But when local party organizations are strong and active, one might expect that the consolidation-mobilization-conversion effects of their campaign activities would elicit greater mass familiarity with the party organization, and its issue concerns, and thus potentially greater identification and elite-mass integration, as well. This should mean comparatively greater, though by no measure *great,* elite-mass consonance in states where local party organization strength exists, with or without commensurate state party organizational strength.

An important caveat must be stated about these PTS data, which by the 1992 election were just over a decade old. It is possible for local parties, and even healthy state party organizations, to rise and/or decline very rapidly. Often the fortunes of party organizations may vary with turnover at the chair level.[3]

Politocultural Variables

Students of public opinion long have recognized the existence of important subpublics that exist between the sociodemographic fault lines of the American political landscape. In a similar vein, American political culture is often characterized as a culture of subcultures (see, e.g., Devine 1972) of varying regional, religious, racial, and ethnic natures. The southern states in particular frequently are referred to as America's most distinctive region, and also serve as the fountainhead of the *traditionalistic* stream of culture that Daniel Elazar (1972) identified as dominant in the southern rim of the United States. The core values of this culture are to a large extent similar to those that are identified in the next section as core concerns of the Christian Right: values of belonging that seem to have been marginalized by a rapidly changing society.

However, as suggested by Leon Epstein's obser-

vation about the capacity of political institutions to generate politocultural attitudes, individual states with their respective histories, institutional frameworks, and laws can have their own unique political subcultures *within* regions or cultural streams, as well. This is part of the thrust of Erikson, Wright, and McIver's seminal work, *Statehouse Democracy: Public Opinion and Policy in the American States* (1993). Opinions about policies in fact are the building blocks of the dependent variable in the present study: the degree to which issue agreement exists among party elites and masses in the southern states. Are there distinct state politocultural attitudes—skewed distributions of ideological predispositions, partisan orientations, civic virtues (i.e., participation), or whatever—that might have a significant impact upon elite-mass issue integration?

For instance, might differences in relative rates of identification with, say, the Democratic party as one goes from less Democratic states to more heavily Democratic states be concordant with proportionately greater mass issue-agreement with Democratic party elites in such states? Would scientific survey evidence of widespread subscription to conservative principles among respondents who identify themselves as Republicans suggest probably greater elite-mass issue integration within a state's Republican party, and less likelihood of cross-party issue-agreement with state Democratic party elites?

Concern with such questions reflects, of course, a conception of "political culture" that is more in keeping with Almond and Verba's (1963) notion of "civic culture" (typical individual attitudes and behaviors) than with Elazar's (1972) more encompassing conception of culture as a set of perceptions, values, and expectations that frame the rules of the political game within a political system. To be perfectly honest, assembling quantitative data for such an Elazarean contextual analysis of eleven states would be extremely difficult (if even possible), and would represent an effort more appropriate to the central thrust of a study than to a book chapter in which state context is merely a control variable.

To control for the states' particular distributions

of partisanship and ideological orientation, on the other hand, is comparably easy. We can use Erikson, Wright, and McIver's (1993) aggregate measures of state party identification, compiled from mass data gathered in 122 CBS/*New York Times* surveys conducted between 1976 and 1988, and pooled state-by-state, plus their aggregate measures of the mean ideology of Republican and Democratic identifiers in each state, as compiled from the same CBS/*New York Times* data, to assess both of those mass political orientations from a perspective that is both recent and longitudinal.

Almost as soon as one views such data, however, the futility of inquiry along such lines becomes so apparent that construction of formal hypotheses about the expected effect of such control variables almost seems a waste of time. It is difficult to see how any of them could affect intraparty cohesion very much, if at all. There is not a lot of within-region variation in the distribution of either partisanship or ideological self-identification.[4] Formerly the "solid South," all eleven states in the region continue to be home to Democratic pluralities of various sizes (ranging from a Democratic margin of 3.3 percent in Virginia to 35.3 percent in Louisiana) relative to Republican identifiers, and only in Virginia do Democratic identifiers not also outnumber independent identifiers (Erikson, Wright, and McIver 1993, 15). And as the fulcrum of the "conservative coalition" that dominated Congress for so long during the middle of the twentieth century, the South continues to find conservative self-identifiers outnumbering liberals in each state by margins ranging from 16.6 percent (Tennessee) to 25.4 percent (Mississippi), and trailing moderate identifiers across the region by an average of only 4.74 percent per state. As Erikson, Wright, and McIver note, the nation's least ideologically polarized states are in the South (Arkansas, Alabama, Louisiana, Mississippi, and North Carolina), and conservatives outnumber liberals within the ranks of Democratic identifiers in each of these states (1993, 41).

Thus while the questions above easily can be formulated into intuitively commendable hypotheses, the range of variation in the data about state-by-state mass contexts is so limited that one does not expect to observe much, if any, relationship between elite-mass issue integration and state-by-state distributions of long-term political orientations. At a range of less than 5 percent, respectively, the distributions of conservative and liberal identifiers across these eleven states is not likely to have any effect when controlled. The chances of such an effect occurring are not much greater for the distribution of mass Republican partisanship (range less than 13 percent) across southern state electorates, and are at best weak for the distribution of mass Democratic partisanship (range less than 23 percent). Therefore, the best measures to be used below as controls are Erikson, Wright, and McIver's *mean state partisanship* index, which is the average difference between the Democratic and Republican percentages of the state electorate during the years 1976–88, and Erikson, Wright, and McIver's mean ideology of partisan identifiers scores (from the same thirteen-year period), which we refer to below as the *liberalism of (Democratic/Republican) party identifiers,* since each party identifier is scored -100 if conservative, 0.0 if moderate, and +100 if liberal (1993, 14–21).

Demographic Variables

Although some of the institutional variables in the first section above interact with certain other institutional variables, the interaction is limited in that the relationships more often than not are recursive in direction. They do not knit together into an overall fabric in which every variable influences or is influenced by every other variable. In contrast, the literature on the demographic variables that influence southern politics suggests much more nonrecursiveness, not unlike a Rube Goldberg ecosystem, except that in this ecosystem, the primary influence—race—is never in doubt. In southern party politics past and present, race seems to be connected with every other demographic factor, and every other demographic factor seems to relate to race.

African American population. The South long has been characterized as the nation's most clearly demarcated region and its most distinctive subculture, as well.

A large part of the reason stems from the presence and influence of the South's African American population. While many nonsouthern states also have sizable African American communities, such populations almost always are metropolitan in location. Compared to the North, however, the African American presence is larger and both a rural and an urban phenomenon. Whether the period is antebellum, Jim Crow, or post–Voting Rights Act, whether the analyst is de Tocqueville, Key (1949), or the brothers Black (1987, 1992), race is a fundamental question in the politics of the South—even more so than in the politics of the United States as a whole, which some influential analysts now characterize as organized and driven by race (see Carmines and Stimson 1989).

African Americans constitute 22.4 percent of the population of the eleven states studied here. The percentage is much higher, at 29.7 percent, in the five Deep South states than it is in the rim South states, for which the average share of 16.4 percent African Americans is smaller than that for many industrial states outside the South. Indeed, the rim-state average would be even smaller, around 15 percent, were it not for North Carolina, which at 22.0 percent African Americans is an outlier among the rim states.

Numerous sources have tried with some success to establish that following the 1965 Voting Rights Act, which enrolled over three million new African American voters, a considerable amount of white flight from the Democratic party to the Republican party took place in the "black-belt" counties of the South. Davison and Krassa (1991a), whose choice and use of data is questioned by some (in particular, Bullock 1991a), make the case that whites of lower socioeconomic attainment in these black-belt counties account for much of the growth of Republican voting in southern congressional races. Others, such as Mackey, indirectly provide support for the white flight hypothesis by showing that industrialization, which some posit as an alternative explanation of the growing Republicanization of the South, has at best "weak and often contradictory associations with electoral change in the South" (Mackey 1991, 109; see also Bartley and Graham 1975).

One political effect of such white flight for Republicans, according to Whitby and Gilliam (1989, 1991), has been the ideological polarization of the parties' southern electoral bases, and, thereby, of the congressional party caucuses. The influx of usually liberal black voters into the Democratic party was met by an outflow of conservative white voters to the Republican party. These opposing effects may have changed the roll-call voting incentives of southern lawmakers in both parties, accounting for part of the rise in congressional party unity voting that has taken place since the 1970s.

If this is indeed the condition of the current southern electorate, then we should expect to find higher levels of elite-mass issue integration in both parties as we move from states with lower percentages of African American population to those with higher percentages of African Americans. In particular, the five Deep South states, with the bulk of the black-belt counties covered by the Voting Rights Act, should contain higher levels of elite-mass issue agreement than is manifest in the rim South states. To make certain that the explanatory power of race has been tested accurately, multiple runs of the data were conducted using not only African American population share, but African American voter registration figures as well, to account for possible cross-state differences in civic virtue or registration accessibility (there proved to be no difference).

Rising levels of education, income, and urbanization. Another possible explanation of southern electoral change that is disputed by advocates of the race explanation is industrialization, or, more broadly defined, modernization. As states develop from traditional, agrarian societies into modern economic and social systems, the resultant socioeconomic diversification should support the growth of meaningful electoral competition. Industrialization, which concentrates capital and labor at a given site for productive purposes, by itself should generate a sufficient divergence of political interests to support party competition. Superimposed upon declining but still potent agrarian power structures (see Thomas and Hrebenar 1991 on the state of agricultural interests in the New South), industrial development endows electoral systems with wealth, on the one hand, and workers on the other. These form the respective bases of two-party competition for political power within metropolitan settings, and serve as coalition-partners on behalf of metropolitan interests in the power competition that takes place within state, regional, and national settings.

Since one end product of the clustering of capital assets (i.e., facilities) and of human capital together at a location is urbanization, one useful indicator of the extent of industrialization of a state is the percentage of the state's population that resides in urban settings. Since another product of industrial development is the creation of wealth, a second useful indicator of its presence in various settings is relatively higher per capita income. Finally, since economic development not only provides more disposable income to be spent on education but also creates greater market demand for an educated, skilled work force, a third concomitant of development is increased educational attainment.

The growth of urbanization, income levels, education levels, and other attributes of socioeconomic modernization are not without consequences for electoral competition and, beyond that, elite-mass linkage. Since the New Deal realignment, there has been a national trend for voters of greater income and educational attainment to support the Republican party. In metropolitan areas the trend resulted in Democratic control of inner cities and Republican control of the suburban collars around them. Within the South, however, as Strong (1955), Lubell (1956), and Sundquist (1973) note, the New Deal realignment of the 1930s took an additional twenty years to complete. Southern presidential Republicanism only took hold in the affluent suburbs of the South's largest metropolitan centers during the 1950s. Prior to the 1950s, Republicanism in the South had been limited to the "mountain Republicans" spawned by the highland-lowland political rivalries of the mid-nineteenth century. Since the 1950s, these "mountain" and "metropolitan" Republicans have been augmented by white flight Republicans in the black-belt counties.

For these reasons, we hypothesize that elite-mass linkage within the respective political parties could be affected in the following ways by the changing demographics of income, urbanization, and education. As per capita income goes up in this region, we might expect to observe less elite-mass issue integration because of a widening gap in the respective conditions and outlooks of the rich and the poor. We expect this contrast to be especially stark within the ranks of the Democratic party and in the Deep South states. Urbanization, on the other hand, although closely linked to per capita income growth, should not have quite the same effect upon party elite-mass cohesion. In the case of the Republican party, the less urban the state, the greater the likelihood of intraparty trifurcation, or at least bifurcation, involving some combination of mountain, metropolitan, and black-belt Republican factions. The more urban the state, the greater the likelihood that metropolitan Republicans, augmented by generational turnover fueled by the popularity of Reagan, will overwhelm mountain and/or black-belt Republicans, whose essentially rural base must shrink as urbanization encroaches. Thus the more urban the state, the more elite-mass integration one should expect to see in the Republican party. Too, the more urban the state, the greater the likelihood that the growing number of Democrats in the industrial cores of metropolitan areas will moot or mute factional rivalry with Democrats in the rural lowlands that have been the slowest to embrace Republicanism.

In contrast, it is much more difficult to anticipate what ascending rates of graduation from college will bring. On the one hand, common sense, reinforced by the literature on political participation, suggests that in those states where college graduation rates are highest, Republican attachments should be higher as well. This correlation should result in correspondingly greater elite-mass integration in both parties. That is, as Republicans increasingly replace Democrats as the party of southern "haves," Democrats should cohere more along lower-middle-class lines than was the case in the days of the solid South. Too, the addition of better educated Generation Xers to the metropolitan wing of southern Republicans should strengthen the middle-class component of that party relative to the mountain Republicans who had been the main core of southern Republicanism prior to the era of Truman and Ike. The gentrification of pockets of mountain Republicans that has taken place as parts of the Blue Ridge Mountains, Smokies, Appalachians, and Ozarks experienced dramatic growth during the 1980s and 1990s reinforces the middle-class image of southern Republicans. On the other hand, if, as Davison and Krassa (1991a) suggest,[5] white flight to the Republican party in black-belt counties has been heaviest among the least-educated whites, then there also is a possibility that we will find that where college graduation rates are highest, the process of partisan change will be comparatively slower than elsewhere in the South. In such circumstances, we would expect a modification of the general trend. Democratic parties should continue to be influenced by educated economic elites, with attendant issue distance between their issue preferences and those of their increasingly black electoral base. The gentrification of the Republicans, however, would not only be slowed but perhaps be offset by racially motivated party switchers whose presence in the Republican party perpetuates issue cleavage within the party.

Fundamentalists and traditional values. The role of the Christian Right in contemporary southern politics is reflexively related to the changes described in each of the foregoing demographic variables. It also may be related to the southern politocultural context to which we now turn, insofar as the emergent political activism of the Christian Right can be interpreted as an attempt to defend traditional, core southern values from the corrosive effects of modernization.

Much of the Christian Right in the South is composed of denominations that are categorized as evangelical protestant. However, not all of the Christian Right is evangelical and not all evangelicals can be considered to belong to the Christian Right. With regard to the former, the Latter-day Saints (Mormons) are sufficiently conservative in political outlook and "nonmainstream" in religious dogma to be treated as part of the Christian Right (Erikson, Wright, and McIver 1993, 65 n. 7). As for the latter,

large numbers of blacks identify themselves in religious censuses as evangelical, but their partisan and ideological tendencies are usually quite opposite those of white evangelical Christians. For these reasons, we assess the impact of the nascent Christian Right upon the issue cohesion of party elites and masses by following Erikson, Wright, and McIver's (1993, 64–67) construct of "fundamentalist Protestants." This group includes all those usually counted as evangelicals (i.e., all denominations coded as "neofundamentalist" in NES code books, as well as generic and "primitive" Baptists)[6] plus Latter-day Saints, but excludes African American denominations self-defined as evangelical.[7]

Theories seeking to explain the rise of the Christian Right promote social group, value-centric, and institutional explanations that tend to mesh together nicely, rather than setting off in separate directions. In a nutshell, a confluence of growing democratic resources (Wolfinger and Rosenstone 1980), equilibrium-disturbing groups and issues (Truman 1951), and interest-group entrepreneurs (Salisbury 1969) each bestirred these fundamentalist worshipers essentially during the same time period.[8]

Traditionally less formally educated, less affluent, and less interested and involved in politics (but more pro-Democrat, insofar as they were involved) than other whites, fundamentalist Christians in the South have been touched by modernization along with the rest of the region. Although they may still lag behind whites of other denominations on most measures of socioeconomic success, as fundamentalists have increased their numbers in the middle class, they have gained access to resources (such as disposable income, information, free time, access to government officials and social networks, and so forth) that facilitate political participation.

Clearly, however, those who now make their political views known through organizational vehicles such as the Moral Majority, the PTL Club, and the Christian Voice have not been mobilized on the basis of what Clark and Wilson (1962) would consider *material* appeals. Rather, they have been mobilized in a *purposive* crusade to defend and promote traditional moral and social values—in essence, values of belonging (to a lifetime mate, to a family, to a community, to a country, to God)—that seem to them to have been marginalized in classroom curricula, in entertainment and news media, in political discourse, and in public policy alike. No less marginalized were the role models and the institutions revered by fundamentalists. John Lennon proclaimed the Beatles "more popular than Christ." Madalyn Murray O'Hair persuaded the Warren Court to secularize what had begun as a "Christian Republic." Soldiers who fought for their country in an unpopular war were reviled by their countrymen as killers. And presidents were hounded from office. Television evangelists who preached the gospel and saved lost souls seemed to be under microscopic scrutiny, while Madonna, rap artists, and heavy metal groups made millions from peddling blasphemy and unwholesome values to impressionable youth. As "black power," "Chicano power," and "gay power" received attention to their symbolic and substantive demands, to white Christians who until then had thought of America as belonging to them, the modern educational and political dogma of multicultural diversity seemed to include everyone but people like themselves.

Even as such marginalization occurred, however, the fundamentalist churches as institutions were modernizing and developing along with their followers. Congregations and their sanctuaries grew bigger. The faithful grew more prosperous. Seminary trained pastors replaced devout, earnest yeomen who merely had "heard the call," and these professional clergy managed the expansion of church missions to include education, day care, and counseling services. Some pioneered in the creation of "electronic churches" that used the airwaves to reach still larger audiences—and to solicit their financial support. All of this served to bring formerly small churches undergoing such institutionalization within the regulatory reach of the state. "The result was a series of classic confrontations between the state's interest in regulating the private provision of social services and the church's claims of immunity under the free exercise clause" (Wald 1987, 208–9). No longer able to escape politics in any case, church leaders have used their parishioners' concern about the condition of modern life, as well as about church-state issues, to build a political movement that would protect the institutional interests of their rapidly growing denominations. Their merger of theology and ideology mobilized the resources of church members to try to set the Republic straight again, by injecting a Christian viewpoint into the national political discourse. As a result, the Christian Right built its voting strength and campaign finance capability to levels that were attractive to the Republican party. Once an integral part of the party's electoral and financial constituencies, the Christian Right fused its own militant form of social conservatism to the traditional Republican agenda of fiscal conservatism.

For our purposes, then, the larger the population of fundamentalist Christians in a state, the more likely it is that the state Republican party will be home to an uneasy coexistence of the Christian Right and the traditional Republican types discussed above. Such a division could mean some intraparty issue cleavage. Therefore, we should expect to see higher elite-mass issue integration in states where fundamentalist Christians are proportionally fewer.

Methods

To test for the impact of environmental influences on the intraparty issue cohesion reported in chapter 3, we employed MANOVA, a technique that allowed us to look at the main effect of a given party elite/mass dyad (or factor) for a given issue when controlled for (1) the presence of a given contextual covariate, and (2) the presence of any interaction effect occurring between that covariate and the factor. The MANOVA model used to examine the effect of the covariate and of the interaction term on the factor is a "regression approach," in which covariates, factors, and interactions are entered and assessed simultaneously and adjusted for each other. We used SPSS (Statistical Package for the Social Sciences) to analyze the data.[9] Readers will recognize the following design statement from SPSS' MANOVA module as one that permits the complex analysis we propose: DESIGN = DV BY FAC (1,2), COV, FAC BY COV.

We performed this analysis, as well as others (see

the Appendixes), for *all* contextual variables across all possible combinations of groups. This conservative strategy, while extremely costly in terms of time and resources, proved prescient. The group means for the various dyadic combinations of the several operational definitions of partisan elites and masses tested in this study proved to be only somewhat sensitive to the influence of environmental covariates when the latter were the only controls,[10] but very responsive when the interactions between these covariates and the elite-mass factors were entered as additional controls. Such environmental influences have been entirely neglected in previously published studies of intraparty issue cohesion.

To make this undertaking more manageable, we confined our analysis to three of the five definitions of mass partisanship used in chapter 3: national and state party identification, and party voted for in the 1992 presidential contest. We retained all three definitions of elite—convention delegate, county party chair, and county party member—thus creating nine possible elite-mass combinations for analysis. Testing all of the covariate effects and covariate-factor interaction effects possible in a study that involves nine elite/mass dyads, multiplied by eleven context variables, multiplied in turn by sixteen issues[11] for which an interaction effect might be registered, was an enormous undertaking.

Equally enormous is the problem of effectively presenting the results of so many analyses of variance. The most economical and germane way to report the findings is to create a scale to measure the impact of the environmental variables upon intraparty cohesion for each of the sixteen issues. We present such a scale, accompanied by a discussion focusing on those cases in which environmental influence seems to have altered, positively or negatively, the level of intraparty issue agreement. In this way we do not lose sight of the broader questions of this chapter and those that follow: does political context condition partisan linkage? Is elite-mass issue cohesion enhanced or diminished by controlling for context? And, finally, which class (endogenous or exogenous?), genus (institutional, politocultural, or

demographic?), and specie (*state party organizational strength* or *percentage black*?) of environmental variable(s) is responsible for such alterations?[12]

In tables 4.1 to 4.16 we report, one issue at a time, the changes that occur, if any, in the distributions of significant versus nonsignificant differences in group means (at $p \leq .05$) for each elite-mass combination when each of the eleven environmental variables is introduced as a covariate and as a source of interaction with that elite-mass combination. This is presented using a simple Dyadic Behavior Scale (DBS), which reports the impact of environmental controls upon elite-mass issue agreement in the following manner.

Cells containing the letter *A* (for "agreement") are those in which elite-mass issue agreement existed in both the base analysis presented in chapter 3 *and* when the specified context variable and its interaction with the elite-mass factor were introduced as controls.

Cells containing the letters *AC* (for "agreement when controlled for covariate and interaction effect") are those in which elites and masses disagreed in the base analysis but agreed *after* the specified context variable and its interaction with the elite-mass factor were introduced as controls.

Cells containing the letters *DC* (for "disagreement when controlled for covariate and interaction effect") are those in which elites and masses agreed during the base analysis but disagreed *after* the specified context variable and its interaction with the elite-mass factor were introduced as controls.

Cells containing the letter *D* (for "disagreement") are those in which elites and masses disagreed both in chapter 3 and *after* the specified context variable and its interaction with the elite-mass factor were introduced as controls.

Results

In tables 4.1 to 4.16 we report, issue by issue, the changes that occur in the distributions of significant versus nonsignificant differences in group means for each elite-mass combination when each of the eleven environmental variables is controlled (1) as a covariate, and (2) for its interaction with the elite-mass factor. Following the order of issue-items established in the previous chapter, we begin with the effect of context upon levels of elite-mass ideological agreement.

Ideology

In table 4.1, we find that elite-mass ideological cohesion is relatively unaffected by controlling for environmental covariates and their interactions with the various elite-mass factors. In the Republican (right-hand) panel of the table we see that in 67 cells—that is, about 75 percent of the cells in the Republican panel—the original base result reported in chapter 3 is not altered by the introduction of environmental covariates and interactions. In 19 cells (21 percent of the panel), the ideological cohesion that prevailed across all but 1 elite/mass dyad in chapter 3 gives way to ideological differences significant at .05 when environmental variables and interactions are introduced. The demographic variables *percentage black, percent urban,* and *percentage fundamentalist* account for fifteen of these nineteen conversions and seem to have affected pairs involving Republican county chairs and party identifiers twice as often as any other dyads. In 4 other cells involving Republican county committee members and Republican voters, however, the base disagreement of chapter 3 gives way to cohesion when *percentage fundamentalist, percentage college graduates,* and the institutional variables *state Republican organizational strength* and *interparty competition* are introduced as controls. Thus while the demographic variables affected Republican intraparty ideological cohesion rather impressively, the ideological cohesion itself was also impressive insofar as it remained intact in 71 percent of the cells in the panel despite the introduction of controls, and was augmented in another 4 percent of the cells in the panel when controls were introduced.

In the Democratic (left) panel of table 4.1, 54 of 90 cells (60 percent) registered no change when the various environmental variables and interactions were introduced as controls. What is really significant is that all 29 cells in which the introduction of controls altered the chapter 3 base result moved from issue disagreement (D) to agreement (AC). No cells register movement in the opposite direction, from a chapter 3 base finding of agreement (A) to disagreement (DC), when context is introduced. Given that there are 33 cells in the panel in which the chapter 3 base finding of agreement was unaffected, controlling for the various context variables has the effect of increasing the level of intraparty ideological agreement within the Democratic party from 37 to 69 percent. Again, the control variables most often associated with conversion of initial intraparty disagreement into cohesion are the demographic variables, especially *percentage college graduates, percentage urban,* and *per capita income,* which by themselves account for over half of the cells containing AC. However, *interparty competition* occasioned as many conversions as any of these, and *state Democratic organizational strength* also performed well. But all of the dyads thus affected were either county Democratic committee members/party identifiers or Democratic convention delegates/masses. Ideological agreement levels among Democratic county chairs and Democratic masses, which were cohesive to begin with, were replaced by significant differences in only 5 of 30 cells possible, usually in response to controlling for *Democratic organizational strength* at the state or local level.

When we look at the two panels of table 4.1 together, it is evident that the Republicans' considerable lead in intraparty ideological cohesion reported in chapter 3 dwindles, but at 6 percent more cells containing A or AC remains slightly stronger than among Democrats, when environmental differences and interactions are controlled. Clearly, controlling for state political context had the effect of teasing out a great deal more ideological cohesion among southern Democratic elites and masses than was apparent in chapter 3.

Turning an eye toward the possible electoral ramifications of these data, it would seem that both southern Republican and Democratic elites in 1992 were in touch ideologically with their respective southern party masses in two-thirds or more of the

TABLE 4.1
DYADIC BEHAVIOR SCALE OF ELITE-MASS COHESION REGARDING IDEOLOGICAL SELF-PLACEMENT

| | DEMOCRATS | | | | | | | | | REPUBLICANS | | | | | | | | |
| | Convention Delegates | | | Party Chairs | | | Committee Members | | | Convention Delegates | | | Party Chairs | | | Committee Members | | |
	NPID	SPID	Voters	NPID	SPID	Voters	NPID	SPID	Voters	NPID	SPID	Voters	NPID	SPID	Voters	NPID	SPID	Voters
Chapter 3 base result	D	D	D	A	A	A	D	D	A	A	A	A	A	A	A	A	A	D
Percentage black	D	D	D	A	A	A	AC	AC	A	DC	DC	A	DC	DC	A	DC	DC	A
Percentage fundamentalist	D	D	D	A	A	A	AC	AC	A	DC	DC	A	DC	DC	A	A	A	AC
Percentage college graduates	AC	AC	AC	A	A	A	AC	AC	DC	A	A	A	DC	DC	A	A	A	AC
Percentage urban	AC	AC	AC	A	A	A	AC	AC	A	A	A	A	DC	DC	DC	DC	DC	D
Per capita income	AC	AC	AC	A	A	A	AC	AC	A	A	A	A	A	A	A	A	A	A
Liberalism of party identifiers index	D	D	D	A	A	A	AC	AC	A	A	A	A	A	A	A	A	A	A
State party identification index	D	D	D	A	A	DC	D	D	DC	A	A	A	A	A	A	A	A	D
Interparty competition index	AC	AC	AC	A	A	A	AC	AC	A	A	A	A	A	A	A	A	A	AC
Local party organizational strength index	D	D	D	DC	DC	A	D	D	A	A	A	A	A	A	DC	A	A	D
State party organizational strength index	D	D	AC	DC	DC	A	AC	AC	A	A	A	A	A	A	A	A	A	AC
(Cross-party) state party organizational strength index	D	D	D	D	D	D	AC	D	D	D	D	D	D	D	D	D	D	D

Note: NPID = national party identifiers; SPID = state party identifiers. In the cells, A = agreement; D = disagreement; AC = agreement when controlled for covariate and interaction effect; DC = disagreement when controlled for covariate and interaction effect.

contexts provided. In contrast, the bottom row of table 4.1 indicates that neither party's elites did a very good job of ideologically reflecting the opposing party's voters and identifiers, even when the context of their own *state party organizational strength* is taken into account. This is consistent with the strong levels of intraparty ideological cohesion within both parties indicated in the rows higher up in the table.

All of this suggests that in an election revolving more around ideology than around specific issues, national conditions, or candidate qualities, both parties could expect to be successful at mobilizing their respective southern voter bases, but neither should expect to be very successful at converting the other's supporters. An election about ideology, of course, is the strategy that worked so well for George Bush versus Michael Dukakis in 1988. The election of 1992, however, was more about issues and national conditions than ideology, as we shall now see.

Gender, Race, and Equality

We turn now from the effects of environment upon general intraparty ideological integration to its effects upon intraparty cohesion across a series of specific issue-items concerning the politics of race, gender, and equality.

Table 4.2 presents the effects of environmental covariates upon elite-mass issue cohesion in government efforts to improve the social and economic situation of women. There we find alteration of the base findings presented in chapter 3 occurring in 50 percent of the cells in the Republican panel, versus only 14 percent of the cells in the Democratic panel. Republican intraparty issue integration increases markedly, from none to 50 percent of the panel, when environmental covariates and interactions are introduced. All 9 possible elite/mass dyads are affected by a minimum of three of the environmental variables, but those involving Republican county committee members and masses (all three types) are 30 percent more likely to be affected than Republican delegate/mass and county chair/mass pairs are. With the exception of *percentage black,* which affects nothing, it is the

demographic variables that occasion almost two-thirds of the cells indicating intra-Republican cohesion concerning government efforts to improve the socioeconomic well-being of women. But the institutional variable *interparty competition* is associated with as many conversions from disagreement to agreement as most of the demographic variables, and the *liberalism of state Republican identifiers* occasions agreement across all 9 elite/mass pairs.

The Democratic panel of table 4.2 is not affected as dramatically by the introduction of state political context variables. However, the 9 cells in which the chapter 3 base result converts from disagreement to agreement do enhance the already healthy rate of intra-Democratic issue cohesion from 62 percent to 72 percent of all cells. All 9 cases involve Democratic convention delegate/mass pairs. Pairs involving both kinds of local Democratic elites with masses were already predisposed to cohere concerning policy toward women; only in 4 of 60 possible cases did controlling for environment convert the base agreement of chapter 3 into disagreement. The context variables effecting the most change are *percentage urban,* which converts all 3 delegate/mass pairs from disagreement to agreement, and *state Democratic organizational strength,* which has the same effect on the delegate/mass pairs but also converts the county chair/voter and county chair/state identifier pairs from agreement to disagreement.

The Democrats' 20-cell edge over the Republicans in the number of cells in table 4.2 that indicate intraparty cohesion suggests better prospects for them to reinforce the views of, and mobilize the votes of, their supporters (especially females). The cells in the Republican panel are evenly divided between elite-mass agreement and disagreement concerning government efforts to provide women socioeconomic help. This, combined with the fact that the bottom row of table 4.2 indicates issue cohesion between both sets of local Democratic elites and all three kinds of Republican masses when *state Democratic organizational strength* is taken into account, suggests that Republicans in the South would find it very hard in 1992 to hold onto the votes of their female supporters, and of any other voters concerned

TABLE 4.2
DYADIC BEHAVIOR SCALE OF ELITE-MASS COHESION REGARDING "THE GOVERNMENT IN WASHINGTON SHOULD MAKE EVERY EFFORT TO IMPROVE THE SOCIAL AND ECONOMIC SITUATION FOR WOMEN"

	DEMOCRATS									REPUBLICANS								
	Convention Delegates			Party Chairs			Committee Members			Convention Delegates			Party Chairs			Committee Members		
	NPID	SPID	Voters	NPID	SPID	Voters	NPID	SPID	Voters	NPID	SPID	Voters	NPID	SPID	Voters	NPID	SPID	Voters
Chapter 3 base result	D	D	D	A	A	A	A	A	A	D	D	D	D	D	D	D	D	D
Percentage black	D	D	D	A	A	A	A	A	A	D	D	D	D	D	D	D	D	D
Percentage fundamentalist	D	D	D	A	A	A	A	A	A	AC	AC	AC	AC	D	D	AC	AC	AC
Percentage college graduates	D	D	AC	A	A	A	A	A	A	D	AC	AC	AC	AC	AC	AC	AC	AC
Percentage urban	AC	AC	AC	A	A	A	A	A	A	D	D	D	AC	AC	AC	AC	AC	AC
Per capita income	D	D	AC	A	A	A	A	A	A	AC	AC	AC	AC	AC	AC	AC	AC	AC
Liberalism of party identifiers index	D	D	D	A	A	A	A	A	A	AC	AC	AC	AC	AC	AC	AC	AC	AC
State party identification index	D	D	D	A	A	A	A	A	A	D	D	D	D	D	D	D	D	D
Interparty competition index	D	D	AC	DC	A	A	DC	A	A	AC	AC	AC	D	AC	D	AC	AC	AC
Local party organizational strength index	D	D	D	A	A	A	A	A	A	D	D	D	D	D	D	D	D	D
State party organizational strength index	AC	AC	AC	A	DC	DC	A	A	A	D	D	D	D	D	D	D	D	D
(Cross-party) state party organizational strength index	D	D	D	AC	AC	AC	AC	AC	AC	D	D	D	D	D	D	D	D	D

Note: NPID = national party identifiers; SPID = state party identifiers. In the cells, A = agreement; D = disagreement; AC = agreement when controlled for covariate and interaction effect; DC = disagreement when controlled for covariate and interaction effect.

about the status of women. Indeed, the more conservative posture taken on this issue by all three types of Republican elites (see table 3.5) not only put them at odds with their own masses in half of the cells but also precluded any ability to draw votes from Democratic rank-and-filers concerned about the status of women, as indicated by the bottom row of the Republican panel of table 4.2.

Table 4.3, which deals with intraparty cohesion concerning government efforts to improve the social and economic position of blacks and other minorities, closely resembles the pattern of table 4.2. Again the introduction of environmental controls converts a significant share (44 percent) of the cells in the Republican panel from disagreement to agreement (AC). Again the changes occur across all 9 dyadic combinations, but slightly more frequently for local Republican committee members than for the other two sets of elites. Again it is *interparty competition, liberalism of state Republican identifiers,* and the demographic variables that associate with these changes, but this time, because it is the socioeconomic status of minorities rather than of women that is in question, we find that *percentage black* is as associated as any of the other demographic variables with the rise in intraparty cohesion. Since table 3.6 revealed that Republican elites were always more conservative than Republican masses on this issue, the association of *percentage black* with rising levels of elite-mass cohesion on this issue does provide some support for the Davison-Krassa (1991) white flight hypothesis of Republican growth in the south. Base disagreement between Republican elites and masses concerning government efforts to help minorities does turn into intra-Republican agreement when the percentage of blacks present is taken into account.

In the Democratic panel of table 4.3, we once again find a healthy predisposition toward intraparty cohesion (56 percent of all cells) on display in the columns beneath the two types of local party activists. This base cohesion is again elevated to 72 percent of all cells by a small number (15 this time) of delegate/mass dyads that went from disagreement to agreement when environment was controlled. A

slightly larger but still small number of cells (10 of 60 possible this time) went in the opposite direction, from base agreement in chapter 3 to disagreement when controlled for environment. Again *state Democratic organizational strength* and *percentage urban* are responsible for many of the changes in both directions, but this time other demographic variables— *per capita income* and *percentage college graduates*— are associated with many of these changes.

Finally, once again the bottom row of table 4.3 shows nothing but significant differences between Republican elites and Democratic masses concerning government efforts to improve the socioeconomic standing of a class of people, whereas both sets of local Democratic elites cohere with all three types of Republican masses when *state Democratic organizational strength* is introduced into the equation. Thus it would appear that in 1992 southern Democratic parties successfully reflected their own mass base— which included large numbers of minorities—on this issue, and at the level of local organizational activists did a good job of representing the Republican masses on this issue, too. In contrast, Republican activists were at odds with their own mass base over this issue in more than 50 percent of the environmental analyses. One therefore expects that the Democrats should have been able to hold their own voter base while also successfully inducing Republican defections, especially among minorities and other Republican voters and identifiers concerned about this issue.

Table 4.4, which reports the effect of environmental covariates upon intraparty cohesion concerning whether women should have an equal role in "running business, industry and government," finds intra-Republican cohesion almost entirely unaffected. Only Republican delegates and both types of Republican identifiers cease to agree on this issue when *liberalism of Republican identifiers* is controlled. Since there was base agreement for both of these delegate/mass pairs in chapter 3, presumably controlling for this politocultural variable and its interaction with each of these factors had the effect of differentiating Republican delegates' attitudes as more conservative, after all, than the attitudes of Republican identifiers on this gender issue.

TABLE 4.3

DYADIC BEHAVIOR SCALE OF ELITE-MASS COHESION REGARDING "THE GOVERNMENT IN WASHINGTON SHOULD MAKE EVERY EFFORT TO IMPROVE THE SOCIAL AND ECONOMIC POSITION OF BLACKS AND OTHER MINORITY GROUPS"

| | DEMOCRATS | | | | | | | | | REPUBLICANS | | | | | | | | |
| | Convention Delegates | | | Party Chairs | | | Committee Members | | | Convention Delegates | | | Party Chairs | | | Committee Members | | |
	NPID	SPID	Voters	NPID	SPID	Voters	NPID	SPID	Voters	NPID	SPID	Voters	NPID	SPID	Voters	NPID	SPID	Voters
Chapter 3 base result	D	D	D	A	A	A	A	A	A	D	D	D	D	D	D	D	D	D
Percentage black	D	D	D	A	A	A	A	A	A	AC	AC	D	D	D	D	AC	AC	AC
Percentage fundamentalist	D	D	D	A	A	A	A	A	A	AC	AC	AC	D	D	D	AC	AC	AC
Percentage college graduates	AC	AC	AC	A	A	DC	DC	A	A	D	D	D	AC	AC	AC	D	D	AC
Percentage urban	AC	AC	AC	A	A	A	A	A	A	D	D	D	D	D	AC	D	D	AC
Per capita income	AC	AC	AC	A	A	A	A	DC	DC	D	D	D	AC	D	AC	AC	D	AC
Liberalism of party identifiers index	D	D	D	A	A	A	A	A	A	AC	AC	AC	AC	AC	AC	AC	AC	AC
State party identification index	D	D	D	A	A	A	A	DC	A	AC	AC	D	D	D	D	D	D	D
Interparty competition index	AC	AC	AC	A	A	A	A	A	A	AC	AC	AC	AC	AC	D	AC	AC	AC
Local party organizational strength index	D	D	D	A	A	DC	A	A	A	D	D	D	D	D	D	D	D	D
State party organizational strength index	AC	AC	AC	A	A	DC	DC	DC	DC	D	D	D	D	D	D	D	D	D
(Cross-party) state party organizational strength index	AC	D	AC	AC	AC	AC	AC	AC	D	D	D	D	D	D	D	D	D	D

Note: NPID = national party identifiers; SPID = state party identifiers. In the cells, A = agreement; D = disagreement; AC = agreement when controlled for covariate and interaction effect; DC = disagreement when controlled for covariate and interaction effect.

TABLE 4.4

DYADIC BEHAVIOR SCALE OF ELITE-MASS COHESION REGARDING "WOMEN SHOULD HAVE AN EQUAL ROLE WITH MEN IN RUNNING BUSINESS, INDUSTRY, AND GOVERNMENT"

| | DEMOCRATS | | | | | | | | | REPUBLICANS | | | | | | | | |
| | Convention Delegates | | | Party Chairs | | | Committee Members | | | Convention Delegates | | | Party Chairs | | | Committee Members | | |
	NPID	SPID	Voters	NPID	SPID	Voters	NPID	SPID	Voters	NPID	SPID	Voters	NPID	SPID	Voters	NPID	SPID	Voters
Chapter 3 base result	D	D	D	A	A	A	A	A	A	A	A	A	A	A	A	A	A	A
Percentage black	D	D	D	A	A	A	A	A	A	A	A	A	A	A	A	A	A	A
Percentage fundamentalist	D	D	D	A	A	A	A	A	A	A	A	A	A	A	A	A	A	A
Percentage college graduates	AC	D	AC	A	A	A	A	A	A	A	A	A	A	A	A	A	A	A
Percentage urban	AC	AC	AC	A	A	A	A	A	A	A	A	A	A	A	A	A	A	A
Per capita income	AC	AC	AC	A	A	A	A	A	A	A	A	A	A	A	A	A	A	A
Liberalism of party identifiers index	D	D	D	A	A	A	DC	DC	A	DC	DC	A	A	A	A	A	A	A
State party identification index	D	D	D	A	A	A	DC	DC	DC	A	A	A	A	A	A	A	A	A
Interparty competition index	D	AC	AC	A	A	A	A	A	A	A	A	A	A	A	A	A	A	A
Local party organizational strength index	D	D	D	A	A	A	A	A	A	A	A	A	A	A	A	A	A	A
State party organizational strength index	AC	D	AC	A	A	A	A	A	A	A	A	A	A	A	A	A	A	A
(Cross-party) state party organizational strength index	D	D	AC	AC	AC	AC	AC	AC	A	A	A	D	D	D	D	D	D	

Note: NPID = national party identifiers; SPID = state party identifiers. In the cells, A = agreement; D = disagreement; AC = agreement when controlled for covariate and interaction effect; DC = disagreement when controlled for covariate and interaction effect.

The Democratic panel of table 4.4 is more affected in a relative sense, but not profoundly, by the introduction of environmental covariates and interactions. The base cohesion that existed between all county activist/mass pairs in chapter 3 is altered in only 5 of 60 cells possible underneath the Democratic county chair and committee member headings. Four of these five conversions from issue agreement to disagreement involve the committee member/national identifier and committee member/state identifier pairs; all five are occasioned by two of Erikson, Wright, and McIver's politocultural variables: *state party identification* index and *liberalism of state Democratic identifiers*. Why local committee members who normally should be expected to be most attuned to mass attitudes should differ significantly from partisan identifiers when these mass politocultural attitudes are controlled is unknown. On the other hand, the base disagreement that existed between the more liberal Democratic national convention delegates and their party's mass base in table 3.7 remains in effect for the most part in table 4.4, despite some environmental modifications. Only 12 of 30 cells possible in the Democratic panel's delegate/mass columns convert from base disagreement to issue cohesion when state contextual controls are introduced. Two-thirds of these changes are brought by demographic variables (*per capita income, percentage urban,* and *percentage college graduates*), but *interparty competition* and *state Democratic organizational strength* also occasion change in 2 of 3 dyads possible.

Overall, table 4.4 suggests that southern Republican parties should have been able to reinforce their mass base on this gender equality issue with greater success than on the distributive gender issue that is the subject of table 4.2. Republican elites and masses cohere with each other on gender equality in 98 percent of the cells in the Republican panel of table 4.4, compared to elite-mass cohesion in 74 percent of the cells in the Democratic panel. On the other hand, the bottom row of table 4.4 indicates that the Democratic elites enjoyed greater cross-party consonance with Republican masses than the Republican elites enjoyed with Democratic masses in 1992. More specifically, it was the local Democratic elites, who are better attuned than Democratic delegates with their own party masses, who cohere with Republican masses on gender equality when *state Democratic organizational strength* is taken into account.

This posed an electoral threat to southern Republican activists, who represented their own mass base well on this issue, but were comparatively weak on the related gender distributive issue. To hold onto the votes of their female adherents in 1992, Republican strategists in the South needed to emphasize their commitment to gender equality and find and develop other issues with which to counter the strong cross-party appeal that Democratic activists enjoyed with Republican masses on both gender issues. In so doing, Republican strategists may have found it wiser to take their cues from their party's national elites rather than its local elites, since it was the former, not the latter, who were in touch with the opposing party's masses, as well, on the question of gender equality. On the other hand, southern Democratic strategy regarding gender equality in 1992 would have done well to heed the cues of the party's local activists, who were better attuned than national delegates to their own party's southern mass base before *and* after state contexts were introduced, and to the Republican party's mass base on this issue, as well.

In table 4.5, which reports the effect of environmental context upon elite-mass attitudes toward affirmative action for blacks in hiring and promotion, we find that the preexistent issue dissonance among Republican elites and masses in chapter 3 is moderated somewhat by environmental influences. In 28 of 90 cells, agreement replaces disagreement when covariates and interactions are introduced. At 31 percent of all possible cells, this does not add up to very much intra-Republican issue agreement concerning affirmative action, but it is a big improvement upon the intraparty issue cleavage over affirmative action that was shown in table 3.8.

The rate of conversion from disagreement to agreement is equally strong among Republican delegate/mass pairs and Republican committee member/mass pairs at 37 percent of all cells within those

TABLE 4.5

DYADIC BEHAVIOR SCALE OF ELITE-MASS COHESION REGARDING "BECAUSE OF PAST DISCRIMINATION BLACKS SHOULD BE GIVEN PREFERENCE IN HIRING AND PROMOTION"

	DEMOCRATS									REPUBLICANS								
	Convention Delegates			Party Chairs			Committee Members			Convention Delegates			Party Chairs			Committee Members		
	NPID	SPID	Voters	NPID	SPID	Voters	NPID	SPID	Voters	NPID	SPID	Voters	NPID	SPID	Voters	NPID	SPID	Voters
Chapter 3 base result	A	A	A	D	D	D	D	D	A	D	D	D	D	D	D	D	D	D
Percentage black	A	A	A	AC	AC	AC	D	D	DC	AC	AC	AC	D	D	AC	AC	AC	AC
Percentage fundamentalist	A	A	A	AC	AC	AC	D	D	DC	AC	AC	AC	D	D	D	D	D	AC
Percentage college graduates	A	A	A	D	D	AC	D	D	A	D	D	D	D	D	D	D	D	D
Percentage urban	A	A	A	AC	AC	AC	AC	AC	A	D	D	D	D	D	AC	D	D	D
Per capita income	A	DC	A	AC	AC	AC	D	D	DC	AC	D	D	AC	AC	AC	AC	AC	AC
Liberalism of party identifiers index	DC	DC	DC	AC	AC	AC	AC	AC	A	AC	D	AC	D	D	AC	D	D	AC
State party identification index	DC	DC	DC	AC	AC	AC	AC	AC	A	D	D	D	D	D	D	D	D	D
Interparty competition index	A	A	A	AC	AC	AC	D	D	A	AC	AC	AC	AC	AC	AC	AC	AC	AC
Local party organizational strength index	A	A	A	D	D	D	D	D	DC	D	D	D	D	D	D	D	D	D
State party organizational strength index	A	A	A	D	D	D	D	D	A	D	D	D	D	D	D	D	D	D
(Cross-party) state party organizational strength index	AC	AC	AC	A	A	A	AC	A	A	D	D	D	D	D	D	D	D	D

Note: NPID = national party identifiers; SPID = state party identifiers. In the cells, A = agreement; D = disagreement; AC = agreement when controlled for covariate and interaction effect; DC = disagreement when controlled for covariate and interaction effect.

columns, respectively, and lags behind at 20 percent of all cells for Republican county chair/mass pairs. The control variables occasioning such influence include two that have not been heard from very much—*percentage fundamentalist* and *percentage black*—along with such recurrent influences as *per capita income, interparty competition,* and *liberalism of state Republican identifiers.* Interestingly, it is the two new control variables that seem to be responsible for the higher cohesion among delegate/mass and committee member/mass pairs, since the conversions occurring in the rows of the recurrent influences seem to be evenly distributed across the 9 dyadic combinations possible.

The environmental impact upon rates of issue consensus and dissensus in the Democratic panel of table 4.5 is even greater. Although the actual number of cells converting from disagreement to agreement is smaller by one (at 27) in this panel than in the Republican panel, it has the effect of raising the total percentage of pairs exhibiting issue agreement from 32 to 62 percent of the pairs in the panel. Then, too, about one-third (11 of 34) of the pairs exhibiting issue disagreement in the Democratic panel of table 4.5 were pairs that converted from base agreement in chapter 3 to disagreement when controls were introduced. As can be seen from a quick glance at the middle of the panel, a majority (21 of 27) of the pairs converting from issue disagreement to agreement involve the 3 Democratic county chair/mass dyads. Seven of the 11 pairs converting in the opposite direction (from agreement to disagreement) involve the 3 Democratic delegate/mass dyads, and the remaining pairs are all to be found in the Democratic committee member/Democratic voter column.

A majority of the pairs converting to issue dissonance (6 of 11) and one-third of the pairs converting to issue agreement (9 of 27) are associated with the politocultural variables *state party identification* index and *liberalism of Democratic identifiers.* Almost half (13 of 27) of the remaining cells that converted to agreement and all but 1 of the remaining cells that converted to disagreement are associated with the demographic control variables, each of which, except

percentage college graduates, influenced a minimum of 4 elite/mass pairs. Of the institutional variables, only *interparty competition* associated with as many as three conversions from the chapter 3 base results.

As far as electoral implications are concerned, it first must be noted that the percentage of cells in table 4.5 indicating elite-mass issue agreement is precisely twice as large for the Democrats as it is for the Republicans. Second, it must be noted that the bottom row of table 4.5 indicates that all three categories of Democratic elites are on the same page with all three categories of Republican rank-and-filers as far as affirmative action is concerned, whereas all three types of Republican elites differ significantly with all three categories of Democratic masses on this issue. Each of these patterns tells us volumes about which party should be successful at reinforcing and then mobilizing their own base of support, as well as making significant inroads into the opposing party's electoral base. Despite Governor Pete Wilson's successful manipulation of resentment of affirmative action in California during the 1990s, the issue seems to have been a plus for Democratic activists and a minus for Republican activists with the southern mass electorates of both parties during the 1992 election.

Domestic Policy

We turn next to the effects of environmental covariates and their interactions with factors upon intraparty cohesion across a wide variety of domestic policy issues prominent in the 1992 presidential campaign (and for the past generation): abortion, school prayer, health care, environmental protection, and employment.

Table 4.6 reports the effects of covariates and interaction terms upon intraparty cohesion concerning the availability of abortion by choice. In the Republican panel of this table, we see that controlling for environment and interaction has the effect of eliciting Republican elite-mass issue cohesion where there had been mostly intraparty disagreement over abortion in table 3.9. Fifty-one cells convert from D to AC when controls are introduced, whereas none

TABLE 4.6

DYADIC BEHAVIOR SCALE OF ELITE-MASS COHESION REGARDING "BY LAW A WOMAN SHOULD BE ABLE TO OBTAIN AN ABORTION AS A MATTER OF PERSONAL CHOICE"

| | DEMOCRATS | | | | | | | | | REPUBLICANS | | | | | | | | |
| | Convention Delegates | | | Party Chairs | | | Committee Members | | | Convention Delegates | | | Party Chairs | | | Committee Members | | |
	NPID	SPID	Voters	NPID	SPID	Voters	NPID	SPID	Voters	NPID	SPID	Voters	NPID	SPID	Voters	NPID	SPID	Voters
Chapter 3 base result	D	D	D	A	D	A	A	A	A	D	D	D	D	D	A	D	D	A
Percentage black	AC	D	D	A	AC	A	A	A	A	AC	AC	AC	AC	AC	A	AC	AC	A
Percentage fundamentalist	AC	D	D	AC	AC	A	A	A	A	AC	D	AC	AC	AC	A	AC	AC	A
Percentage college graduates	AC	AC	AC	AC	AC	A	A	A	A	AC	AC	AC	AC	AC	A	AC	AC	A
Percentage urban	AC	D	AC	AC	AC	A	A	A	A	AC	AC	D	AC	AC	A	AC	AC	A
Per capita income	AC	AC	AC	AC	AC	A	A	A	A	AC	AC	AC	AC	AC	A	AC	AC	A
Liberalism of party identifiers index	D	D	D	AC	AC	A	A	A	A	AC	D	AC	AC	AC	A	AC	AC	A
State party identification index	AC	D	D	AC	AC	A	A	A	A	AC	D	AC	AC	AC	A	AC	AC	A
Interparty competition index	AC	AC	AC	AC	AC	A	A	A	A	AC	AC	AC	AC	AC	A	AC	AC	A
Local party organizational strength index	D	D	D	D	D	A	A	A	A	D	D	D	D	D	A	D	D	A
State party organizational strength index	D	D	AC	AC	AC	A	A	A	DC	D	D	AC	D	AC	A	D	AC	A
(Cross-party) state party organizational strength index	AC	AC	AC	AC	AC	AC	AC	AC	AC	D	D	D	D	D	D	D	D	D

Note: NPID = national party identifiers; SPID = state party identifiers. In the cells, A = agreement; D = disagreement; AC = agreement when controlled for covariate and interaction effect; DC = disagreement when controlled for covariate and interaction effect.

convert from A to DC. Controlling for environment thus has the effect of raising the total percentage of cohesive pairs in the Republican panel from 22 to 79 percent and diminishing the total percentage of dissonant pairs from 78 to 21 percent—a complete about-face on the issue. Obviously, when this much transformation takes place within the grid, most of the control variables must be affecting most of the elite/mass dyads in the panel. Only 2 dyads—the Republican county chair/voter and Republican committee member/voter combinations which already cohered in the chapter 3 base result—experienced no changes when the context variables were introduced. And only two context variables—the *local* and *state Republican organizational strength* variables— were associated with few or no conversions from disagreement to agreement. Indeed, several variables, including *percentage black, percentage college graduates, per capita income,* and *interparty competition,* occasioned conversions for every elite/mass pair that was not already cohesive.

The Democratic panel of table 4.6 reveals some gain in cohesion between Democratic elites and masses, but not as much as occurred in the Republican panel. The introduction of state contextual controls saw intra-Democratic cohesion on the abortion question increase by 72 percent, from 39 to 67 pairs (and thus 74 percent of the pairs possible in the panel) when the AC cells are added to the A cells. In contrast, only 1 cell in the entire panel (in the county committee members/ voters column) converted from intraparty agreement to disagreement when context was introduced. Almost two-thirds of the cells converting to agreement involved the county chair/Democratic identifier dyads, and the rest of the conversions are evenly divided between the delegate/voter column, on the one hand, and the two delegate/party identifier columns on the other hand. The Democratic county committee member/mass dyads and the Democratic county chair/voter dyad already saw eye-to-eye on abortion before the control variables were introduced.

At first blush the southern Republican parties would appear to have been able to hold their own with the Democrats as far as the abortion issue in 1992 was concerned. Table 4.6 seems to suggest that the Republican elites were slightly more in tune with their mass base than the Democratic activists were with theirs. Furthermore, since the South is home to the Southern Baptist Convention and other conservative religious pillars of the so-called Bible Belt, it may have seemed reasonable that Republicans could make inroads into the swing vote and even the Democratic base throughout the region because of the abortion issue.

However, the bottom row of table 4.6 suggests otherwise. When the *state party organizational strength* of the respective parties is controlled, we see that the abortion views of the southern Republican elites in 1992 had no cross-party affinity with those of mass Democrats, whereas the southern Democratic elites' abortion views were consonant in each instance with those of the Republicans' mass base. Republican activists were guilty, then, not only of "preaching to their choir" but also of allowing Democratic activists to share their pulpit. In so many words, the 1992 Republican electoral strategy built in part on the crude assumption of anti-abortion sentiment among religious conservatives in the South and elsewhere was a disastrous miscalculation. With more than one "acceptable" product on the shelf, the Republican party should not have counted on its product holding its own share of the market, much less expanding its market share. As a recent study by Princeton Survey Research Associates notes, women (who are the ones affected most by this issue) tend nowadays to "maintain a `shopping cart' approach to religion, accepting many of their denomination's teachings, but discarding others that do not fit with their personal needs and experiences" (Center for Gender Equality 1999). Campaign strategists should have expected no less subtle consumer discretion on an issue that had been part of the public discourse for two decades already.

In table 4.7, which reports the effect of environmental influences upon intraparty cohesion regarding school prayer, we find that the agreement that had existed in the base analysis under the Republican committee member/voter and Republican delegate/voter and delegate/state identifier pairings is almost tripled when controls are introduced. Fifty of

TABLE 4.7
DYADIC BEHAVIOR SCALE OF ELITE-MASS COHESION REGARDING "PRAYER SHOULD BE ALLOWED IN THE PUBLIC SCHOOLS"

	DEMOCRATS									REPUBLICANS								
	Convention Delegates			Party Chairs			Committee Members			Convention Delegates			Party Chairs			Committee Members		
	NPID	SPID	Voters	NPID	SPID	Voters	NPID	SPID	Voters	NPID	SPID	Voters	NPID	SPID	Voters	NPID	SPID	Voters
Chapter 3 base result	D	D	D	A	A	A	A	A	A	D	A	A	D	D	D	D	D	A
Percentage black	D	D	D	A	A	A	A	A	A	AC	A	A	AC	AC	AC	AC	AC	A
Percentage fundamentalist	D	D	D	A	A	A	A	A	A	AC	A	A	AC	AC	AC	AC	AC	A
Percentage college graduates	AC	AC	AC	A	A	A	A	A	DC	AC	A	A	AC	AC	AC	AC	AC	A
Percentage urban	AC	AC	AC	A	A	A	A	A	A	AC	A	A	AC	AC	AC	AC	AC	A
Per capita income	AC	AC	AC	A	A	A	A	DC	DC	AC	A	A	AC	AC	AC	AC	AC	A
Liberalism of party identifiers index	D	D	A	DC	A	A	DC	DC	DC	AC	DC	A	AC	AC	AC	AC	AC	A
State party identification index	D	D	D	DC	DC	A	DC	DC	A	AC	A	A	AC	AC	AC	AC	AC	A
Interparty competition index	AC	AC	AC	DC	DC	DC	A	A	A	AC	A	A	AC	AC	AC	AC	AC	A
Local party organizational strength index	D	D	D	A	A	A	A	A	A	D	D	D	D	D	D	D	D	A
State party organizational strength index	D	D	AC	DC	DC	A	A	A	A	D	A	AC	AC	AC	AC	D	D	DC
(Cross-party) state party organizational strength index	AC	AC	AC	AC	AC	AC	AC	AC	D	D	D	D	D	D	D	D	D	D

Note: NPID = national party identifiers; SPID = state party identifiers. In the cells, A = agreement; D = disagreement; AC = agreement when controlled for covariate and interaction effect; DC = disagreement when controlled for covariate and interaction effect.

the 90 cells in the Republican panel convert from issue dissensus to consensus, raising Republicans' intraparty cohesion level on school prayer from 31 to 87 percent of all cells. The changes are dramatic in every column except those in which the original base result was cohesion, and every context variable except the two *Republican organizational strength* variables is associated with such conversions. In contrast, only 2 pairs shift in the opposite direction (from agreement to disagreement) in response to controlling for the *liberalism of Republican identifiers* and *state Republican organizational strength*, respectively.

In the Democratic panel of table 4.7, we see less environmental influence at work. Only fourteen conversions from the base agreement in table 3.10 occur in the six columns containing the county party elite/ mass pairs, and half of these are brought out by just the two politocultural variables (*liberalism of Democratic identifiers* and *party identifier index*). In contrast, conversions from disagreement to cohesion occur in 13 of the 21 pairs possible underneath the delegate/mass headings, and almost three-fourths of these changes are associated with the demographic variables *per capita income, percentage urban,* and *percentage college graduates.* Issue cohesion for the whole Democratic panel thus incurs a net loss of one cell due to environmental covariates and interactions, and stands at 66 percent of all possible pairs.

Normally, the Republicans' 21 percent edge over the Democrats in intraparty cohesion should make an issue a winner for Republicans, especially since in this case the issue is prayer in schools and the electoral battleground in question is the southern heart of the "Bible Belt," where the size of Republicans' mass voter base is almost even with that of the Democrats. However, while the school prayer issue receives a lot of lip service, it does not agitate voters on either side of the issue to the same degree that abortion or even affirmative action does, and therefore may not carry as much weight as these or other issues in many voters' decision calculus. Furthermore, it again must be noted that the bottom row of table 4.7 indicates that while Republican activists may have been very much in step in 1992 with their own base of electoral sup-

port, their posture on school prayer had no cross-party appeal with Democratic masses. In contrast, Democratic party activists' positions on school prayer in 1992 were consonant with those of the Republican rank and file across 8 of 9 pairs. Consequently, Republican strategists should not have assumed in 1992, or probably any other year, that advocacy of school prayer would generate for them a net advantage in votes, all other things considered.

In table 4.8, which reports the effects of environmental covariates upon intraparty cohesion concerning the health-care coverage issue that was at the heart of the 1992 campaign, we find that the context variables occasioned conversions from disagreement to agreement in 47 of 90 cells possible in the Republican panel. Since all 9 elite-mass Republican pairs held significantly different attitudes in the base results reported in table 3.11, no changes in the opposite direction (from cohesion to disagreement) could possibly take place. The conversions to cohesion took place across all 9 possible elite/mass dyads, but the county chair/mass and county committee member/ mass dyads each were host to 38 percent of the conversions, compared to only 23 percent taking place at the nexus of Republican national convention delegates and masses.

Each demographic control variable was associated with conversions in at least 4 of the 9 elite/mass dyads possible, so demographics on the whole occasioned 57 percent of the conversions to cohesion. However, only one demographic variable—*percentage fundamentalist*—was associated with conversion to agreement across all 9 dyads, whereas none of the others came closer than 5 of 9. *Interparty competition* and *liberalism of Republican identifiers* also were associated with conversion to cohesion across all 9 dyads, but no other politocultural or institutional variable occasioned change in more than 2 of 9 dyads—indeed, 2 out of 3 resulted in no changes at all when introduced to the equation.

In the Democratic panel of table 4.8, we find that the introduction of environmental covariates and interactions had the effect of elevating the level of intraparty cohesion concerning the health-care

TABLE 4.8

DYADIC BEHAVIOR SCALE OF ELITE-MASS COHESION REGARDING "THE GOVERNMENT OUGHT TO HELP PEOPLE GET DOCTORS AND HOSPITAL CARE AT LOW COST"

	DEMOCRATS									REPUBLICANS								
	Convention Delegates			Party Chairs			Committee Members			Convention Delegates			Party Chairs			Committee Members		
	NPID	SPID	Voters	NPID	SPID	Voters	NPID	SPID	Voters	NPID	SPID	Voters	NPID	SPID	Voters	NPID	SPID	Voters
Chapter 3 base result	D	D	D	A	A	A	D	D	D	D	D	D	D	D	D	D	D	D
Percentage black	D	D	D	A	A	A	AC	AC	AC	D	D	AC	AC	D	D	AC	AC	AC
Percentage fundamentalist	D	D	D	A	A	A	AC	AC	AC	AC	AC	AC	AC	AC	AC	AC	AC	AC
Percentage college graduates	AC	AC	AC	A	A	A	AC	AC	AC	D	AC	D	AC	AC	AC	D	AC	D
Percentage urban	AC	AC	AC	A	A	A	AC	AC	AC	D	D	D	AC	AC	AC	AC	AC	D
Per capita income	AC	AC	AC	A	A	A	AC	AC	AC	D	D	D	AC	AC	AC	D	AC	D
Liberalism of party identifiers index	D	D	D	A	A	A	D	D	AC	AC	AC	AC	AC	AC	AC	AC	AC	AC
State party identification index	D	D	D	DC	DC	DC	D	D	D	D	D	D	D	D	D	D	D	D
Interparty competition index	D	D	AC	DC	A	A	AC	AC	AC	AC	AC	AC	AC	AC	AC	AC	AC	AC
Local party organizational strength index	D	D	D	A	A	A	AC	AC	AC	D	D	D	D	D	D	D	D	D
State party organizational strength index	AC	AC	AC	A	A	A	AC	AC	AC	D	D	D	D	D	D	D	AC	AC
(Cross-party) state party organizational strength index	AC	D	AC	AC	AC	AC	AC	AC	AC	D	D	D	D	D	D			D

Note: NPID = national party identifiers; SPID = state party identifiers. In the cells, A = agreement; D = disagreement; AC = agreement when controlled for covariate and interaction effect; DC = disagreement when controlled for covariate and interaction effect.

coverage issue by almost 150 percent. In the base result of chapter 3, only Democratic county chairs and masses agreed on this issue: both Democratic delegates and county committee members were significantly more liberal than their electoral base on health-care coverage. Democratic delegates continued to differ significantly from their base in 17 of 30 cells possible when state political context was controlled; however, the county committee members converted to issue agreement with Democratic masses in all but 5 of the 30 cells possible, resulting in a total of 42 cells marked AC. In contrast, only 4 of the 30 county chair/mass pairs developed significant differences when the control variables were introduced, leaving 26 cells marked A. All told, the introduction of context resulted in intraparty issue cohesion in 71 percent of all cells in the Democratic panel.

Demographic variables—especially *per capita income, percentage urban,* and *percentage college graduates,* each of which brings intraparty cohesion to every dyad not already cohesive—account for 63 percent of all of the newly generated cohesion in the Democratic panel. However, *state Democratic organizational strength* also converted every delegate/mass dyad and committee member/mass dyad to cohesion, and the other institutional variables converted 50 percent or more of the dyads in these same categories. The politocultural variables, on the other hand, made little or no contribution to intra-Democratic cohesion; indeed, *state party identification* index had quite the opposite effect.

Yet once again the bottom row of table 4.8 reveals that when the strength of their respective state party organizations is controlled, the Republican activists' positions on health-care coverage are significantly different from those of the Democratic identifiers and presidential voters, whereas the Democratic elites' positions are, in 8 of 9 pairs, compatible with those of the Republican masses. Thus on yet another issue the Republican party held a slight edge over its opponents in terms of partisan linkage in the southern states in 1992, only to be confronted by (1) an apparent inability to expand its voting support beyond its original partisan base

and (2) the apparent vulnerability of its own base to cross-party appeals by the opponents.

Table 4.9 reports the effect of environmental covariates upon intraparty cohesion concerning spending for environmental protection. Here we find that very little of the preexistent issue cohesion between local Republican elites and masses reported in chapter 3 is undone by the introduction of environmental controls. Fifty-three of the 60 pairs possible in the Republican chair/mass and committee member/mass columns remain agreed; only 7 cells—5 of which involve county chairs and masses—convert to issue disagreement. In contrast, 19 of 30 cells possible converted from base disagreement to agreement in the Republican delegate/mass pairs. Twelve of these 19 were occasioned by the demographic variables *per capita income, percentage urban, percentage college graduates,* and *percentage fundamentalist,* although *interparty competition* and *liberalism of Republican identifiers* matched these demographics in that all 3 delegate/mass pairs converted to agreement when the latter two were controlled as well. All in all, controlling for environment increased intraparty cohesion in the Republican panel of table 4.9 from 59 to 80 percent of the pairs in the panel.

The Democratic panel of table 4.9 is reminiscent of its counterpart in table 4.8. The chapter 3 base result for both tables logged disagreement across all 3 Democratic delegate/mass pairs and Democratic committee member/mass pairs, sandwiching issue agreement across the 3 Democratic county chair/mass categories located in the middle of the panel. None of the cohesive chair/mass pairs in table 4.9 converts to disagreement, compared to only 4 pairs that did so in table 4.8. Sixty percent of the delegate/mass and committee member/mass pairs in table 4.9 convert from disagreement to agreement when controls are introduced, compared to 63 percent of the 60 pairs possible in those categories in the preceding table. In both tables *percentage black* and *percentage fundamentalist* affect only the Democratic committee member/mass pairs, whereas the other three demographic variables affect those pairs plus the 3 Democratic delegate/mass pairs, as well. *State Democratic organizational strength* also

TABLE 4.9

DYADIC BEHAVIOR SCALE OF ELITE-MASS COHESION REGARDING "GOVERNMENT SPENDING ON IMPROVING AND PROTECTING THE ENVIRONMENT SHOULD BE INCREASED"

| | DEMOCRATS | | | | | | | | | REPUBLICANS | | | | | | | | |
| | Convention Delegates | | | Party Chairs | | | Committee Members | | | Convention Delegates | | | Party Chairs | | | Committee Members | | |
	NPID	SPID	Voters	NPID	SPID	Voters	NPID	SPID	Voters	NPID	SPID	Voters	NPID	SPID	Voters	NPID	SPID	Voters
Chapter 3 base result	D	D	D	A	A	A	D	D	D	D	D	D	A	A	A	A	A	A
Percentage black	A	D	D	A	A	A	AC	AC	AC	DC	DC	A	A	DC	A	A	DC	A
Percentage fundamentalist	A	D	D	A	A	A	AC	AC	AC	A	A	A	A	A	A	A	A	A
Percentage college graduates	A	AC	AC	A	A	A	AC	AC	AC	A	AC	AC	A	A	A	A	A	A
Percentage urban	A	AC	AC	A	A	A	AC	AC	AC	A	AC	AC	A	A	A	A	A	A
Per capita income	A	AC	AC	A	A	A	AC	AC	AC	A	AC	AC	A	A	A	A	A	A
Liberalism of party identifiers index	A	D	D	A	A	A	D	D	D	DC	AC	AC	DC	DC	DC	A	A	A
State party identification index	A	D	D	A	A	A	D	D	D	A	A	A	A	A	A	A	A	A
Interparty competition index	A	D	D	A	A	A	AC	AC	AC	A	AC	AC	A	A	A	A	A	A
Local party organizational strength index	A	D	D	A	A	A	AC	AC	AC	A	A	A	A	A	A	A	A	A
State party organizational strength index	A	AC	AC	A	A	A	AC	AC	AC	A	A	A	A	A	A	A	A	DC
(Cross-party) state party organizational strength index	AC	AC	D	A	D	D	AC	AC	D	D	D	D	D	D	D	AC	AC	D

Note: NPID = national party identifiers; SPID = state party identifiers. In the cells, A = agreement; D = disagreement; AC = agreement when controlled for covariate and interaction effect; DC = disagreement when controlled for covariate and interaction effect.

affects all 6 of these pairs in both tables, whereas the other two institutional variables affect only the 3 committee member/mass pairs, excepting 1 Democratic delegate/voter cell in table 4.8. Finally, controlling for politocultural control variables does not facilitate intraparty cohesion in either table. As a result, 73 percent of the pairs possible in the Democratic panel of table 4.9 register elite-mass agreement on spending to protect the environment, compared to 71 percent of the Democratic pairs in the preceding table.

Once again, then, southern Republicans enjoy a small lead of 7 percent over southern Democrats in terms of intraparty cohesion when state context is taken into account. This, plus the fact that the bottom row shows that the Democratic activists' cross-party harmony with Republican masses on this issue was considerably curtailed, while the Republican activists were not quite as hopelessly out of touch with the Democratic base on it, suggests that the issue of spending for environmental protection was probably a wash in terms of electoral advantage in the South for either party in 1992.

Table 4.10 reports the effect of environmental covariates and their interactions with the factors upon intraparty cohesion concerning the statement "The government in Washington should see to it that every person has a job and a good standard of living." Such controlled analyses uncovered a goodly amount of intra-Republican cohesion where the chapter 3 base results indicated there was none, due to the significantly greater conservatism of Republican elites on such a redistributive issue. Twenty-five of the 90 cells in the Republican panel convert from D to AC under controlled conditions. However, these changes are so scattered across all 9 elite/mass dyads in the panel—every pair except 1 converts to AC for only two or three out of ten variables—that it is impossible to characterize any particular dyads as prone to cohesion on this issue. It is possible, however, to observe that when the *liberalism of Republican identifiers* index score for each southern state is taken into account, elite-mass cohesion on this issue results across all 9 pairs possible. Taking the *per capita income* of the states and the degree of *interparty competition* in each into account also brings intraparty cohesion about across most of the dyads.

In the Democratic panel of table 4.10, we find an even greater amount of conversion to cohesion taking place. The Democrats started out with some base agreement on this issue between national convention delegates (who are more liberal than local elites on this issue) and the Democratic masses. Like the Republican elites, however, county Democratic chairs and committee members in the South were more conservative than mass Democrats on this combination redistributive/"big government" issue. When the environmental variables were introduced to the analysis, almost one-third of the delegate/mass pairs in the panel converted from base cohesion to significant differences, and 62 percent of the county elite-mass cells converted from base disagreement to cohesion, raising the overall level of cohesion in the Democratic panel from 33 to 64 percent. Here, too, the *interparty competition, per capita income,* and *liberalism of Democratic identifiers* variables were most strongly associated with bringing about issue agreement between Democratic masses and the more conservative local party elites (both types). All of the other politocultural, demographic, and institutional variables (except *local Democratic organizational strength*) seemed to be effectively associated with conversion to cohesion among the county committee member/mass dyads, but did not similarly affect the county chair/mass dyads.

The issue of governmental responsibility for employment availability and living conditions is one that should and did work to the Democrats' electoral advantage in 1992 for multiple reasons. First, southern Democrats enjoyed a better than two-to-one advantage over southern Republicans in intraparty issue cohesion in table 4.10. Second, despite the fact that local Democratic elites in the South somewhat tended, like their Republican elite counterparts, to be more conservative than their party's voter base on this particular issue, most voters associate the Democratic party label with federal job-creation programs during the 1930s (e.g., WPA, CCC, TVA, etc.) and with federal welfare legislation thereafter (e.g., Aid to Families with

TABLE 4.10

DYADIC BEHAVIOR SCALE OF ELITE-MASS COHESION REGARDING "THE GOVERNMENT IN WASHINGTON SHOULD SEE TO IT THAT EVERY PERSON HAS A JOB AND A GOOD STANDARD OF LIVING"

	DEMOCRATS									REPUBLICANS								
	Convention Delegates			Party Chairs			Committee Members			Convention Delegates			Party Chairs			Committee Members		
	NPID	SPID	Voters	NPID	SPID	Voters	NPID	SPID	Voters	NPID	SPID	Voters	NPID	SPID	Voters	NPID	SPID	Voters
Chapter 3 base result	A	A	A	D	D	D	D	D	D	D	D	D	D	D	D	D	D	D
Percentage black	DC	DC	A	D	AC	D	AC	AC	AC	D	D	D	D	D	D	D	D	D
Percentage fundamentalist	DC	DC	A	AC	AC	D	AC	AC	AC	D	D	D	D	D	D	D	D	D
Percentage college graduates	A	A	A	D	D	D	AC	AC	AC	D	D	D	D	D	AC	D	D	D
Percentage urban	A	A	A	D	AC	AC	AC	AC	AC	AC	D	D	AC	D	D	AC	D	AC
Per capita income	A	A	A	AC	AC	D	AC	AC	AC	AC	AC	AC	D	AC	AC	D	D	AC
Liberalism of party identifiers index	DC	DC	DC	AC	D	AC	AC	AC	AC	AC	AC	AC	AC	AC	AC	AC	AC	AC
State party identification index	A	DC	DC	AC	D	D	AC	AC	AC	D	D	D	D	D	D	D	D	D
Interparty competition index	A	A	A	AC	AC	AC	AC	AC	AC	AC	AC	AC	D	AC	AC	AC	AC	AC
Local party organizational strength index	A	A	A	D	D	D	D	D	D	D	D	D	D	D	D	D	D	D
State party organizational strength index	A	A	A	D	D	AC	AC	AC	D	D	D	D	D	D	D	D	D	D
(Cross-party) state party organizational strength index	AC	AC	D	A	A	A	A	A	AC	D	D	D	D	D	D	D	D	D

Note: NPID = national party identifiers; SPID = state party identifiers. In the cells, A = agreement; D = disagreement; AC = agreement when controlled for covariate and interaction effect; DC = disagreement when controlled for covariate and interaction effect.

Dependent Children, food stamps, etc.). Southern Democratic elites were far more conservative during the decades bookended by those federal acts than they are during the 1990s, and yet that conservatism did not dampen the appeal of Democratic tickets to southern electors until the desegregation-era elections of 1964 and 1968. Third, the bottom row of table 4.10 reveals that, once again, southern Republican elites were on a different page than the more liberal Democratic masses, whereas southern Democratic elites (especially the local variety, who were somewhat more conservative on this issue than Democratic delegates and masses) did not differ significantly from the views of Republican masses in 8 of 9 pairs. Finally, rightly or wrongly, the voting public usually assigns responsibility for current economic conditions to the incumbent President and his party, and these were not good at all during the first three quarters of 1992. Many voters all over the country interpreted President Bush's laissez-faire response to the recession as indifference to their economic insecurity and hopes.

Political Economy

We turn now from the effects of environment upon the narrower, micro-level concern of governmental responsibility for the employment and economic viability of individuals to broader, macro-level questions of government fiscal policy: government spending, taxes, and budget balancing.

Table 4.11 deals with environmental impact upon intraparty agreement concerning cuts in federal services "in order to reduce government spending." In the base result reported in chapter 3's table 3.14, none of the Republican elite/mass pairs had agreed on this issue because the party elites were significantly more conservative than the party masses on this issue. However, as the Republican panel of table 4.11 shows, 31 of 90 pairs in the panel convert to issue agreement when context variables and their interactions with the pairs are controlled. Almost 50 percent of these conversions occur among the Republican committee member/mass pairs, with the remaining cases almost evenly divided between the

delegate/mass and county chair/mass pairs. The context variables most likely to be associated with such conversions to cohesion were, in descending order, *liberalism of Republican identifiers, interparty competition, per capita income,* and *percentage college graduates.* The remaining variables accounted for only one or two cases apiece, or, as in the case of the two *party organizational strength* variables and *state party identification* index, none at all. An interesting pattern was that *per capita income* seemed to bring about change in the pairs involving both kinds of Republican identifiers with all three kinds of Republican elites, but never in the pairs involving the latter with Republican presidential voters.

The Democratic panel of table 4.11 involves relatively few changes in either direction, and indicates a high rate of intra-Democratic cohesion on the issue of cutting services in order to cut spending. The base result in chapter 3 was that local Democratic elites were cohesive with Democratic masses on this issue, whereas Democratic convention delegates were more liberal than the party base. When state political context is introduced as a control, 14 of the 30 delegate/mass pairs possible converted from disagreement to agreement, whereas only 6 of 60 county elite/mass pairs possible converted from base agreement to disagreement. As a result, intraparty cohesion on the issue rises from 67 to 76 percent, counting the changes in both directions. *State Democratic organizational strength* and three demographic variables—*per capita income, percentage urban,* and *percentage college graduates*—account for all but two of the conversions from disagreement to agreement. The *interparty competition* index induced change from agreement to disagreement in all three Democratic chair/mass categories, and the *state party identification* index affected two of those same three categories similarly.

Obviously, this is yet another issue in which southern Democrats enjoyed a big advantage over southern Republicans in 1992. Table 4.11 shows that Democratic activists enjoyed a greater than two-to-one advantage over their Republican counterparts in cohesion with their party electoral base on the classic Reaganomics approach of cutting government

TABLE 4.11

DYADIC BEHAVIOR SCALE OF ELITE-MASS COHESION REGARDING "THE GOVERNMENT IN WASHINGTON SHOULD PROVIDE FEWER SERVICES, EVEN IN AREAS SUCH AS HEALTH AND EDUCATION, IN ORDER TO REDUCE GOVERNMENT SPENDING"

| | DEMOCRATS | | | | | | | | | REPUBLICANS | | | | | | | | |
| | Convention Delegates | | | Party Chairs | | | Committee Members | | | Convention Delegates | | | Party Chairs | | | Committee Members | | |
	NPID	SPID	Voters	NPID	SPID	Voters	NPID	SPID	Voters	NPID	SPID	Voters	NPID	SPID	Voters	NPID	SPID	Voters
Chapter 3 base result	D	D	D	A	A	A	A	A	A	D	D	D	D	D	D	D	D	D
Percentage black	D	D	D	A	A	A	A	A	A	D	D	D	D	D	D	D	D	AC
Percentage fundamentalist	D	D	D	A	A	A	A	A	A	D	D	D	D	D	D	D	D	AC
Percentage college graduates	AC	AC	AC	A	A	A	A	A	A	AC	D	AC	D	D	D	AC	AC	D
Percentage urban	AC	AC	AC	A	A	A	A	A	A	D	D	D	D	D	D	AC	AC	D
Per capita income	AC	AC	AC	A	A	A	A	A	A	AC	AC	D	AC	AC	D	AC	AC	D
Liberalism of party identifiers index	D	D	D	A	A	A	A	A	A	AC	AC	AC	AC	AC	AC	AC	AC	AC
State party identification index	D	D	D	A	DC	DC	A	A	A	D	D	D	D	D	D	D	D	D
Interparty competition index	AC	D	D	A	DC	DC	A	A	A	D	AC	AC	AC	AC	AC	AC	AC	AC
Local party organizational strength index	D	D	AC	A	A	A	A	A	A	D	D	D	D	D	D	D	D	D
State party organizational strength index	AC	AC	AC	A	A	A	A	A	DC	D	D	D	D	D	D	D	D	D
(Cross-party) state party organizational strength index	AC	AC	AC	AC	AC	AC	AC	AC	AC	D	D	D	D	D	D	D	D	D

Note: NPID = national party identifiers; SPID = state party identifiers. In the cells, A = agreement; D = disagreement; AC = agreement when controlled for covariate and interaction effect; DC = disagreement when controlled for covariate and interaction effect.

services and spending. Moreover, the bottom row of the table shows that once again, when the organizational strength of the respective state parties is controlled, Democratic activists saw eye-to-eye with Republican masses on this issue, whereas Republican activists, who saw eye-to-eye with their own party base in about one-third of the cells (and then only *after* contextual controls were introduced), differed significantly from Democratic masses across all 9 pairs possible. In the context of recession and economic uncertainty, voters in 1992 wanted more action, not less, from their national government. The era of Reaganomics was over.

Table 4.12, which deals with the question of passing a Constitutional amendment to balance the federal budget, starts out with the same chapter 3 base results that we saw in the last table: Republican elites and masses disagree across the board, while local Democratic activists and masses agree but Democratic delegates are significantly more liberal. From this point on, however, table 4.12 diverges from the preceding table in that its distribution of cells includes quite a few more cases of conversion from disagreement to agreement in the Republican panel, and even more cases of conversion from agreement to disagreement in the Democratic panel. With controls for context, exactly one-half of the cells in the Republican panel of table 4.12 register elite-mass agreement on the balanced budget amendment. Such cohesion is quite a bit stronger between Republican committee members and masses, for whom two-thirds of the 30 pairs possible agree. In contrast, about 40 percent of the Republican chair/mass pairs and 43 percent of the Republican delegate/mass pairs cohere. Demographic variables alone account for 58 percent of all cohesive pairs in the panel—a performance that is the more impressive given that one demographic (*percentage black*) accounted for no more than 1 pair. However, *liberalism of Republican identifiers* associated with conversions to cohesion across all 9 dyads, and *interparty competition* associated with such conversions across 7 of 9 dyads.

The Democratic panel of table 4.12 reveals that sixteen conversions from issue agreement to disagreement in the local elite/mass pairs more than offset the fourteen conversions from disagreement to agreement that took place among the delegate/mass pairs when controls were introduced. Net agreement for the panel was thus reduced by about 3 percent when the control variables and interactions were added, but still came to about 64 percent of all possible cells.

Over half of the conversions to disagreement occurred in the two county chair/Democratic identifier columns; the rest either occurred in the committee member/state identifier column or the county chair/voter column. The variables most associated with the displacement of cohesion were *state party identification* index, *percentage black* and *percentage fundamentalist*. The conversions from disagreement to cohesion, of course, had to take place entirely within the nexus of convention delegates and masses, and were occasioned in almost two-thirds of the cases by a different set of demographic variables—*per capita income, percentage urban,* and *percentage college graduates.* However, *state Democratic organizational strength* was associated with change to cohesion across all 3 dyads possible, and *interparty competition* was associated with changes in 2 of 3 dyads.

Looking at the Democrats' 14 percent edge in cells indicating intraparty cohesion, and their across-the-board superiority in cross-party issue representation indicated by the bottom row of table 4.12, it appears as if the balanced budget amendment, a venerable staple of Republican campaigns since the 1970s, was not particularly useful to Republicans in the South in 1992. Republican elites and masses were only on the same page in 50 percent of the pairings—and even this was true only when state political contexts were added to the analysis. Some of this intraparty dissensus no doubt stemmed from H. Ross Perot's successful expropriation of this issue from Republicans in 1992, as well as from President Bush's notorious 1990 about-faces on the subject of a tax increase for deficit reduction, which provided much of the impetus not only for Perot's presidential bid but also for Patrick Buchanan's highly divisive challenge for the Republican nomination.

Table 4.13, which deals with whether states

TABLE 4.12

DYADIC BEHAVIOR SCALE OF ELITE-MASS COHESION REGARDING "A CONSTITUTIONAL AMENDMENT TO BALANCE THE NATIONAL BUDGET SHOULD BE PASSED"

| | DEMOCRATS | | | | | | | | | REPUBLICANS | | | | | | | | |
| | Convention Delegates | | | Party Chairs | | | Committee Members | | | Convention Delegates | | | Party Chairs | | | Committee Members | | |
	NPID	SPID	Voters	NPID	SPID	Voters	NPID	SPID	Voters	NPID	SPID	Voters	NPID	SPID	Voters	NPID	SPID	Voters
Chapter 3 base result	D	D	D	A	A	A	A	A	A	D	D	D	D	D	D	D	D	D
Percentage black	D	D	D	DC	DC	DC	A	A	A	D	D	D	D	D	D	D	D	AC
Percentage fundamentalist	D	D	D	DC	DC	DC	A	A	A	AC	AC	AC	AC	D	D	AC	AC	AC
Percentage college graduates	AC	AC	AC	A	A	A	A	DC	A	AC	D	AC	AC	AC	AC	AC	AC	AC
Percentage urban	AC	AC	AC	A	A	A	A	DC	A	D	D	D	AC	D	AC	AC	AC	D
Per capita income	AC	AC	AC	A	A	A	A	A	A	AC	D	AC	AC	AC	AC	AC	AC	AC
Liberalism of party identifiers index	D	D	D	A	A	A	A	DC	A	AC	AC	AC	AC	AC	AC	AC	AC	AC
State party identification index	D	D	D	DC	DC	A	DC	DC	A	D	D	D	D	D	D	AC	AC	AC
Interparty competition index	AC	D	AC	A	DC	A	A	A	A	AC	AC	AC	D	D	AC	AC	AC	AC
Local party organizational strength index	D	D	D	DC	DC	A	A	A	A	D	D	D	D	D	D	D	D	D
State party organizational strength index	AC	AC	AC	A	A	A	A	A	A	D	D	D	D	D	D	D	D	D
(Cross-party) state party organizational strength index	AC	AC	AC	AC	AC	AC	AC	AC	A	D	D	D	D	D	D	D	D	D

Note: NPID = national party identifiers; SPID = state party identifiers. In the cells, A = agreement; D = disagreement; AC = agreement when controlled for covariate and interaction effect; DC = disagreement when controlled for covariate and interaction effect.

TABLE 4.13

DYADIC BEHAVIOR SCALE OF ELITE-MASS COHESION REGARDING "IF THIS STATE FACES A FINANCIAL CRISIS, THE STATE LEGISLATURE SHOULD RAISE TAXES RATHER THAN REDUCE SPENDING"

	DEMOCRATS									REPUBLICANS								
	Convention Delegates			Party Chairs			Committee Members			Convention Delegates			Party Chairs			Committee Members		
	NPID	SPID	Voters	NPID	SPID	Voters	NPID	SPID	Voters	NPID	SPID	Voters	NPID	SPID	Voters	NPID	SPID	Voters
Chapter 3 base result	D	D	A	A	A	A	A	A	A	D	D	D	D	D	D	D	D	D
Percentage black	AC	AC	A	A	A	A	A	A	A	D	D	D	D	D	D	D	D	D
Percentage fundamentalist	AC	AC	A	A	A	A	A	A	A	D	D	D	D	D	D	D	D	D
Percentage college graduates	AC	AC	DC	A	A	A	A	A	A	D	AC	D	AC	AC	AC	AC	AC	AC
Percentage urban	AC	AC	A	A	A	A	A	A	A	D	AC	D	AC	AC	AC	AC	AC	D
Per capita income	AC	AC	DC	A	A	A	A	A	A	AC	AC	D	D	D	AC	AC	AC	AC
Liberalism of party identifiers index	AC	AC	A	A	A	A	A	A	A	AC	AC	AC	AC	AC	AC	AC	AC	AC
State party identification index	AC	AC	A	A	A	A	A	A	A	D	D	D	D	D	D	D	D	D
Interparty competition index	D	AC	A	DC	DC	A	A	A	A	AC	AC	AC	D	D	D	AC	AC	AC
Local party organizational strength index	AC	AC	A	A	A	A	DC	DC	A	D	D	D	D	D	D	D	D	D
State party organizational strength index	AC	AC	DC	A	A	A	A	A	A	D	D	D	D	D	D	D	D	D
(Cross-party) state party organizational strength index	D	D	D	D	D	AC	AC	AC	AC	D	D	D	D	D	D	D	D	D

Note: NPID = national party identifiers; SPID = state party identifiers. In the cells, A = agreement; D = disagreement; AC = agreement when controlled for covariate and interaction effect; DC = disagreement when controlled for covariate and interaction effect.

should meet fiscal crises by raising taxes rather than reducing spending, starts out much the same as tables 4.11 and 4.12. Once again, the base result in chapter 3 was disagreement over this issue among Republican elites and masses (who were less conservative than the elites), and between Democratic delegates and two of three categories of Democratic masses (who were less liberal than the delegates), while local Democratic elites and masses saw eye-to-eye. Only 34 of 90 cells in the Republican panel convert to agreement this time, leaving the percentage of issue cohesion across all pairs in the panel at 38 percent. Again the rate of conversion is higher (at 41 percent) for Republican committee member/mass pairs than it is for delegate/mass and chair/mass pairs (29 percent each). The conversions associate most frequently with *liberalism of Republican identifiers* (at 9 out of 9 pairs) and then *percentage college graduates* (7 of 9 pairs), followed by *per capita income, percentage urban,* and *interparty competition* (all at 6 of 9 pairs). None of the other variables were associated with switches to issue agreement.

The Democratic panel of table 4.13 is also easily reported. All of the Democratic delegate/mass pairs except one (delegates/national identifiers, controlled for *interparty competition*) converted from base disagreement to agreement when the control variables and interactions were introduced. Since almost all possible cases converted to cohesion, all of the control variables except the one mentioned had the same effect. On the other hand, only 4 scattered cells out of 60 possible underneath the local elite-mass headings switched to disagreement when context was introduced, and another 3 pairs within the delegate/voter column did likewise. Institutional variables were responsible for 5 of these breakdowns of cohesion, but since the cases are so few it is a stretch to suggest that some variables associate more than others with such incidents.

The overall cohesion in the Democratic panel of table 4.13 is quite impressive, then, at 80 percent of all pairs. This is more than double the incidence of cohesive pairs in the Republican panel of the table. Moreover, the bottom row of the table shows that

Republican activists once again differed significantly in attitude from the positions national and state Democratic identifiers and Democratic presidential voters held on this issue in 1992. After twelve years of domestic spending cuts and devolutionary federalism under Reagan and Bush, many supporters of both parties were not ready for their state governments to do less, especially during hard times. The only upside for Republicans is that at least on this issue, Democratic delegates and Democratic county chairs (two of three times) were out of step with the Republican masses as well.

Foreign Policy and National Security

Finally, we come to the effects of environmental covariates and interaction terms upon intraparty cohesion regarding national security and foreign policy issues prominent in the first post–Cold War presidential election: defense spending, prioritization of domestic versus foreign policy, and cooperation with the new Russia.

In the first of these tables, we find that environmental and interaction effects increase intraparty cohesion by a net gain of 18 cells. In chapter 3's table 3.17, county Republican activists were significantly more conservative than the Republican rank and file on defense spending. Only Republican convention delegates cohered with the party's mass base on this issue. The Republican panel of table 4.14 reveals that 26 of the 60 county elite/mass pairs possible converted from disagreement to agreement when context was manipulated. These conversions in all but three cases occurred in response to just four variables—*liberalism of Republican identifiers, per capita income, percentage urban,* and *percentage college graduates*—and came within 1 cell of involving all 6 possible county elite/mass pairs for every variable except the latter. In contrast, only 8 Republican delegate/mass pairs out of the 30 possible developed significantly different means when context was introduced. *Liberalism of Republican identifiers* and *percentage college graduates* accounted for 6 of these 8 pairs (and thus "ran the table," so to speak), while

TABLE 4.14

DYADIC BEHAVIOR SCALE OF ELITE-MASS COHESION REGARDING "DEFENSE SPENDING SHOULD BE INCREASED"

	DEMOCRATS									REPUBLICANS								
	Convention Delegates			Party Chairs			Committee Members			Convention Delegates			Party Chairs			Committee Members		
	NPID	SPID	Voters	NPID	SPID	Voters	NPID	SPID	Voters	NPID	SPID	Voters	NPID	SPID	Voters	NPID	SPID	Voters
Chapter 3 base result	D	D	D	A	A	A	A	A	A	A	A	A	D	D	D	D	D	D
Percentage black	AC	D	D	A	A	A	A	A	A	A	A	A	D	D	D	D	D	D
Percentage fundamentalist	AC	D	D	A	A	A	A	A	A	DC	DC	A	D	D	D	D	D	AC
Percentage college graduates	D	AC	AC	A	A	A	DC	DC	DC	DC	DC	DC	AC	AC	AC	AC	AC	D
Percentage urban	AC	D	AC	A	A	A	A	A	DC	A	A	A	AC	AC	AC	AC	AC	AC
Per capita income	AC	AC	AC	A	A	A	DC	DC	DC	A	A	A	AC	AC	AC	AC	AC	AC
Liberalism of party identifiers index	D	D	D	A	A	A	DC	DC	DC	DC	DC	DC	AC	AC	AC	AC	AC	AC
State party identification index	D	D	D	A	A	A	A	A	A	A	A	A	D	D	D	D	D	D
Interparty competition index	AC	AC	AC	A	A	A	A	A	A	A	A	A	D	D	AC	D	D	AC
Local party organizational strength index	D	D	D	A	A	A	A	A	A	A	A	A	D	D	D	D	D	D
State party organizational strength index	D	D	AC	A	A	A	A	DC	DC	A	A	A	D	D	D	D	D	D
(Cross-party) state party organizational strength index	D	D	D	A	AC	A	A	A	A	A	A	A	D	D	D	D	D	D

Note: NPID = national party identifiers; SPID = state party identifiers. In the cells, A = agreement; D = disagreement; AC = agreement when controlled for covariate and interaction effect; DC = disagreement when controlled for covariate and interaction effect.

percentage fundamentalist was associated with the other 2. All in all, then, partisan cohesion for Republicans as a whole on this issue was 53 percent of all cells in the panel.

The pattern of the chapter 3 base results for Democrats on this issue was exactly the opposite of that for the Republicans: Democratic county elites were in step with their party's base, and the too liberal Democratic delegates were not. Controlling for context converted 12 of the 60 county elite/mass pairs to disunity and 11 of the 30 delegate/mass pairs to unity, so the effect of environment on partisan linkage on this issue was essentially nil (which left the Democrats in good shape, however, at just shy of 66 percent partisan cohesion for the whole panel). All 12 of the county elite-mass cells that developed issue differences occurred in the committee member/ mass categories, which were affected by *per capita income, percentage college graduates, liberalism of Democratic identifiers,* and, to a lesser extent, *state Democratic organizational strength. Per capita income* also was associated with the delegate/mass pairs that developed issue solidarity, as were *interparty competition* and, to a lesser degree, *percentage urban* and *percentage college graduates.*

Historically, pushing for more defense spending has served Republican presidential candidates well in the postwar period, especially during the 1980s. But that decade ended with communism falling in Europe, sparking widespread popular discussion of how America should spend its "peace dividend." President Bush's efforts to make the point that the international scene was more unpredictable for the disappearance of the USSR simply did not resonate with the popular mind, or for that matter with the media. Note how elite-mass agreement on defense spending in the Republican panel of table 4.14 leads disagreement by only 53 to 47 percent of the cells, even though the South has been the region most supportive of the U.S. military—and has benefited economically from military spending (Sale 1975)—during the postwar period. The issue was a loser for Republicans in the South in 1992, even though the bottom row of the table indicates that for a change

the Republican elites were not without some cross-party appeal on an issue.

Table 4.15 reports the effect of environment upon a hallmark theme of the 1992 Democratic campaign, which was "This country should pay more attention to problems at home and less attention to problems in other parts of the world." The chapter 3 base findings for the two parties are almost totally opposite one another, and so is the effect of environment upon those base findings. The base analysis reported in table 3.18 turned up intra-Democratic consensus across all 9 elite/mass dyads, as opposed to almost complete dissensus among the Republican dyads. But table 4.15 reveals considerable environmental alteration of the Republicans' dissensus, and almost no revision whatsoever of the Democrats' internal consensus.

The only base agreement among Republicans occurred between Republican county committee members and Republican presidential voters—and this pair remains cohesive across every control variable introduced except *per capita income, percentage urban,* and *local Republican organizational strength.* But intraparty cohesion jumps enormously when covariates and interactions are added to the analysis of the 8 dissonant Republican elite/mass pairs. Fifty-seven of 80 cells possible convert to agreement, resulting in intraparty cohesion in a total of 64 out of 90 cells (71 percent). Such large-scale change means, of course, that most dyads are affected by most environmental variables. Scanning the panel reveals that the fewest cells affected for any dyad is 5 out of 10 (which is about par for the three Republican delegate/mass dyads), whereas the norm for the Republican chair/mass dyads and Republican committee member/identifier dyads is that 8 of 18 cells are converted to cohesion by controlling for context. Every control variable except *local Republican organizational strength* is associated with such conversions; the variables that have this effect across all 8 dyads possible are *percentage college graduates, interparty competition,* and *liberalism of Republican identifiers,* with *per capita income* affecting all but 1 cell and *percentage black* and *percentage fundamentalist* affecting all but 2 cells.

In the Democratic panel of table 4.15, there is

TABLE 4.15

DYADIC BEHAVIOR SCALE OF ELITE-MASS COHESION REGARDING "THIS COUNTRY SHOULD PAY MORE ATTENTION TO PROBLEMS AT HOME AND LESS ATTENTION TO PROBLEMS IN OTHER PARTS OF THE WORLD"

| | DEMOCRATS | | | | | | | | | REPUBLICANS | | | | | | | | |
| | Convention Delegates | | | Party Chairs | | | Committee Members | | | Convention Delegates | | | Party Chairs | | | Committee Members | | |
	NPID	SPID	Voters	NPID	SPID	Voters	NPID	SPID	Voters	NPID	SPID	Voters	NPID	SPID	Voters	NPID	SPID	Voters
Chapter 3 base result	A	A	A	A	A	A	A	A	A	D	D	D	D	D	D	D	D	A
Percentage black	DC	A	A	A	A	A	A	A	A	D	D	AC	AC	AC	AC	AC	AC	A
Percentage fundamentalist	DC	A	A	A	A	A	A	A	A	D	D	AC	AC	AC	AC	AC	AC	A
Percentage college graduates	A	A	A	A	A	A	A	A	A	AC	AC	AC	AC	AC	AC	AC	AC	A
Percentage urban	A	DC	A	A	A	A	A	A	A	AC	AC	D	AC	AC	D	D	D	D
Per capita income	A	DC	A	A	A	A	A	A	A	AC	AC	AC	AC	AC	D	AC	AC	D
Liberalism of party identifiers index	A	A	A	A	A	A	A	A	A	AC	AC	AC	AC	AC	AC	AC	AC	A
State party identification index	A	A	A	A	A	A	A	A	A	D	D	D	AC	AC	AC	AC	AC	A
Interparty competition index	A	A	A	A	A	A	A	A	A	AC	AC	AC	AC	AC	AC	AC	AC	A
Local party organizational strength index	A	A	A	A	A	A	A	A	A	D	D	D	D	D	D	D	D	D
State party organizational strength index	A	A	A	A	A	A	A	A	A	D	D	D	AC	AC	AC	AC	AC	A
(Cross-party) state party organizational strength index	D	D	AC	AC	AC	AC	AC	AC	AC	D	D	D	D	D	D	D	D	D

Note: NPID = national party identifiers; SPID = state party identifiers. In the cells, A = agreement; D = disagreement; AC = agreement when controlled for covariate and interaction effect; DC = disagreement when controlled for covariate and interaction effect.

very little change in response to the introduction of environmental covariates and interactions with the factors. Only 4 cells convert from the chapter 3 base agreement to disagreement. The Democratic delegate/national identifier pair loses cohesion when *percentage black* and *percentage fundamentalist* are controlled, respectively, and the Democratic delegate/ state identifier pair differs significantly when *percentage urban* and *per capita income* are controlled, respectively. The cohesion rate for the panel is thus 96 percent of all possible cells.

This issue, more than any other, speaks to the theme of the 1992 Democratic campaign and the mandate that was earned. "More attention to problems at home" summarizes not only the 1992 American electorate's insecurities about the performance of the economy, their employability, and their health-care vulnerability, but also the agenda of the first two years of the Clinton presidency.[13] As table 4.15 shows, southern Republican activists creditably represented their partisan base on this issue, but not nearly as extensively as southern Democratic activists were able to represent the Democratic masses, and not nearly enough to be able to counteract the Democratic activists' cross-party attraction to potential defectors from the Republican mass base.

The last table deals with the effects of environmental covariates upon intraparty cohesion regarding the proposition "The United States should continue to cooperate with Russia." Table 4.16 is only the fourth table in the chapter in which the chapter 3 base result was that intraparty cohesion was more typical of the Republicans than of the Democrats. In the Republican panel of this table, we see that four demographic variables—*per capita income, percentage urban, percentage college graduates,* and *percentage fundamentalist*—account for 12 of the 14 cells in which the base agreement between delegates and masses gives way to disagreement when environment is controlled. On the other hand, the first three of these variables also have the effect, when controlled, of converting issue disagreement among county elite/mass pairs to agreement in almost all cells. *Interparty competition, state Republican organizational strength,* and *liberalism of Republican*

identifiers also convert disagreement to agreement across 5 of 6 or all 6 county elite/mass dyads. As a result, intra-Republican elite-mass cohesion concerning policy toward Russia exists in 55 of 90 cells (about 61 percent) in the Republican panel.

This is not quite as much cohesion, however, as that which existed in the Democratic panel of table 4.16 once state context was controlled. Fifty-six of 90 cells in the Democratic panel converted from base disagreement to cohesion, especially in response to *interparty competition, per capita income,* and *percentage urban,* each of which was associated with changes across all 9 dyads. Other variables which brought cohesion to a majority of the 9 dyads included *percentage black, percentage fundamentalist,* and *percentage college graduates.* The dyads most resistant to the influence of the variables that performed less well were the 2 that involved Democratic convention delegates with national and state Democratic identifiers.

The Democrats' lead over the Republicans in cohesion in table 4.16 consisted of only 1 cell. That narrow margin, plus the fact that the bottom row of the table shows the southern Republican activists to have more in common with the Democratic rank and file than the latter party's activists have with the Republican masses, is just enough to concede the Republicans a slight electoral advantage on this issue in 1992. After all, since Russian communism collapsed during the Republicans' watch, the Republican party should have been able to take electoral credit as the party best able to manage our relationship with Russia. This entry on the positive side of the Republicans' ledger was of small comfort in 1992, however, for as we saw in the data of the preceding table and in the campaign discourse of that election, 1992 is the election year in which the electorate finally heeded George McGovern's 1972 plea to "Come home, America."

It is clear from our analysis that political context affects southern intraparty issue cohesion in complex ways and with a frequency that should be taken into account in all future studies of intraparty elite-mass

TABLE 4.16

DYADIC BEHAVIOR SCALE OF ELITE-MASS COHESION REGARDING "THE UNITED STATES SHOULD CONTINUE TO COOPERATE WITH RUSSIA"

| | DEMOCRATS | | | | | | | | | REPUBLICANS | | | | | | | | |
| | Convention Delegates | | | Party Chairs | | | Committee Members | | | Convention Delegates | | | Party Chairs | | | Committee Members | | |
	NPID	SPID	Voters	NPID	SPID	Voters	NPID	SPID	Voters	NPID	SPID	Voters	NPID	SPID	Voters	NPID	SPID	Voters
Chapter 3 base result	D	D	D	D	D	D	D	D	D	A	A	A	D	D	D	D	D	D
Percentage black	D	AC	AC	AC	AC	AC	D	AC	AC	A	A	A	AC	AC	AC	D	D	AC
Percentage fundamentalist	D	D	AC	AC	AC	AC	AC	AC	AC	DC	DC	DC	D	D	D	D	D	D
Percentage college graduates	D	D	D	AC	AC	AC	AC	AC	AC	DC	DC	DC	AC	AC	AC	AC	AC	AC
Percentage urban	AC	AC	AC	AC	AC	AC	AC	AC	AC	DC	DC	DC	AC	AC	AC	AC	AC	AC
Per capita income	AC	AC	AC	AC	AC	AC	AC	AC	AC	DC	DC	DC	D	AC	AC	AC	AC	AC
Liberalism of party identifiers index	D	D	D	D	D	D	D	D	D	A	A	A	AC	AC	AC	AC	AC	AC
State party identification index	D	D	D	D	D	AC	D	D	AC	A	A	A	D	D	AC	D	AC	D
Interparty competition index	AC	AC	AC	AC	AC	AC	AC	AC	AC	A	A	A	AC	AC	AC	AC	AC	AC
Local party organizational strength index	D	D	D	D	D	D	AC	AC	AC	DC	A	DC	D	D	D	D	D	D
State party organizational strength index	D	D	D	D	D	AC	AC	AC	AC	A	A	A	AC	AC	AC	AC	AC	D
(Cross-party) state party organizational strength index	D	D	D	D	D	AC	A	A	A	AC	AC	A	A	A	A	D	D	D

Note: NPID = national party identifiers; SPID = state party identifiers. In the cells, A = agreement; D = disagreement; AC = agreement when controlled for covariate and interaction effect; DC = disagreement when controlled for covariate and interaction effect.

issue linkage—and probably in extraparty studies of elite-mass linkage, as well. This should not come as a great surprise. Environments are not inert things. By definition, ecosystems are manifestations of the scientific principle that each action causes an opposite reaction. Interaction between party actors and their surrounding political environments should be expected. Indeed, this is explicit in Epstein's statement that "the parties are less what they make of themselves than what the environment makes of them."

Specific findings that provide support for this intuition include the relative distributions of the AC and DC categories of the Dyadic Behavior Scale used in this chapter, which illustrate that the effect of environment, when fully controlled, is far more often to elicit issue cohesion than to promote issue distance. Thirty percent of the 2,880 cells in tables 4.1 to 4.16 changed from disagreement to agreement when controls were introduced, whereas only 5 percent moved in the opposite direction.

Why such dramatic changes from the base levels of issue agreement and disagreement established in chapter 3? Unlike that chapter, in which party elites and masses from across the South are linked together in a regionwide analysis, in this chapter the thrust of the analysis ties party elites to party masses more closely, because of controls for *state-based* demographics, institutions, political culture, and so on. The levels of issue cohesion are thus higher in this chapter because the elites and masses of any given state share the same habitat, and should more closely reflect one another at the state level than is typical at the regional level. Hypothetically, intrastate elite-mass cohesion should be higher than interstate elite-mass cohesion. In the comparatively few cases in which elite/mass pairs convert from base agreement in chapter 3 to disagreement when controlled for specific environmental conditions in chapter 4, the regional linkage for that pair has proven stronger than the linkage for that specific state context.

The aforementioned rates of environmental modification of the chapter 3 base levels of partisan linkage differed considerably from one party to the other. In the Republican panels of these sixteen tables, 35 percent of the cells moved from disagreement to agreement and only 3 percent moved in the opposite direction, while in the Democratic panels 25 percent of the cells moved from dissensus to cohesion, and 8 percent lost cohesion. Expressed as ratios, intra-Republican cohesion thus grew at a rate of ten to one, compared to a growth rate of only three to one for intra-Democratic cohesion, when environment was controlled.

It is clear from this and from other summary data that controlling for environment influences the intraparty cohesion of the two parties differently. Overall, Republican elite-mass factors were more susceptible, by a margin of 546 cells to the Democrats' 468 cells, to the influence of contextual covariates and their interaction with the factors. On ten of the sixteen issues studied, elite-mass linkage was altered in more cells in the Republican panels than in the Democratic panels. The number of cells containing AC is greater among Republicans for eleven issues, and greater among Democrats for five issues. However, Democrats in the end still usually enjoyed more intraparty issue cohesion across all possible elite-mass combinations. Republicans were more cohesive than Democrats for only five of sixteen issues—ideological self-placement, equality for women in business and government, abortion, school prayer, and spending for environmental protection.

The significance of the latter distributions for electoral competition in the South in 1992 is heightened when paired with the respective parties' rates of successful cross-party representation of each other's mass bases in the bottom rows of the tables above. The Republicans not only trailed the Democrats in terms of intraparty cohesion on eleven of sixteen issues, but also trailed the Democrats in terms of cross-party representation on all but one issue (cooperation with Russia). Even on the five issues for which Republican intraparty cohesion exceeded Democratic intraparty cohesion, Democratic activists nevertheless represented Republican identifiers and voters better than Republican activists were able to represent Democratic activists and identifiers.

This is important because the electoral bases of

both parties in the South are presently close to even in size, which means that victory depends on more than each party's ability to reinforce and mobilize its own voting base—it also depends on each party's ability to capture swing votes, and to elicit defections or at least depress turnout among voters in the opposing party's base. The southern Democratic activists' almost uniformly better performance at cross-party representation suggests that they probably enjoyed even greater superiority over the Republicans in the performance of the latter two tasks in 1992 than they did in terms of linkage with their own electoral base. In a regional presidential electorate consisting of conservative white "core Republicans," moderate white "swing voters," a small bloc of liberal white "core Democrats," and black Democrats (Black and Black 1992, 25, 357–60), logic suggests that the moderate white swing vote should be drawn more to the party whose issue positions have demonstrable appeal across party lines than to the party whose activists lack such cross-party attraction.

Democrats and Republicans also differed somewhat as far as which elite/mass pairs displayed the most issue cohesion once environmental influences had been taken into account. Reviewing all 16 issues × all 10 environmental variables for each pair, we find that the percentage of total cells in which issue cohesion exists runs 6 percent higher among both Republican delegate/identifier pairs than among Democratic delegate/identifier pairs, and 2 percent higher among Republican delegate/voter pairs, as well. For every category of local elite/mass pairs, however, intraparty cohesion runs higher among Democrats. Democratic county committee member/state identifier pairs experience 16 percent more cohesive cells than their Republican counterparts, Democratic committee member/voter pairs are 18 percent more cohesive than Republican committee member/voter pairs, and Democratic committee member/national identifier pairs are 19 percent more cohesive than their Republican counterparts. Democratic county chair/mass pairs, in turn, cohere 22 percent (with state identifiers), 27 percent (with national identifiers), and

28 percent (with voters) higher, respectively, than Republican county chair/mass pairs.

Perhaps such a pattern should have been expected, given the higher incidence of "dual" or "segmented" partisan identification that Hadley (1985), Maggiotto and Wekkin (1992), Cotter and Stovall (1992) and others have noted in the South. For years now a certain proportion of the southern electorate has apportioned its partisan loyalties, or at least its votes, to Republicans as far as contests for national office are concerned, to Democrats in races for state office, and to Democrats or independents in races for local office. Higher issue consistency between electors and Republican delegates, on the one hand, and between electors and Democratic county activists, on the other hand, is not a disparity when the concept of federally differentiated partisan affect is applied to these data.

Students of multiple partisan identification will be disappointed, however, to learn that the same calculations used to show higher delegate/mass cohesion among Republicans and higher local activist/mass cohesion among Democrats do not reveal higher issue cohesion, in either party, between delegates—that is, national party activists—and national partisan identifiers than exists for delegate/state identifier pairs. The percentage of issue cohesion for Republican delegate/national identifier pairs and for Republican delegate/state identifier pairs is exactly the same at 53 percent of all cells for each dyad in tables 4.1 to 4.16. At 47 percent, the percentage of cohesive cells for Democratic delegate/national identifiers is 1 percent higher than that for Democratic delegate/state identifiers. Nor is there any significant difference, for either party, in the distribution of cohesive pairs for county elites and identifiers, when theoretically state partisan identifiers should have more views in common with county chairs and committee members than would national partisan identifiers.

Finally, Democrats and Republicans also differed somewhat with regard to which environmental variables influenced their cohesion the most. Although both sets of party factors were influenced consistently by the introduction of the *interparty competition* index and of the modernization-related demographics (*per capita income, percentage college graduation,* and *percentage urbanization*), the Republican factors were much more responsive than their Democratic counterparts were to the *state liberalism of party identifier* indexes, and the Democratic factors were slightly more responsive than Republican factors were to the *party organizational strength* variables.

Percentage black and *percentage fundamentalist,* on the other hand, were "the dogs that did not bark" in this study. Despite their preeminence in many analyses of southern politics, neither had as much effect upon intraparty issue cohesion within the ranks of either party as did the aforementioned variables. Indeed, the overshadowing of these variables by the modernization-related demographics *percentage urban, per capita income,* and *percentage college graduate* is theoretically significant, for it suggests the presence within southern state party ranks of the political processes implied by the "modernization" and "top-down" theories of the growth of two-party competition in the South, rather than the political processes implied by the white flight hypothesis.

We turn next to a more in-depth analysis of the influence of each environmental context variable on intraparty issue cohesion, to see if further light can be shed on the aforementioned theoretical controversy regarding southern partisan change, the theoretical controversy regarding the interrelationships between parties and their environments, as well as the democratic question of partisan linkage between elites and governed.

Chapter 5

Partisan Linkage and Party Environments

In the previous chapter, in which the analysis was organized and presented issue by issue, there were many instances in which the intraparty cohesion of both parties was improved dramatically by controls for the influence of cross-state per capita incomes, percentages of urban population, percentages of college graduates, and incidence of two-party electoral competition. In addition, issue cohesion was elevated by party organizational strength (especially state rather than local) or the ideological orientation of the state's partisan identifiers in many instances for the Democratic party and in some instances for the Republican party. There were far fewer instances in which controlling for race or religious orientation mattered very much to the intraparty cohesion of either party.

Altogether, the rates at which these respective variables interacted with partisan linkage within each party leave the impression that the building of the current party system of the South has had as much or more to do with the ongoing processes of economic development (i.e., "modernization") and of political development (i.e., "party building") than

with age-old demographic tensions between the races or more recent ones between less tolerant evangelicals and more tolerant non-evangelicals. If that is indeed the case, these data would lend support to the theoretical stances on southern partisan change taken by Bullock and by Bartley and Graham versus the race-driven models of Key, Black and Black, and Davison and Krassa.

All of this suggests implications for the party-environment nexus that may be important for understanding the place of political parties in politics and society, at least in the South and perhaps in the United States as a whole. Some of the context variables that influenced intraparty cohesion on issue after issue in chapter 5 are, conceptually speaking, endogenous to the political parties—for example, *state party organizational strength* and the index of *interparty competition*. Others that were influential were exogenous to the political parties—for example, *per capita income, urbanism,* and *percentage college graduates*. Then, too, there were endogenous as well as exogenous variables that seldom influenced intraparty issue agreement: *local party strength* and *state party identifier* index as examples of the former, and *percentage black* and *percentage fundamentalist* as examples of the latter.

In this chapter we reorganize and reexamine the data of the last chapter with more of an eye on the importance of which contexts influence intraparty issue cohesion, rather than on the importance of the issue cohesion itself. Tables 5.1 to 5.6 deal with those covariates that are endogenous to political parties, as conceptualized by V. O. Key Jr.: Cotter et al.'s *state party organizational strength* (5.1 and 5.2) and *local party organizational strength* (5.3); Fleury's update of Ranney's index of *state interparty competition* (5.4), which when folded is a kind of indication of the competitive strength of the respective "parties-in-office" in each state; and Erikson, Wright, and McIver's indexes of *state partisan identification* (5.5) and of the *liberalism of each state party's identifiers* (5.6), which indicate the strength and policy direction of the respective "parties-in-the-electorate" in each state.

Tables 5.7 to 5.11 deal with all of the exogenous variables. Table 5.7 reports issue agreement obtained when state *percentage of black population* is controlled, table 5.8 reports the results obtained when state *percentage of fundamentalist* Christians is controlled, and tables 5.9, 5.10, and 5.11 report results for *per capita income, percentage college graduates,* and *percentage urban,* respectively, as controls.

Results Using Endogenous Covariates

Table 5.1 indicates a moderate amount (42 percent of all cells) of issue agreement among the Democratic party's various elite/mass dyads before and after controlling for the effects of a covariate and its interaction with the several elite-mass factors. But when *state party organizational strength* is introduced as a covariate and an interaction with the various elite-mass factors, the group means in 44 cells respond by converting from significant to insignificant levels of difference. This results in an impressive amount of consensus, as indicated by the nonsignificant differences in 74 percent of all Democratic cells.

Of course, for some issues, the variable either has

no effect or actually contributes to the loss of cohesion. Grouping the issues on the Y axis of table 5.1 by topic area, we find that *state Democratic organizational strength* had (1) a moderate, evenhanded effect (8 AC cells versus 6 DC cells produced) on the four issues of race, gender, and equality; (2) a larger and definitely cohesive effect (19 AC cells versus 3 DC cells produced) on the five domestic policy issues; (3) a moderate but definitely cohesive effect (9 AC cells versus 1 DC cell) on the three political economy issues; (4) a moderate, overall cohesive effect (6 AC cells versus 2 DC cells) on the three foreign policy/national security issues; and (5) a considerable but divided effect (3 AC cells versus 3 DC cells) on ideological self-placement.

Issue cohesion among Democratic county chair/voter pairs and delegate/national identifier pairs was affected in a very positive manner (across ten and eight of sixteen issues, respectively) by *state Democratic organizational strength,* but cohesion between Democratic voters and the other two elite categories was just as likely to decrease as increase in response to this variable.

The Republican side of table 5.1 is a different matter. Although the rate of change wrought by the introduction of the covariate and interaction effect is about the same for Republicans as for Democrats, the Republican party begins with far fewer cells containing insignificant differences. The Republican panel contains only 32 cells (22 percent of the total) indicating issue agreement before and after the introduction of controls. This then increases to a not inconsiderable, but not overly impressive, 35 percent of all cells when the covariate and interaction were introduced. This is more consistent with our a priori expectations; but, then, Republican state organizations in the South are as a rule weaker than those of the Democrats.

State Republican organizational strength did not affect intraparty cohesion in either direction on any of the gender, race, and equality variables or political economy variables, and barely affected ideological self-placement (1 AC cell to zero DC cells). Domestic policy issues were affected moderately in the

TABLE 5.1

MANOVA RESULTS FOR ALL ELITE-MASS FACTORS, WITH COVARIATE = STATE PARTY ORGANIZATIONAL STRENGTH SCORES

| | DEMOCRATS | | | | | | | | | REPUBLICANS | | | | | | | | |
| | Delegates | | | Chairs | | | Members | | | Delegates | | | Chairs | | | Members | | |
	NPID	SPID	Voters	NPID	SPID	Voters	NPID	SPID	Voters	NPID	SPID	Voters	NPID	SPID	Voters	NPID	SPID	Voters
Ideological self-placement	D	D	AC	DC	DC	A	AC	AC	A	A	A	A	A	A	A	A	A	AC
More for women's SES	AC	AC	AC	A	DC	DC	A	A	A	D	D	D	D	D	D	D	D	D
More SES for minorities	AC	AC	AC	A	A	DC	DC	DC	DC	D	D	D	D	D	D	D	D	D
Equal power for both sexes	AC	D	AC	A	A	A	A	A	A	A	A	A	A	A	A	A	A	A
Keep affirmative action	A	A	A	D	D	D	D	D	A	D	A	D	D	D	D	D	D	D
Abortion by choice	D	D	AC	AC	AC	A	A	A	DC	D	D	AC	D	AC	AI	D	AC	A
Allow school prayer	D	D	AC	DC	DC	A	A	A	A	D	A	A	D	AC	AC	D	D	DC
Help people get health care	AC	AC	AC	AC	A	A	AC	AC	AC	D	AC	D	D	D	D	D	AC	AC
More spending to protect environment	AC	AC	AC	A	A	A	AC	AC	AC	D	D	AC	A	A	A	A	A	DC
Guarantee jobs and good living	A	A	A	D	D	AC	AC	AC	D	D	D	D	D	D	D	D	D	D
Cut services and spending	AC	AC	AC	A	A	A	A	A	DC	D	AC	D	D	D	D	D	D	D
Pass balanced budget amendment	AC	AC	AC	A	A	A	A	A	A	D	D	D	D	D	D	D	D	D
More state taxes, not cuts	AC	AC	DC	A	A	A	A	A	A	D	D	D	D	D	D	D	D	D
More defense spending	D	D	AC	A	A	A	A	DC	DC	D	A	A	D	D	D	D	D	D
America first, overseas second	A	A	A	A	A	A	A	A	A	AC	A	D	AC	AC	AC	AC	AC	A
Continue cooperation with Russia	D	D	D	D	AC	AC	AC	AC	AC	AC	A	A	AC	AC	AC	AC	AC	D

Note: NPID = national party identifiers; SPID = state party identifiers. In the cells, A = agreement; D = disagreement; AC = agreement when controlled for covariate and interaction effect; DC = disagreement when controlled for covariate and interaction effect.

direction of cohesion (8 AC cells to 2 DC cells), and foreign policy/national security issues were affected moderately, but definitely in the direction of cohesion (9 AC cells to zero DC cells). On the other hand, no Republican elite/mass dyad was affected by this control variable, positively or negatively, across more than four of sixteen issues.

The difference in the relative representativeness of the respective parties' elite activists is even more pronounced when we look at the cross-party comparisons reported in table 5.2. Neither party was very much representative of the other party's mass base when only the elite-mass factors were analyzed in chapter 3. But when state party organizational strength is introduced as a covariate and as an interaction with the factor, the Democratic elites-with-Republican-masses side of the table skyrockets from 4 percent pairs agreed before and after controls to 73 percent agreed, whereas the Republican elites-with-Democratic-masses combinations only increase by 4 cells, from 7 percent to 10 percent agreed pairs. Indeed, the only issue for which Republican activists seem to have had any real cross-party appeal was cooperation with Russia, although Republican delegates at least managed to find common ground with all three Democratic mass categories on defense spending and gender equality in business and industry.

Looking at the Democratic panel of table 5.2 by topic area, we find that *state Democratic organizational strength* affected Democratic elite/Republican mass pairs across the board, promoting cohesion for every dyad on at least 7 and as many 13 of the 16 issues. However, Democratic committee member/Republican mass pairs clearly were affected the most, gaining cohesion on an average of 11 of 16 issues, compared to 9.7 of 16 issues for Democratic chair/Republican mass chairs and 7.7 issues for Democratic delegate/Republican mass pairs. The issues for which cross-party cohesion takes place most often were the political economy, domestic policy, and gender/race equality questions, in that order. *State Democratic organizational strength* had (1) a frequent and overwhelmingly cohesive effect (21 AC cells versus zero

DC cells) on the three political economy issues; (2) a similar but slightly less frequent effect (33 AC cells versus zero DC cells) on the five domestic policy issues; and (3) a somewhat less frequent but no less one-sided effect (22 AC cells versus zero DC cells) on the four race/gender equality issues. It should be noted that included in these areas are three defining Republican issues on which Democratic elites proved to be extremely in touch with the Republican rank and file (25 AC cells out of 27 possible), despite Republican campaign efforts to the contrary: abortion, school prayer, and balancing the federal budget.

In contrast, Democratic elite/Republican mass conversions to cohesion were far less frequent on the three foreign policy/national security issues (8 AC cells to zero DC cells) and were all but non-existent as far as ideological self-identification is concerned. It goes without saying that these are the election battlegrounds on which George Bush bested Michael Dukakis in 1988, and toward which the Republicans need to steer future election discourse.

All in all, it must be granted that the *state party organizational strength* variable seems to affect intraparty cohesion importantly. Recall that in the discussion of theoretical expectations at the beginning of chapter 4, we hypothesized that the relative weakness of southern state party organizations in general should make for little intraparty issue integration. What we find instead is that, for Democrats, at least, state party organizational strength matters. In states in which party organizational vitality provides a favorable setting, higher intraparty agreement is possible on the indicated issues.

This is not as true of the other measure of formal party organizational presence within a state political setting. As table 5.3 suggests, the PTS group's index of *local party organizational strength* is not similarly productive when introduced as a control variable. Only 3 out of 144 cells in the Republican panel are affected, and in the direction of disagreement rather than agreement. Issue cohesion is affected only slightly less marginally in the Democratic panel, where the net increases in cohesive cells are -2 across the three race/gender equality issues, +6 across five domestic policy

TABLE 5.2

CROSS-PARTY MANOVA RESULTS FOR ALL ELITE-MASS FACTORS, WITH COVARIATE = STATE PARTY ORGANIZATIONAL STRENGTH SCORES

| | DEMOCRATS | | | | | | | | | REPUBLICANS | | | | | | | | |
| | Delegates | | | Chairs | | | Members | | | Delegates | | | Chairs | | | Members | | |
	NPID (Rep.)	SPID (Rep.)	Voters (Rep.)	NPID (Rep.)	SPID (Rep.)	Voters (Rep.)	NPID (Rep.)	SPID (Rep.)	Voters (Rep.)	NPID (Dem.)	SPID (Dem.)	Voters (Dem.)	NPID (Dem.)	SPID (Dem.)	Voters (Dem.)	NPID (Dem.)	SPID (Dem.)	Voters (Dem.)
Ideological self-placement	D	D	D	D	D	D	AC	D	D	D	D	D	D	D	D	D	D	D
More for women's SES	D	D	D	AC	AC	AC	AC	AC	AC	D	D	D	D	D	D	D	D	D
More SES for minorities	D	AC	D	AC	AC	AC	AC	AC	AC	D	D	D	D	D	D	D	D	D
Equal power for both sexes	D	D	D	AC	A	AC	AC	AC	AC	A	A	A	D	D	D	D	D	D
Keep affirmative action	AC	AC	AC	A	A	A	A	A	A	D	D	D	D	D	D	D	D	D
Abortion by choice	AC	AC	AC	AC	AC	AC	AC	AC	AC	D	D	D	D	D	D	D	D	D
Allow school prayer	AC	AC	AC	AC	AC	AC	AC	AC	D	D	D	D	D	D	D	D	D	D
Help people get health care	AC	D	AC	AC	AC	AC	AC	AC	AC	D	D	D	D	D	D	D	D	D
More spending to protect environment	AC	AC	D	AC	D	AC	AC	AC	D	D	D	D	D	D	D	AC	AC	D
Guarantee jobs and good living	AC	AC	D	A	A	A	AC	A	AC	D	D	D	D	D	D	D	D	D
Cut services and spending	AC	AC	AC	AC	AC	AC	AC	AC	AC	D	D	D	D	D	D	D	D	D
Pass balanced budget amendment	AC	AC	AC	AC	AC	AC	AC	AC	A	D	D	D	D	D	D	D	D	D
More state taxes, not cuts	D	D	D	D	AC	AC	D	AC	AC	D	D	D	D	D	D	D	D	D
More defense spending	D	D	D	AC	A	A	A	A	A	D	D	D	D	D	D	D	D	D
America first, overseas second	D	D	AC	AC	AC	AC	AC	AC	AC	A	A	A	D	D	D	D	D	D
Continue cooperation with Russia	D	D	D	D	D	D	AC	AC	AC	AC	AC	AC	A	A	A	D	D	D

Note: NPID = national party identifiers; SPID = state party identifiers. In the cells, A = agreement; D = disagreement; AC = agreement when controlled for covariate and interaction effect; DC = disagreement when controlled for covariate and interaction effect.

issues, -1 across the three political economy issues, +3 across the three foreign policy/national security issues, and -2 for ideological self-identification. The 57 percent intra-Democratic cohesion and 21 percent intra-Republican cohesion levels in this table for the most part preexisted, and survived, the impact of our environmental analysis. Such findings are not a strong recommendation for the respective national party committees' much touted local organization-building programs (e.g., Project 2000, Working Partners, the State Party Works, etc.) of the 1980s. But then, our theoretical expectation was that local party organizational strength would not matter as much at the state level of analysis as would state party organizational strength, about which we also had reservations.

But the levels of intraparty issue agreement achieved when the folded *interparty competition* index is controlled are even higher than for *state party organizational strength*, especially for the Republicans. Consistent with the top-down theory of Republican growth in the South, much higher levels of Republican elite-mass issue agreement are achieved when the parties' respective levels of success in state electoral competition replace party formal organizational presence as the control variable. As table 5.4 shows, the elite/mass pairs agreeing on issues jump from 47 to 83 percent for Democrats, and from 24 to 89 percent for Republicans, when the *interparty competition* index score is introduced as a covariate and as an interaction with the various elite-mass factors. These are impressive levels of intraparty agreement for both parties. Note that the rate of change for the Republicans induced by the environmental analysis is nearly twice that for the Democrats. This reflects not only that the Republicans enjoyed a better than two-to-one advantage in intraparty agreement prior to the introduction of the covariate and interaction term but also that these controls had the effect of converting 11 Democratic pairs from issue agreement to disagreement. It is noteworthy that 10 of the 11 pairs thus altered involved Democratic county chairs, whereas the number (26) of Democratic delegate/mass pairs converting to cohesion was more than

twice that among county chair/mass pairs (11), and nearly twice that committee member/mass pairs (14).

Most of those 11 disagreed Democratic pairs also revolved around political economy issues, where DC cells outnumbered AC cells by a margin of six to four. However, intraparty cohesion proliferated strongly in each of the other issue areas, led by domestic policy (21 AC cells versus 3 DC cells, out of 45 cells possible) and followed by foreign policy/national security (12 AC cells versus zero DC cells, out of 27 cells), ideology (5 of 9 cells AC, zero DC), and race/gender equality (8 AC cells versus 2 DC cells, out of 36 cells possible).

But this very respectable showing paled next to the boost intra-Republican cohesion received as a result of controlling for *interparty competition*. In the Republican panel, 32 out of 45 cells possible for the five domestic policy issues converted to cohesion, as did 21 of the 27 cells possible for the political economy issues, 24 of the 36 cells possible for the race/gender equality issues, and 16 of 27 cells possible for the foreign policy/national security issues. The affirmative action and health-care issues each saw conversions to cohesion across all 9 elite/mass dyads possible; cutting government services and spending, government assistance for minorities, and dealing with domestic problems ahead of foreign problems each witnessed conversions to cohesion in 8 of 9 cells. Not one cell in any of these issue clusters contained a DC (i.e., went from agreement to disagreement). Only for the ideological self-identification item did a cell convert to disagreement, only to be canceled out by a cell moving in the opposite direction.

Such data patterns provide clear evidence that, under conditions of strong two-party competition for public office, partisan linkage between elites and masses can be strong as well. As we stated in the theoretical discussion at the start of chapter 4, stiff competition for the median voter forces party elites to position themselves at, or near, the median in the pursuit of electoral success. Where one party dominates elections, on the other hand, party elites can get away with ignoring mass perspectives at little or no cost to their prospects for victory at the polls.

TABLE 5.3
MANOVA RESULTS FOR ALL ELITE-MASS FACTORS, WITH COVARIATE = LOCAL PARTY ORGANIZATIONAL STRENGTH, BY STATE

| | DEMOCRATS | | | | | | | | | REPUBLICANS | | | | | | | | |
| | Delegates | | | Chairs | | | Members | | | Delegates | | | Chairs | | | Members | | |
	NPID	SPID	Voters	NPID	SPID	Voters	NPID	SPID	Voters	NPID	SPID	Voters	NPID	SPID	Voters	NPID	SPID	Voters
Ideological self-placement	D	D	D	DC	DC	A	D	D	A	A	A	A	A	A	DC	A	A	D
More for women's SES	D	D	D	A	A	A	A	A	A	D	D	D	D	D	D	D	D	D
More SES for minorities	D	D	D	A	A	DC	A	A	A	D	D	D	D	D	D	D	D	D
Equal power for both sexes	D	D	D	A	A	A	A	A	A	A	A	A	A	A	A	A	A	A
Keep affirmative action	AC	AC	AC	D	D	D	D	D	DC	D	D	D	D	D	D	D	D	D
Abortion by choice	D	D	D	D	D	A	A	A	A	D	D	D	D	A	A	D	D	A
Allow school prayer	D	D	D	A	A	A	A	A	A	D	A	A	D	D	D	D	D	A
Help people get health care	D	D	D	A	A	A	AC	AC	AC	D	D	D	D	D	D	D	D	D
More spending to protect environment	D	D	D	A	A	A	AC	AC	AC	A	A	A	A	A	A	A	A	A
Guarantee jobs and good living	A	A	A	D	D	D	D	D	D	D	D	D	D	D	D	D	D	D
Cut services and spending	D	D	AC	A	A	A	A	A	A	D	D	D	D	D	D	D	D	D
Pass balanced budget amendment	D	D	D	DC	DC	D	A	A	A	D	D	D	D	D	D	D	D	D
More state taxes, not cuts	AC	AC	AC	A	A	A	DC	DC	A	D	D	D	D	D	A	D	A	D
More defense spending	D	D	D	A	A	A	D	D	A	D	D	D	D	D	A	D	D	D
America first, overseas second	A	A	A	A	A	A	A	A	A	D	D	D	D	D	D	D	D	D
Continue cooperation with Russia	D	D	D	D	D	D	AC	AC	AC	DC	A	DC	D	D	D	D	D	D

Note: NPID = national party identifiers; SPID = state party identifiers. In the cells, A = agreement; D = disagreement; AC = agreement when controlled for covariate and interaction effect; DC = disagreement when controlled for covariate and interaction effect.

TABLE 5.4

MANOVA RESULTS FOR ALL ELITE-MASS FACTORS, WITH COVARIATE = RANNEY INTERPARTY COMPETITION INDEX SCORES, BY STATE

	DEMOCRATS									REPUBLICANS								
	Delegates			Chairs			Members			Delegates			Chairs			Members		
	NPID	SPID	Voters	NPID	SPID	Voters	NPID	SPID	Voters	NPID	SPID	Voters	NPID	SPID	Voters	NPID	SPID	Voters
Ideological self-placement	AC	AC	AC	A	A	A	AC	AC	A	A	A	A	A	A	A	DC	A	AC
More for women's SES	D	D	AC	DC	A	A	DC	A	A	AC	AC	AC	D	AC	D	AC	AC	AC
More SES for minorities	AC	AC	AC	A	A	A	A	A	A	AC	AC	AC	AC	AC	D	AC	AC	AC
Equal power for both sexes	D	AC	AC	A	A	A	A	A	A	A	A	A	A	A	A	A	A	A
Keep affirmative action	A	A	A	AC	AC	AC	D	D	A	AC	AC	AC	AC	AC	AC	AC	AC	AC
Abortion by choice	AC	AC	AC	AC	AC	A	A	A	A	AC	AC	AC	AC	AC	A	AC	AC	A
Allow school prayer	A	AC	AC	A	DC	DC	A	A	A	AC	A	A	AC	AC	AC	AC	AC	A
Help people get health care	D	D	AC	DC	A	A	AC	AC	AC	AC	AC	AC	AC	AC	AC	AC	AC	AC
More spending to protect environment	D	D	D	A	A	A	AC	AC	AC	A	AC	AC	A	A	A	A	A	A
Guarantee jobs and good living	A	A	A	AC	AC	AC	AC	AC	AC	AC	AC	AC	D	AC	D	AC	AC	AC
Cut services and spending	AC	D	D	DC	DC	DC	A	A	A	D	AC	AC	AC	AC	AC	AC	AC	AC
Pass balanced budget amendment	AC	D	AC	A	A	A	A	A	A	AC	AC	AC	D	D	AC	AC	AC	AC
More state taxes, not cuts	D	AC	A	DC	DC	A	A	A	A	AC	AC	AC	D	D	D	AC	AC	AC
More defense spending	AC	AC	AC	A	A	A	A	A	A	A	A	A	D	D	AC	D	D	AC
America first, overseas second	A	A	A	A	A	A	A	A	A	AC	AC	AC	AC	AC	AC	AC	AC	A
Continue cooperation with Russia	AC	AC	AC	AC	AC	AC	AC	AC	AC	A	A	A	AC	AC	AC	AC	AC	AC

Note: NPID = national party identifiers; SPID = state party identifiers. In the cells, A = agreement; D = disagreement; AC = agreement when controlled for covariate and interaction effect; DC = disagreement when controlled for covariate and interaction effect.

The percentage of cells indicating issue agreement is only roughly half that for table 5.4 when Erikson, Wright, and McIvers's *state partisan identification* index is substituted as the control variable. This is partly due to the fact that this variable actually has the effect of reducing issue cohesion in the Democratic panel, which contains 24 DC cells compared to only 12 AC cells. Given this net loss, the total cohesion levels of 48 percent for the Democrats and 38 percent for the Republicans are still quite respectable, especially when we recall that in chapter 4 we did not expect this variable to have much of an impact because of its low range of variability across the eleven southern states.

As table 5.5 reveals, once the covariate and interaction term are introduced, Democratic elite/mass pairs experience more losses than gains of cohesion in every issue category except foreign policy/national security, where they pick up 2 AC cells on the cooperation with Russia issue. On issues of race/gender equality, 5 Democratic county activist/mass pairs gain cohesion on affirmative action, but 3 delegate/mass pairs lose cohesion on the same issue, and 4 more county committee member/mass pairs lose cohesion on the issues of equality for women with men in business and industry and of government doing more for blacks and other minorities. On the political economy questions, 6 assorted Democratic pairs went from agreement to disagreement over the balanced budget amendment and/or cutting government services and spending, compared to only 2 delegate/identifier pairs that reached agreement on state tax increases rather than spending cuts. Across the five domestic policy issues, only 5 Democratic elite/mass cells converted to cohesion, compared to 7 cells that lost cohesion. Finally, 2 pairs of county activists and Democratic voters ceased to agree ideologically when controls were introduced.

The Republicans are not as cohesive overall in table 5.5 as the Democrats are, but a much larger proportion of their issue integration is generated by controlling for *state partisan identification* index. There are 21 AC cells, no DC cells, and 33 A cells in the panel. The control variable thus not only did not

reduce net cohesion in any way but was responsible for generating 39 percent of the issue integration in the panel. Two-thirds of these gains in cohesion occurred among county elite/mass pairs and involved the Republican boilerplate issues of abortion and school prayer, along with paying more attention to problems at home rather than overseas.

It is difficult to speculate as to how and why the respective proportions of Democratic self-identifiers and Republican self-identifiers in the electorate of each southern state should create intraparty cohesion among Republican pairs and destabilize cohesion among Democratic pairs. Inspection of residuals, like the reporting of actual coefficients, was an early casualty of the vast amount of data manipulation involved in this environmental analysis. However, one possibility that comes to mind is the racial (overwhelmingly white) and ideological (conservative) homogeneity of southern Republican identifiers, which is more easily represented than the heterogeneous combination of moderate and liberal whites and largely liberal blacks found among southern Democratic identifiers. Both such compositional tendencies should, in theory, be accentuated in states where the Republican share of the electorate is smaller, and the Democrats' share is larger. Consequently, as the index score indicating the respective sizes of the two parties' electoral bases changes (i.e., grows in Democratic share) from state to state, we should see that Republicans advantaged by inherent homogeneity are able to come together on issues that were highlighted at their 1992 convention in Houston; whereas Democrats encumbered by inherent heterogeneity should be more inclined to disagree than agree across a number of issues.

The Republicans gain the upper hand in intraparty cohesion by a wide margin when the final endogenous measure, which also pertains to the party in the electorate, is introduced as a covariate and an interactor. Table 5.6 shows that after controlling for Erikson, Wright, and McIver's *liberalism of party identifiers,* Republican cohesion is reflected in 89 percent of cells, and Democratic cohesion in only 54 percent.

Democratic gains and losses are balanced at

TABLE 5.5
MANOVA RESULTS FOR ALL ELITE-MASS FACTORS, WITH COVARIATE = STATE PARTISAN IDENTIFICATION INDEX

| | DEMOCRATS | | | | | | | | | REPUBLICANS | | | | | | | | |
| | Delegates | | | Chairs | | | Members | | | Delegates | | | Chairs | | | Members | | |
	NPID	SPID	Voters	NPID	SPID	Voters	NPID	SPID	Voters	NPID	SPID	Voters	NPID	SPID	Voters	NPID	SPID	Voters
Ideological self-placement	D	D	D	D	A	D	D	D	DC	A	A	A	A	A	A	A	A	D
More for women's SES	D	D	D	A	A	A	A	A	A	D	D	D	D	D	D	D	D	D
More SES for minorities	D	D	D	A	A	A	A	DC	A	AC	AC	D	D	D	D	D	D	D
Equal power for both sexes	D	D	D	A	A	A	DC	DC	DC	A	A	A	A	A	A	A	A	A
Keep affirmative action	DC	DC	DC	AC	AC	AC	AC	AC	A	D	D	D	D	D	D	D	D	D
Abortion by choice	D	D	D	AC	AC	A	A	A	A	D	D	AC	AC	AC	A	AC	AC	A
Allow school prayer	D	D	D	DC	DC	A	DC	DC	A	AC	A	A	AC	AC	AC	AC	AC	A
Help people get health care	D	D	D	DC	DC	DC	D	D	D	D	D	D	D	D	D	D	D	D
More spending to protect environment	D	D	D	A	A	A	D	D	D	D	D	D	A	A	A	A	A	A
Guarantee jobs and good living	A	DC	D	D	D	D	AC	AC	AC	D	D	D	D	D	D	D	D	D
Cut services and spending	D	D	D	A	DC	DC	A	A	A	D	D	D	D	D	D	D	D	D
Pass balanced budget amendment	D	D	D	DC	DC	A	DC	DC	A	D	D	D	D	D	D	D	AC	AC
More state taxes, not cuts	AC	AC	A	A	A	A	A	A	A	A	A	A	A	D	D	D	D	D
More defense spending	D	D	D	A	A	A	A	A	A	D	D	D	D	D	D	D	D	D
America first, overseas second	A	A	A	A	A	A	A	A	A	D	D	A	AC	AC	AC	AC	AC	A
Continue cooperation with Russia	D	D	D	D	D	AC	D	D	AC	A	A	A	D	D	AC	D	D	D

Note: NPID = national party identifiers; SPID = state party identifiers. In the cells, A = agreement; D = disagreement; AC = agreement when controlled for covariate and interaction effect; DC = disagreement when controlled for covariate and interaction effect.

fifteen conversions in each direction: AC and DC. Democrats became more cohesive in ideological self-placement (2 AC cells versus zero DC cells) and political economy (2 AC cells versus 1 DC cell). On issues of race/gender equality, the Democrats gained 4 cohesive pairs and lost cohesion in 5 pairs (again, Democrats were divided over affirmative action and equality for women in business and industry). On domestic policy issues, they gained 7 pairs but lost 6. On foreign policy/national security matters, they lost cohesion in 3 pairs and gained cohesion in none.

In the Republican panel, on the other hand, all 9 elite/mass dyads were influenced in the direction of cohesion on at least ten of the sixteen issues. The gains brought by controlling for the ideology of Republican identifiers were exceptional in every issue category except ideological self-placement (which, of course, may have been a case in which the control variable and dependent variable were substantially the same). Political economy issues led the parade in that all 27 cells possible across these issues converted to cohesion when the *liberalism of state Republican identifiers* was controlled. The three foreign policy/national security issues were not far behind (20 AC cells versus 3 DC cells, out of 27 possible). Domestic policy concerns were next (32 AC cells versus 4 DC cells, out of 45 possible), followed by race/gender equality issues (22 AC cells versus 2 DC cells, out of 36 possible). In addition to the three political economy issues, other concerns for which all 9 elite/mass pairs possible converted to cohesion included health care, government assistance for (1) women and (2) minorities, and government guarantees of employment and standards of living.

In short, the patterns of the data in table 5.6 are similar to, although much stronger than, the patterns of table 5.5: the control variable brings about huge increases in issue integration within the Republican party, but results in neither gains nor losses of cohesion, as opposed to modest losses, within the Democratic party. The similarity is not so surprising, since both variables are mass politocultural ones. Perhaps this cell behavior occurs because while Black and Black (1992) are correct about "liberal" whites and

blacks comprising most of the electoral base of the Democratic party in the South, Erikson, Wright, and McIver establish that between 1976 and 1988 southern Democratic identifiers were relatively more conservative than their counterparts outside the South, as indicated by the negative scores for mass Democrats in every southern state except Virginia (1993, table 2.8). This could mean that as our analysis for this variable proceeded from Democratic elite/mass pairs in states lower in the Erikson, Wright, and McIver *liberalism of identifiers* scale through those from states higher on that scale, the diversity of ideology within the Democratic rank and file progressively widened. That is, the distributions of the data Erikson, Wright, and McIver used conceivably may cluster more around the state mean in those states farther down the *liberalism of partisan identifiers* scale, and be widely dispersed around the mean in states farther up the scale. Southern Republican masses, on the other hand, all scored so close together and so far down the Erikson, Wright, and McIver *liberalism of identifiers* scale (i.e., -30.0 or lower) that it seems highly unlikely that their scores on that scale could mask very much mass ideological diversity.

Viewed in tandem with our earlier discovery of greater intraparty cohesion among Republicans than among Democrats with respect to the ideological self-placement issue, the electoral consequences of the findings in table 5.6 are indeed formidable. The electoral weak link of the Democratic party in the South is ideology. In the partisan war to mobilize your own electoral base, carry the swing vote, and raid or at least depress turnout within the opponent's electoral base, it is a mixed blessing to be an ideologically diverse party. The Democrats' intraparty ideological diversity can be advantageous in terms of facilitating party attraction of swing voters and voting defections from the opposing party; that is why the Democrats outshine their opponents in cross-party issue cohesion in table 5.2. But that same intraparty ideological diversity also can be a Democratic "Trojan Horse": exploited effectively, as it was in 1988, such diversity can complicate and frustrate even the first task of campaigning, which is to secure your own base

TABLE 5.6
MANOVA RESULTS FOR ALL ELITE-MASS FACTORS, WITH COVARIATE = LIBERALISM OF PARTISAN IDENTIFIERS, BY STATE

| | DEMOCRATS | | | | | | | | | REPUBLICANS | | | | | | | | |
| | Delegates | | | Chairs | | | Members | | | Delegates | | | Chairs | | | Members | | |
	NPID	SPID	Voters	NPID	SPID	Voters	NPID	SPID	Voters	NPID	SPID	Voters	NPID	SPID	Voters	NPID	SPID	Voters
Ideological self-placement	D	D	D	A	A	A	AC	AC	A	A	A	A	A	A	A	A	A	A
More for women's SES	D	D	D	A	A	A	A	A	A	AC	AC	AC	AC	AC	AC	AC	AC	AC
More SES for minorities	D	D	D	A	A	A	A	A	A	AC	AC	AC	AC	AC	AC	AC	AC	AC
Equal power for both sexes	D	D	D	A	A	A	DC	DC	A	DC	DC	A	A	A	A	A	A	A
Keep affirmative action	DC	DC	DC	D	AC	AC	AC	AC	A	AC	AC	AC	D	D	D	AC	D	AC
Abortion by choice	D	D	D	AC	AC	A	A	A	A	D	D	AC	AC	AC	A	AC	AC	A
Allow school prayer	D	D	D	A	A	A	DC	DC	DC	AC	DC	AC	AC	AC	AC	AC	AC	A
Help people get health care	D	D	D	A	A	A	D	D	AC	AC	AC	AC	AC	AC	AC	AC	AC	AC
More spending to protect environment	D	D	D	A	A	A	D	D	D	AC	AC	AC	DC	DC	DC	A	A	A
Guarantee jobs and good living	DC	DC	DC	D	D	AC	AC	AC	AC	AC	AC	AC	AC	AC	AC	AC	AC	AC
Cut services and spending	D	D	D	A	A	A	A	A	A	AC	AC	AC	AC	AC	AC	AC	AC	AC
Pass balanced budget amendment	D	D	D	A	A	A	D	DC	A	AC	AC	AC	AC	AC	AC	AC	AC	AC
More state taxes, not cuts	AC	AC	A	A	A	A	A	A	A	AC	AC	AC	AC	AC	AC	AC	AC	AC
More defense spending	D	D	D	A	A	A	DC	DC	DC	DC	DC	DC	AC	AC	AC	AC	AC	AC
America first, overseas second	A	A	A	A	A	A	A	A	A	AC	AC	AC	AC	AC	AC	AC	AC	A
Continue cooperation with Russia	D	D	D	D	D	D	D	D	D	A	A	A	AC	AC	AC	AC	AC	AC

Note: NPID = national party identifiers; SPID = state party identifiers. In the cells, A = agreement; D = disagreement; AC = agreement when controlled for covariate and interaction effect; DC = disagreement when controlled for covariate and interaction effect.

against the opponent. From what we have seen in this table, and in the first table (ideological self-placement) of the last chapter, it seems that not all of the conservative whites in the South are Republicans, yet, and not all of the moderate whites are the "swing voters" that Black and Black (1993) characterized to be crucial to controlling the southern Electoral College vote. Rather, more than a few white conservatives and moderates are still nominally Democrats, whether ideologically comfortable under that label and its portents or not. Focusing the campaign on ideological differences—Lee Atwater's "L-word" gambit of 1988—still appears viable as a Republican strategy for carrying the South in presidential elections.

In sum, regardless of from which party element—party organization, party in office, or party in the electorate—one draws the covariate, the overall finding is that party-specific variables endogenous to the question of intraparty issue cohesion have the effect of increasing the level of such cohesion when their main and interaction effects are controlled. Where state party organizations are strong, where two-party competition is intense, the setting is present for high issue agreement between party elites and masses to take place. Where the liberalism of the respective partisan electoral bases varies, the ability of party elites to represent the issue views of those electoral bases is also variable, with potent consequences for electoral strategy. The clear implication is that political parties indeed matter as far as democratic linkage is concerned. Let us turn now to the presentation of results from the exogenous variables, to see whether the case they make for themselves is as strong.

Results Using Exogenous Covariates

As the data in table 5.7 reveal, when *percentage black* is controlled, it affects issue agreement in the same direction that the endogenous, party-centric covariates did, but not as strongly as several of the latter. The 67 percent of cells indicating issue agreement in the Democratic panel of table 5.7 is a strong showing, but still one that falls short of the 74 and 83 per-

cent levels obtained for *state party organizational strength* and *interparty competition*, respectively. Moreover, the 47 percent share of issue agreement in the Republican panel of table 5.7 indicates that state racial composition has a not inconsiderable impact upon Republican intraparty issue cohesion, but has nowhere near the effect that endogenous variables such as the *interparty competition* index and the *liberalism of state Republican identifiers* had.

Conversion to cohesion, though more frequent among county Democratic elite/mass pairs than Democratic delegate/mass pairs by a three-to-one margin, did not really occur in sufficient volume to qualify as "typical" of any dyad. The leading pair, Democratic committee member/state identifiers, only experienced conversions to cohesion in 5 of 16 cells (perhaps because as was true of the rest of the county elite/mass dyads, it had 10 or so cells in which there was agreement before and after controlling for racial presence). The only policy area in which even a moderate rate of conversions to cohesion occurred was domestic policy issues (12 AC cells versus 3 DC cells, out of 45 cells possible). Foreign policy/national security issues had a not unimpressive rate of change (6 AC cells versus 1 DC cell, out of 27 cells possible), but the political economy issues (2 AC cells versus 3 DC cells, out of 27 possible), the race/gender equality issues (3 AC cells to 1 DC, out of 36 possible), and ideological self-placement (2 AC cells) were affected very little.

The Republican panel of table 5.7, like the Democratic panel, contains no dyads for which conversion to cohesion was the norm but nonetheless was comparably more responsive to *percentage black*. Domestic issues (17 AC cells to 3 DC cells), foreign policy/national security issues (10 AC cells to zero DC cells), and race/gender equality issues (11 AC cells to zero DC cells) all witnessed moderate or better improvements in cohesion. Indeed, these conversions, plus two more that occurred within the political economy section, accounted for 60 percent of the cohesive cells within the Republican panel. Moreover, controlling for racial presence within each state had the effect of dissolving ideological cohesion in 6 cells involving

TABLE 5.7
MANOVA RESULTS FOR ALL ELITE-MASS FACTORS, WITH COVARIATE = STATE PERCENTAGE OF BLACKS

| | DEMOCRATS | | | | | | | | | REPUBLICANS | | | | | | | | |
| | Delegates | | | Chairs | | | Members | | | Delegates | | | Chairs | | | Members | | |
	NPID	SPID	Voters	NPID	SPID	Voters	NPID	SPID	Voters	NPID	SPID	Voters	NPID	SPID	Voters	NPID	SPID	Voters
Ideological self-placement	D	D	D	A	A	A	AC	AC	A	DC	DC	A	DC	DC	A	DC	DC	A
More for women's SES	D	D	D	A	A	A	A	A	A	D	D	D	D	D	D	D	D	D
More SES for minorities	D	D	D	A	A	A	A	A	A	AC	AC	D	D	D	D	AC	AC	AC
Equal power for both sexes	D	D	D	A	A	A	A	A	A	A	A	A	A	A	A	A	A	A
Keep affirmative action	A	A	A	AC	AC	AC	D	D	DC	AC	AC	AC	D	D	D	AC	AC	AC
Abortion by choice	D	D	D	AC	AC	A	A	A	A	AC	AC	A	AC	AC	A	AC	AC	A
Allow school prayer	D	D	D	A	A	A	A	A	A	AC	A	A	AC	AC	AC	AC	AC	A
Help people get health care	D	D	D	A	A	A	AC	AC	AC	D	D	AC	D	D	D	AC	AC	AC
More spending to protect environment	D	D	D	A	A	A	AC	AC	AC	D	D	D	A	A	A	D	D	A
Guarantee jobs and good living	DC	DC	A	AC	AC	D	AC	AC	AC	D	D	D	D	D	D	D	D	D
Cut services and spending	D	D	D	A	A	A	A	A	A	D	AC	D	AC	AC	AC	D	D	AC
Pass balanced budget amendment	D	D	D	DC	DC	DC	A	A	A	D	D	D	D	D	D	D	D	AC
More state taxes, not cuts	AC	AC	A	A	A	A	A	A	A	A	A	A	A	A	A	A	A	D
More defense spending	D	D	D	A	A	A	A	A	A	D	D	D	D	D	D	D	D	D
America first, overseas second	DC	A	A	A	A	A	A	A	A	D	A	AC	AC	AC	AC	AC	AC	A
Continue cooperation with Russia	D	D	AC	AC	AC	AC	D	AC	AC	A	A	A	A	AC	AC	D	D	AC

Note: NPID = national party identifiers; SPID = state party identifiers. In the cells, A = agreement; D = disagreement; AC = agreement when controlled for covariate and interaction effect; DC = disagreement when controlled for covariate and interaction effect.

national and state Republican identifiers with each type of Republican elite. This last datum suggests that as racial presence increases, the ideological response among both kinds of Republican identifiers is *decreased* conservatism, which hardly seems consistent with the racist backlash predicted by white flight theorists of Republican growth, such as Davison and Krassa (1991).

Based on the ecological data of the latter authors, the recent works of Black and Black (1987, 1993) and Carmines and Stimson (1989), and the original work of V. O. Key Jr., we had expected to see higher levels of elite-mass issue integration in both parties as the analysis progressed from states with the fewest African Americans to states with the most African Americans. Higher levels did, in fact, come about as a result of racial presence; however, (1) they were not as high, overall, as the cohesion levels associated with several of the party-endogenous variables; (2) they were not nearly as frequently the product of post-control conversions to cohesion as was true in the case of several party-endogenous variables; and (3) they certainly were not up to the levels one expects of a variable that is said by so many to drive partisan change and electoral strategy in the South.

When the *percentage of fundamentalists* per state was inserted as the control variable, the incidence of issue agreement among Republicans increased a little relative to table 5.7, to 55 percent of all cells in the Republican panel of table 5.8, whereas cohesion among Democrats in table 5.8 stood pat at 67 percent of all cells. Once again, these fruits have been bested, as noted previously, by several of the endogenous variables. Indeed, all of the latter except *local party organizational strength* matched or outperformed *percentage fundamentalists* at generating intraparty cohesion among Democrats.

But what is most remarkable about table 5.8 is the close consonance of the distributions for the Democratic panels of this table and table 5.7. Except for the AC in the committee member/national identifier cell for the cooperation with Russia issue and the AC in 3 committee member/mass cells for the

issue of gender equality in business and industry, the Democratic panel of table 5.8 is a mirror image of its predecessor.

The Republican panel of table 5.8 is also uncanny in that here, too, we find *percentage fundamentalists* having exactly the same effect that *percentage black* had in table 5.7 upon the distributions for six issues: cutting federal services and spending, school prayer, state tax increases rather than cuts, government guarantees of jobs and standards of living, equal power for women in business and industry, and solving problems at home before problems overseas. Most of the other issues had cell distributions closely similar to those in table 5.7, as well.

In brief, *percentage black* and *percentage fundamentalist* have almost exactly the same effect upon intraparty cohesion—an effect which, once again, was nothing to shout about. How profound an effect can a variable be said to have, if not only certain other variables surpass that effect, but still another demographic virtually duplicates its effect? We reject the possibility that fundamentalist presence and racial presence are interrelated: only white evangelicals were included in the Erikson, Wright, and McIver formulation of *fundamentalism* that we control for in this study, and we are unaware of any scientific evidence that the rise of Christian fundamentalism is a reaction to racial presence (and/or empowerment). We prefer for the present to attribute this similarity of effect to ecological accident.

When state *per capita income* differences are controlled, at last the number of cells indicating issue agreement are competitive with those generated by the strongest of the party-endogenous variables. Table 5.9 shows that controlling for *per capita income* drives up the incidence of issue agreement in the Democratic panel from 47 percent agreed before and after to 89 percent of all cells, and the percentage of issue agreement in the Republican panel from 22 percent agreed before and after to 78 percent of all cells. Sixty cells converted to cohesion in the Democratic panel, accounting for 47 percent of the issue cohesion in that panel, and 81 cells converted to cohesion in the Republican panel,

TABLE 5.8

MANOVA RESULTS FOR ALL ELITE-MASS FACTORS, WITH COVARIATE = STATE PERCENTAGE OF FUNDAMENTALIST CHRISTIANS

	DEMOCRATS									REPUBLICANS								
	Delegates			Chairs			Members			Delegates			Chairs			Members		
	NPID	SPID	Voters	NPID	SPID	Voters	NPID	SPID	Voters	NPID	SPID	Voters	NPID	SPID	Voters	NPID	SPID	Voters
Ideological self-placement	D	D	D	A	A	A	AC	AC	A	DC	DC	A	DC	DC	A	A	A	AC
More for women's SES	D	D	D	A	A	A	A	A	A	AC	AC	AC	D	D	D	AC	AC	AC
More SES for minorities	D	D	D	A	A	A	A	A	A	AC	AC	AC	D	D	D	AC	AC	AC
Equal power for both sexes	D	D	D	A	A	A	AC	AC	AC	A	A	A	A	A	A	A	A	A
Keep affirmative action	A	A	A	AC	AC	AC	D	D	DC	AC	AC	AC	AC	D	D	D	D	AC
Abortion by choice	D	D	D	A	AC	A	A	A	A	D	D	AC	AC	AC	A	AC	AC	A
Allow school prayer	D	D	D	A	A	A	A	A	A	AC	A	A	AC	AC	AC	AC	AC	A
Help people get health care	D	D	D	A	A	A	AC	AC	AC	AC	AC	AC	AC	AC	AC	AC	AC	AC
More spending to protect environment	D	D	D	A	A	A	AC	AC	AC	AC	AC	AC	A	A	A	A	A	A
Guarantee jobs and good living	DC	DC	A	AC	AC	D	AC	AC	AC	D	D	D	D	D	D	D	D	D
Cut services and spending	D	D	D	A	A	A	A	A	A	D	D	D	D	D	D	D	D	AC
Pass balanced budget amendment	D	D	D	A	DC	DC	A	A	DC	AC	AC	AC	D	D	D	AC	AC	AC
More state taxes, not cuts	AC	AC	A	A	A	A	A	A	A	D	D	D	D	D	D	D	D	D
More defense spending	D	D	D	A	A	A	A	A	A	DC	DC	A	D	D	D	D	D	AC
America first, overseas second	DC	A	A	A	A	A	A	A	A	D	D	AC	AC	AC	AC	AC	AC	A
Continue cooperation with Russia	D	D	AC	AC	AC	AC	AC	AC	AC	DC	DC	DC	D	D	D	D	D	D

Note: NPID = national party identifiers; SPID = state party identifiers. In the cells, A = agreement; D = disagreement; AC = agreement when controlled for covariate and interaction effect; DC = disagreement when controlled for covariate and interaction effect.

accounting for 71 percent of its total cohesion. Stronger environmental impact than this would be difficult to find.

For the Democrats, the strongest environmental impact was felt on the five domestic policy issues (25 AC cells versus 2 DC cells), followed by the three foreign policy/national security issues (12 AC cells versus 4 DC cells), the four race/gender equality issues (10 AC cells versus 3 DC cells), the three political economy issues (8 AC cells versus 1 DC cell), and personal ideology (5 AC cells to zero). Fully 60 percent of these conversions took place among the delegate/mass pairs, followed by 23 percent involving committee member/mass pairs and 17 percent involving county chair/mass pairs.

The number of conversion cells in the Republican panel of table 5.9 was higher by one-third, so every issue area was affected profoundly except the ideological self-placement item, which was cohesive across all 9 dyads before and after controlling for *per capita income*. Conversions to issue cohesion came in 25 of 45 possible cells for domestic issues, 20 of 27 possible cells for political economy issues, and 18 of 36 possible cells for race/gender equality issues, without a single DC cell occurring for any of the twelve issues thus covered. The three foreign policy/national security issues also moved toward issue agreement in 18 of 27 possible cells, but also had 3 Republican delegate/mass cells move toward disagreement on cooperation with Russia. The distribution of these changes across the 9 elite/mass dyads was pretty even, with every column hosting at least six conversion pairs and none hosting more than 11 out of 16 possible, but the six county elite/mass pairs were a little more involved in that the three delegate/mass pairs accounted for only one-quarter, instead of one-third, of the conversions to cohesion.

Only a little less impressive than the results of table 5.9 are those of table 5.10 (*percentage college graduates*) and table 5.11 (*percentage urban*). Whereas the effect of introducing these two variables into the analysis of the various Democratic pairings is to increase the percentage of overall issue cohesion to extreme heights, their outstanding performances in the Republican panel only serve to lift overall Republican cohesion to strong, but not spectacular, levels. Controlling for *percentage of college graduates* in each state drives up the percentage of issue agreement from 49 to 86 percent of the cells in the Democratic panel of table 5.10, just as controlling for *urbanism* raises issue agreement from 45 to 95 percent of all cells in the Democratic panel of table 5.11. However, the impact of these two variables upon the Republican panels of tables 5.10 and 5.11 is nullified by the considerably lower bases of before-and-after agreement available to be built upon. Issue agreement in the Republican panel of table 5.10 rises from a starting point of 19 percent to 69 percent of all cells when *college graduation* is controlled, and Republican issue agreement in table 5.11 rises from a starting point of 18 percent to 58 percent of all cells when *percentage urban* is controlled. Such showings are sufficiently strong to place the overall impact of these variables just a notch or two below that of the Ranney *interparty competition* index and *per capita income*.

In the Democratic panel of table 5.10, *percentage of college graduates* is associated with a high number of conversions to cohesion for domestic policy issues (22 AC cells versus 1 DC cell) and for ideology (6 AC cells out of 9 possible), and moderate rates of increased cohesion for political economy issues (9 AC cells to 1 DC cell), foreign policy/national security issues (8 AC cells to 3 DC cells), and race/gender equality issues (7 AC cells to 2 DC cells). Well over 50 percent of these postcontrol increases affect the delegate/mass dyads. But the variable outdoes this performance in the Republican panel of the table, where the rate of conversion to cohesion is high not only for domestic policy (22 AC cells, zero DC cells), but also for political economy (19 AC cells, zero DC cells) and foreign policy/national security (19 AC cells versus 6 DC cells), and is moderately influential (12 AC cells to zero DC cells) for race/gender equality, as well. Only ideological self-placement is not boosted significantly by *percentage of college graduates*.

In table 5.11, as in tables 5.10 and 5.9, it is the Democratic delegate/mass pairs that are influenced most heavily when *percentage urban* is controlled.

TABLE 5.9
MANOVA RESULTS FOR ALL ELITE-MASS FACTORS, WITH COVARIATE = STATE PER CAPITA INCOME

	DEMOCRATS									REPUBLICANS								
	Delegates			Chairs			Members			Delegates			Chairs			Members		
	NPID	SPID	Voters	NPID	SPID	Voters	NPID	SPID	Voters	NPID	SPID	Voters	NPID	SPID	Voters	NPID	SPID	Voters
Ideological self-placement	AC	AC	AC	A	A	A	AC	AC	A	A	A	A	A	A	A	A	A	A
More for women's SES	D	D	AC	A	A	A	A	A	A	AC	AC	AC	AC	AC	AC	AC	AC	AC
More SES for minorities	AC	AC	AC	A	A	A	A	DC	DC	D	D	D	AC	D	AC	AC	D	AC
Equal power for both sexes	AC	AC	AC	A	A	A	A	A	A	A	A	A	A	A	A	A	A	A
Keep affirmative action	D	A	AC	AC	AC	D	D	D	D	D	D	AC	AC	AC	AC	AC	AC	
Abortion by choice	AC	AC	AC	AC	AC	A	A	A	A	AC	AC	A	A	AC	A	AC	AC	A
Allow school prayer	AC	AC	AC	A	A	A	A	DC	DC	AC	A	A	AC	AC	AC	AC	AC	A
Help people get health care	AC	AC	AC	AC	A	A	AC	AC	AC	AC	D	AC	AC	AC	AC	D	AC	D
More spending to protect environment	AC	AC	AC	A	A	A	AC	AC	AC	AC	AC	A	A	A	A	A	A	A
Guarantee jobs and good living	A	A	A	AC	AC	D	AC	AC	AC	D	D	AC	AC	AC	D	D	D	AC
Cut services and spending	AC	AC	AC	A	A	A	A	A	A	AC	AC	D	AC	AC	D	AC	AC	D
Pass balanced budget amendment	AC	AC	AC	A	A	A	A	A	A	AC	D	AC	AC	D	AC	AC	AC	AC
More state taxes, not cuts	AC	AC	DC	A	A	A	A	A	A	AC	AC	D	D	D	AC	AC	AC	AC
More defense spending	AC	AC	AC	A	A	A	DC	DC	DC	A	A	A	AC	AC	AC	AC	AC	AC
America first, overseas second	A	DC	A	A	A	A	A	A	A	AC	DC	AC	AC	D	D	AC	AC	D
Continue cooperation with Russia	AC	AC	AC	AC	AC	AC	AC	AC	AC	DC	DC	DC	AC	AC	AC	AC	AC	AC

Note: NPID = national party identifiers; SPID = state party identifiers. In the cells, A = agreement; D = disagreement; AC = agreement when controlled for covariate and interaction effect; DC = disagreement when controlled for covariate and interaction effect.

TABLE 5.10
MANOVA RESULTS FOR ALL ELITE-MASS FACTORS, WITH COVARIATE = STATE COLLEGE GRADUATION RATE

| | DEMOCRATS | | | | | | | | | REPUBLICANS | | | | | | | | |
| | Delegates | | | Chairs | | | Members | | | Delegates | | | Chairs | | | Members | | |
	NPID	SPID	Voters	NPID	SPID	Voters	NPID	SPID	Voters	NPID	SPID	Voters	NPID	SPID	Voters	NPID	SPID	Voters
Ideological self-placement	AC	AC	AC	A	A	A	AC	AC	DC	A	A	A	DC	DC	A	A	A	AC
More for women's SES	D	D	AC	A	A	A	A	A	A	D	AC	AC	AC	AC	AC	AC	AC	AC
More SES for minorities	AC	AC	AC	A	A	DC	DC	A	A	D	D	D	AC	AC	AC	D	D	AC
Equal power for both sexes	AC	D	AC	A	A	A	A	A	A	A	A	A	A	A	A	A	A	A
Keep affirmative action	A	A	A	D	D	AC	D	D	A	D	D	D	D	D	D	D	D	D
Abortion by choice	D	AC	AC	AC	AC	A	A	A	A	AC	AC	AC	AC	AC	AC	AC	AC	A
Allow school prayer	AC	AC	AC	A	A	A	A	A	DC	AC	A	A	AC	AC	AC	AC	AC	A
Help people get health care	AC	AC	AC	A	A	A	AC	AC	AC	D	AC	D	AC	AC	AC	D	AC	D
More spending to protect environment	AC	AC	AC	A	A	A	AC	AC	AC	AC	AC	AC	A	A	A	A	A	A
Guarantee jobs and good living	A	A	A	D	D	D	AC	AC	AC	D	D	D	D	D	AC	D	D	D
Cut services and spending	AC	AC	AC	A	A	A	A	A	A	AC	D	AC	D	D	D	AC	AC	D
Pass balanced budget amendment	AC	AC	AC	A	A	A	A	DC	A	AC	D	AC	AC	AC	AC	AC	AC	AC
More state taxes, not cuts	AC	AC	DC	A	A	A	A	A	A	D	AC	D	AC	AC	AC	AC	AC	AC
More defense spending	AC	AC	A	A	A	DC	DC	DC	DC	DC	DC	AC	AC	AC	AC	AC	D	
America first, overseas second	A	A	A	A	A	A	A	A	A	AC	AC	AC	AC	AC	AC	AC	AC	A
Continue cooperation with Russia	D	D	D	AC	AC	AC	AC	AC	AC	DC	DC	DC	AC	AC	AC	AC	AC	AC

Note: NPID = national party identifiers; SPID = state party identifiers. In the cells, A = agreement; D = disagreement; AC = agreement when controlled for covariate and interaction effect; DC = disagreement when controlled for covariate and interaction effect.

TABLE 5.11
MANOVA RESULTS FOR ALL ELITE-MASS FACTORS, WITH COVARIATE = STATE PERCENTAGE OF URBAN POPULATION

	DEMOCRATS									REPUBLICANS								
	Delegates			Chairs			Members			Delegates			Chairs			Members		
	NPID	SPID	Voters	NPID	SPID	Voters	NPID	SPID	Voters	NPID	SPID	Voters	NPID	SPID	Voters	NPID	SPID	Voters
Ideological self-placement	AC	AC	AC	A	A	A	AC	AC	A	A	A	A	DC	DC	DC	DC	DC	D
More for women's SES	AC	AC	AC	A	A	A	A	A	A	D	D	D	AC	AC	AC	AC	AC	AC
More SES for minorities	AC	AC	AC	A	A	A	A	A	A	D	D	D	D	D	AC	D	D	AC
Equal power for both sexes	AC	AC	AC	A	A	A	A	A	A	A	A	A	A	A	A	A	A	A
Keep affirmative action	A	A	A	AC	AC	AC	AC	AC	A	D	D	D	D	D	D	D	D	D
Abortion by choice	D	D	AC	AC	AC	A	A	A	A	D	AC	D	AC	AC	A	AC	AC	A
Allow school prayer	AC	AC	AC	A	A	A	A	A	A	AC	A	A	AC	AC	AC	AC	AC	A
Help people get health care	AC	AC	AC	A	A	A	AC	AC	AC	D	D	D	AC	AC	AC	AC	AC	D
More spending to protect environment	AC	AC	AC	A	A	A	AC	AC	AC	AC	AC	AC	A	A	A	A	A	A
Guarantee jobs and good living	A	A	A	AC	AC	AC	AC	AC	AC	D	D	D	AC	D	D	AC	D	AC
Cut services and spending	AC	AC	AC	A	A	A	A	A	A	D	D	D	D	D	D	AC	AC	D
Pass balanced budget amendment	AC	AC	AC	A	A	A	A	DC	A	D	D	D	D	AC	D	AC	AC	D
More state taxes, not cuts	AC	AC	A	A	A	A	A	A	A	D	AC	D	AC	AC	AC	AC	AC	D
More defense spending	AC	D	AC	A	A	A	A	A	DC	A	A	A	AC	AC	AC	AC	AC	AC
America first, overseas second	A	DC	A	A	A	A	A	A	A	AC	AC	D	AC	AC	D	D	D	D
Continue cooperation with Russia	AC	AC	AC	AC	AC	AC	AC	AC	AC	DC	DC	DC	AC	AC	AC	AC	AC	AC

Note: NPID = national party identifiers; SPID = state party identifiers. In the cells, A = agreement; D = disagreement; AC = agreement when controlled for covariate and interaction effect; DC = disagreement when controlled for covariate and interaction effect.

Thirty-two of the 61 cases of conversion to cohesion in the panel—twice as many as for either the county chair/mass dyads or committee member/mass dyads—involve delegate/mass pairs. Again, the five domestic policy issues (23 AC cells versus zero DC cells) are affected impressively, followed by a strong impact upon ideology (5 AC cells, zero DC cells) and moderate impacts upon race/gender equality (14 AC cells, zero DC cells), foreign policy/national security (11 AC cells, 2 DC cells), and political economy (8 AC cells to 1 DC cell).

In the Republican panel of table 5.11, *percentage urban* performs nearly as well as in the Democratic panel, but the conversion cells are distributed differently across the various elite/mass dyads. For each type of elite, cells converting to cohesion are most numerous in the national identifier column and least numerous in the party voter column. Again a large, one-sided pattern of influence is found for the domestic issues (22 AC cells, zero DC cells), joined this time by foreign policy/national security issues (16 AC cells, 3 DC cells). Moderate environmental influence is present for the political economy issues (12 AC cells, zero DC cells) and for race/gender equality issues (8 AC cells, zero DC cells). Especially noteworthy, but not surprising, is the finding that 5 of 6 county elite/mass cells cease to agree ideologically when *percentage urban* is introduced as a control. Erikson, Wright, and McIver (1993, 230) note in their cross-state study of political culture that "state urbanism is an important predictor of state liberalism." We should not be surprised, then, to find that the Republican electorate begins to reflect increased ideological heterogeneity, thus making it more difficult for the party's usually more conservative elites to find common ground with their grassroots, as the percentage of urban population increases from state to state. Perhaps this also helps to explain why overall Republican cohesion in this table was 11 percent lower than it was when *percentage college graduates* was controlled in table 5.10: Erikson, Wright, and McIver (1993, 230) go on to add that "to a much lesser extent, education consistently predicts conservatism."

Whatever the differences of effect for these final three demographic variables, our theoretical view is that they walk hand-in-hand as important indicators of the economic and social development of the various southern states. As such, they provide a test of the modernization explanation of the growth of two-party competition in the South, which holds that economic and social development generate pluralism, that is, a proliferation of interests sufficient to provide the bases for more than one party coalition. From the data presented in tables 5.9, 5.10, and 5.11, it is possible to say that as income, educational attainment, and urbanization each increase, intraparty issue cohesion increases within both political parties on a large scale—much larger than for variables such as *percentage black* and *percentage fundamentalist*, and on a par with the major party endogenous variables, *state Democratic organizational strength, interparty competition,* and *liberalism of (Democrat/Republican) party identifiers.*

Are the Findings Artifacts of Direct Effects?

To be certain that the findings in this chapter and the last are not artifacts of direct contextual influence upon issue distributions, we tested for such direct causation using, first, simple bivariate Pearson's correlations[1] between the issue responses and the context variables, and then simple multiple regression, entering all state political context variables as independent variables. Such tests uncovered very little evidence of direct environmental explanation of issue distributions (see tables in Appendix B). Bivariate tests turned up very few significant Pearson coefficients. Further, those coefficients that did meet the $p < .05$ test of significance clustered much nearer 0.0 than 1.0, indicating that even these relationships were very weak. As one might expect, the sample sizes involved typically were very large in those cases in which the null hypothesis was rejected despite pallid coefficients. Only for the samples of Democratic and Republican county committee members, respectively, each of which contains more than four thousand respondents, did significant relationships between political context variables and issue distributions occur with any frequency. Even then, none of the significant correlations for the Republican county committee members achieves $r > .10$, and only two coefficients for Democratic county committee members are larger than .20.

Multiple regression results not only confirmed these findings, but uncovered considerable multicollinearity, further reducing the incidence of significant covariations by more than half (see tables B.15 and B.16 in Appendix B). Moreover, in the few remaining cases of significant covariation, slope coefficients were diminutive (data not shown in Appendix B) for all but one variable. The lone exception was *state party organizational strength,* which covaried significantly with a handful of issues within both parties, and within every operationalization of party elite and mass except one. It also nearly always registered sizable slope coefficients in such cases, although these did not convert into sizable standardized coefficients in the case of the Republican samples (see table B.15). However, even this variable, like its less robust contextual counterparts, ultimately contributes very little to the total explained variance of the issue distributions. For further details about this and other multiple regression or bivariate results, see the tabular data in Appendix B.

Looking back at the data above, it is apparent that nearly all contextual variables, even the exogenous variables seemingly least likely to affect the distributions of opinions among elites and masses, do in fact affect intraparty issue cohesion. The effect of each covariate and companion interaction term is to bring about a usually positive and significant increase in issue cohesion, more often than not at a large or even very large rate of gain.

State party organizational strength performed very well in this analysis but was not the strongest contextual variable at work here. That title would go to Fleury's updated Ranney index of *interparty competition.* Overall, the theoretical expectation that endogenous, party-centric variables would have more effect than exogenous variables upon intraparty co-

hesion received empirical support. The existence of two-party competition, party organizational strength, and the ideological and partisan orientations of party identifiers all facilitate greater intraparty issue agreement, and, thereby, the democratic linkage of the governed to the activists who help to frame electoral choices and to screen those who govern.

The party variables more than held their own against standard demographic covariates that are staple ingredients of social science. Bear in mind that this performance by party-centric variables takes place in the American South, a region historically characterized by candidate-centered politics and weak-to-nonexistent formal party organizations. This in effect resurrects, for future research, the question of whether political parties are captives, or captors, of their environments. There is evidence above for both interpretations. In our concluding chapter we shall visit this question more thoroughly.

But certain demographic variables have been shown here to influence intraparty integration more than other demographic variables, with consequences for competing theories of partisan change in the South. Party elite-mass agreement on issues responded considerably more strongly to development-related variables such as *per capita income, percentage urban,* and *percentage college graduates* than to *percentage black* and *percentage fundamentalist.* This is more consistent with economic development or modernization theories of the Republicanization of the South than with the race-driven white flight theory of Republican growth. For that matter, the party-endogenous variables had more influence upon intraparty integration, as well, indicating that scholarly participants in the partisan change debate should take the efforts of the parties themselves more seriously.

Moreover, under conditions in which state political context is taken into account, Republican party elites fare much better than the literature acknowledges at the critical electoral and democratic task of providing substantive representation to their party's mass following. For the most part, as we pointed out in the conclusion to chapter 4, they still trail the

Democratic elites in this regard, though not by much, and not always: a great deal depends on which environmental variable is controlled. In this chapter, however, we uncovered the Democrats' potential weakness in an area of Republican strength—intraparty ideological cohesion. The potential exists for Republicans to nullify the Democrats' representational edge on so many issues by keeping the Democrats off balance throughout the South with campaign discourse focused on ideological differences.

Finally, by tracking throughout this chapter which of the three types of party elites were most representative of the party masses on each issue, we can also state here that within the Democratic party, the local party elites (county chairs and committee members) clearly are more closely representative of the masses on the issues than are the national party elites (national convention delegates). Perusing the tables above reveals that the delegate columns record the lowest percentage of issue harmony with Democratic mass categories under every environmental condition except when *per capita income* is controlled. No such clear pattern occurs within the Republican panels of the above tables. In fact, Republican national convention delegates sometimes lead the Republican elites, or are close to the lead, in the number of cells indicating agreement with the party masses.

Chapter 6

Political Parties and the Representation Puzzle

In this book we have pushed the seminal work of Herbert McClosky (McClosky, Hoffman, and O'Hara 1960) ahead on three fronts. First, we have conceptually refined McClosky, Hoffman, and O'Hara and subsequent works in that vein by using multiple operational definitions of party elites and party masses, a conceptual advance that allowed us to discern differences between and within parties on the degree of *intraparty* issue cohesion. *What is true for one operationalization of "elite" and "mass" is not necessarily true for other operationalizations, as we have shown repeatedly in this study.* For example, despite identifiable ideological "wings" among all save convention delegates, elite and mass southern Democrats were more homogeneous in their issue preferences. To be sure, convention delegates were more liberal. Even so, rarely were Democratic elites out of step with each other or with the rank and file. On the other hand, southern Republicans professed greater ideological unity but demonstrated greater issue diversity. Republican elites evidenced less cohesion on issue preferences than Democratic elites, and they were separated from the Republican rank and file by a greater distance than could be found among Democrats.

Yet despite the fact that each of the parties' followers, however defined, typically shared modal preferences on issues, and despite the success of southern Democratic elites in representing their own mass partisans, Democratic elites were not noticeably better representatives of the southern Republican rank and file than were Republican elites, as the asymmetry of the McClosky distribution predicted. Moreover, the ability of county Democratic party chairs and committee members to reflect more closely than Democratic convention delegates the views of the rank and file was not uniformly shared by Republicans. Interparty differences between elites and intraparty diversity among Republicans prevented rank-and-file Republicans from experiencing from either party organization the type of issue representation provided to Democratic partisans by the Democratic party. Interestingly, however, the extant intraparty cohesiveness increased when the variability of the surrounding political context provided by each state was taken into account.

Second, we have furthered the research agenda of McClosky, Hoffman, and O'Hara (1960) by analyzing the various operationalizations of elites and masses in light of the demographic composition of each group, which McClosky, Hoffman, and O'Hara promised to do in subsequent research reports but which apparently never was completed or released. In our analysis of the relationship between the demographic backgrounds of elites and masses on the one hand and their respective issue preferences on the other, we found many similarities between the parties. To be sure, there were more African Americans and Catholics among rank-and-file Democrats, as well as proportionately more women. There were more poor and poorly educated Democrats than Republicans. Rank-and-file Republicans were younger and newer to their communities. But it is not true that there were no poor Republicans and no well-educated Democrats.

To those who would suggest that elites closest to the rank and file locally should be most similar sociodemographically to the rank and file, our data provide weak supporting evidence. More obvious, however, are the similarities across organizational levels and across party boundaries. Party activists of both parties are predominantly middle-aged, male, better educated, reasonably secure financially, and white. Among Democratic elites, we found proportionately more blacks, more longtime residents, and more women among their convention delegates. But this is not the sociological divide to which stratification theorists would point as the seedbed of political differences. However, it does indicate that, excepting race, both parties are diverse enough compositionally to provide visceral, as well as intellectual, expression to the agendas of politically relevant groups.

Third, we have introduced and assessed at length broader analytical questions concerning the political contexts that frame and give perspective to the issue opinions of elites and masses and the level of intraparty issue agreement that occurs. We found that elite-mass issue agreement not only holds up when political environmental variables are controlled, but that such issue agreement increases in their presence.

Indeed, we have seen in the preceding chapters that the issue integration of party elites—especially local party elites—and masses increases markedly when state politocultural, demographic, institutional, and other contextual differences are controlled. Neither simple means tests like those used in our earlier chapters and in McClosky, Hoffman, and O'Hara nor the subsequent literature (e.g., Luttbeg 1981; Kirkpatrick 1975, 1978; Montjoy, Shaffer, and Weber 1980) tell the whole story. With political context variables taken into account not only as covariates but as covariate-by-factor interaction terms, we found that party elites provided a fair degree of substantive representation. That is, elites held issue positions that were not significantly different from the predominant issue preferences of the political party's mass following. What is more, several of the context variables that seem to matter most to elite-mass agreement were endogenous, or of partisan content, rather than exogenous. This indicates that the political parties themselves have a place in the linkage process.

The comparatively small size of the mass sample that is used in this study is a drawback that undoubtedly will (and should) stimulate calls for further study. Our use of analysis of variance techniques that are better suited for continuous data will earn criticism as well from methodological purists. Nevertheless, one simple, straightforward outcome of this study cannot escape notice. Inclusion of state political context in the analyses converted a remarkable number of *significant* differences of means into *insignificant* differences, resulting in much *greater* intraparty issue integration than was measured previously (see tables 5.1–5.11). Furthermore, despite the acknowledged limitations of the mass data and of the instrument employed, our refinement of the design, which incorporates multiple operational definitions of "elite" and of "mass," purchases us greater latitude for generalization than ordinarily would be the case for this kind of study. Therefore, with more confidence than we would normally claim, we can say that elite representation of the parties' rank and file is more complicated than the McClosky distribution acknowledges.

Our multivariate findings have important theoretical implications for the literatures on southern politics, political parties, and representation (or democratic linkage). Regarding southern politics, our findings indicate that state-specific distributions of race or religion have less impact upon intraparty elite-mass issue integration than do state-specific partisan variables and modernization/development variables. This suggests that race and religion—two variables usually credited with helping to refashion southern politics—may be playing a more modest role in the politics of party representation toward the end of the twentieth century than they did earlier. Moreover, the modernization/development variables, which at least have been touted by some authors as an alternative to the race-centric explanation of partisan change in the South, were not any more associated with intraparty elite-mass issue agreement than were the strongest party-endogenous variables, *state party organizational strength, interparty competition,* and *liberalism of party identifiers.* Yet no one until the present moment has posited a "party-building" or political development explanation of the Republicanization of the South. Clearly, more research is required to investigate more complex explanations of partisan change in the South, involving additional variables and/or their interactions.

Concerning political parties, our research revealed that partisan variables had as much, if not more, impact than exogenous variables upon the measurement of elite-mass issue integration. This result questions the wisdom that parties are less what they make of themselves than what the environment makes of them. Rather, our findings suggest that the party-environment nexus is causally more complex than either Schattschneider or Epstein suggested. Although neither scholar was so naive as to represent the causal relationship between party and environment as strictly a "one-way street," all too often reviews of the literature on political parties effectively present the perspectives of Schattschneider and Epstein in such a reductionist manner. Our evidence suggests that the party-environment connection is not only a two-way street, along which traffic in each

direction is affected by traffic headed the other way, but a complex thoroughfare about which political scientists still know very little.

On representation, our findings reveal that it ultimately matters little whether state political parties are merely the products of their respective environments. What matters is whether they effectively communicate to each other and to the larger polity the political aspirations of the sovereign populace. As we will elaborate, virtually all of the constitutionally provided roles for states in the composition and operation of our federal system face serious challenges. Functional constituencies, organized on the basis of economic specialization and/or socioeconomic cleavage, now compete with subnational polities for the attention of the national government. To the extent that our political system remains a "federal" one, it is due to political parties in the states, and the extent to which party elites echo the aspirations of their parties' mass affiliates.

Federalism, Representation, and Political Parties

Representation—what it consists of, and how best to achieve it—is one of the oldest debates in the history of human political thought. In its most recent form, the debate has migrated away from the elected representative and what decision rule(s) should guide his/her legislative behavior. In that earlier formulation, one model of behavior centered entirely upon the representative, who was charged to vote his/her own best judgment. The opposing model introduced the constituent into the debate as an independent variable that *should* structure and order the representative's legislative decision making.

Central to the debate between these two models is, of course, the question of linkage between the masses and the elites who govern them with the consent of the governed. The latter model is structured to ensure that democratic linkage exists. If representatives vote as their constituents would have them, then government outputs—laws and policies—should reflect popular preferences. Substantive representation is thus achieved. The result, according to marketplace theorists of democracy, is service of "the greatest good of the greatest number."

Critics of this "instructed delegate" model and its attempt to ensure linkage by structuring attentiveness to constituency have faulted it on numerous grounds: the ignorance and inattentiveness of large numbers of constituents, their resulting political marginalization, and the upper-class accent of the policies that ensue from listening to the constituents who are enlightened enough to participate. "The people" are thus better served, revisionist democrats argue, if political elites choose for themselves the fiduciary role of "trustee," and thus allow themselves to be guided by their own enlightened sociopolitical compasses. Leninists and many social democrats, although not rowing their boats in the same direction, tend to agree with this revisionist critique of the delegate model and the classical democracy it espouses.

This is where more recent contributions have broadened the dialogue between these two models of representation. Citing the political marginalization of the inattentive (who are often "have-nots") as well as Davidson's (1969) empirical research showing that most members of Congress episodically employ the decision rules of both models, many modern students of representation insist that democratic linkage requires the ruling elite to expand its membership systematically to include members of special publics that otherwise would be marginalized. Only by assuring such "descriptive representation" can trustee behavior be engineered to include in sufficient degree the perspectives and wants of the marginalized.

A second, more thoughtful and more troubling critique of the delegate model begins by asking who is it that officeholders are supposed to represent? Influenced by the pluralist notions of Dahl (1961) and Banfield (1961), the interest-group notions of Truman (1951), and the corporatist notions of Schmitter (1974) and others (e.g., Wiarda 1977; Anderson 1979), many scholars now argue that elites holding federal government offices effectively represent "functional" (i.e., interest-based) constituencies. Functional constituencies operate within elites' geospatial districts or contribute to their reelection campaigns from without (see

Beer 1978; Piltes and Niemi 1993). They are distinct from "topocratic" constituencies, consisting of states and of substate, population-based districts, as prescribed by the Constitution. Another challenge to the holistic view of topocratic constituencies is Fenno's (1978) "homestyles" analysis, which revealed congressional sensitivity to the political stratification of constituencies. Who was represented—and how well—depended upon their centrality to the member's core of support.

In short, a wide and varied literature now exists suggesting that extraterritorial constituencies are more important to democratic linkage than geographic districts or states. Among these are the organized collective action entities of industries, corporations, growers' coops, ethnic and racial groups, single-issue groups, and so forth. As presented, the "functionalist" school of democratic linkage shares some common ground with those who prescribe "descriptive representation." Each asserts the primacy of non-geocentric constituencies at the expense of territorial ones. Each thus has the effect, intended or not, of contributing to the centralization of power within the American system by competing with the territorial constituencies for influence, while also seeking to enlarge the roles and powers of national government institutions. The "Great Compromise" and other constitutional guarantees of territorial voice within the national government may have thus been countered, if not eclipsed.

The goal of descriptive representation, of course, is to extend the fruits of democracy and of capitalism to those existing on the margins of society, who, frequently being nonparticipants and tax-consumers rather than voters and tax-payers, are ill positioned to reach either fruit.

It is difficult to gainsay such a laudable goal, of course, or any of the *value*-words—such as diversity, inclusiveness, multiculturalism, and so on—frequently employed in support of descriptive representation and related goals. But it is even more difficult to reconcile the preferred tactics of the descriptive democrats with such goals and values. Indeed, those who espouse descriptive representation in the interest of recognizing our national diversity and multiculturalism embrace as a tool the very centralization of power and policy that our Founding Fathers rejected as a threat to diversity in the first place. Who wants uniformity of treatment and of condition, wants unitary government, with power to make policy invested in the national authority and little left at lower levels. The federal structure brokered at Philadelphia decentralizes policy authority in a manner that foils uniformity and protects diversity. Yet because that decentralization can be an impediment to social and political change, as it was during desegregation, *or* a facility for such change, as it was during Progressivism, modern proponents of democratic diversity have chosen to pursue their agenda through national policy, and usually are advocates of the authority of that level.

In doing so, the proponents of descriptive representation are following in the footsteps of a long political history of centralizing impulses, beginning with Hamilton and Marshall and culminating in the "centralized federalism" of the Great Society. Policy power in the twentieth century has gravitated from the states to Washington, and therein from the other branches to the executive branch. What preserved the influence of state and local governments within the context of such centralization perhaps more than anything was electoral federalism. Voters at the grass roots are critical to the reelection of both federal and state and local elected officials—and the "feds" are on less intimate terms with their "bosses" than are state and local political elites. As Banfield and Wilson (1963, 2) wrote of that period, "In the United States, the connection between local and national politics is particularly close . . . Congressmen and senators are essentially local politicians, and those of them who forget it soon cease to be politicians at all." Consequently, the collective wisdom of political science accepted that "the parties are responsible for both the existence and form of the considerable measure of decentralization that exists in the United States" (Grodzins 1966, 254; see also Riker 1964, 91–101; and Truman 1967, 81–109).

While election campaigns today admittedly are candidate-centered, media-intensive affairs that no longer pivot around the party organization, it never-

theless remains true that political parties still effectively provide linkage between local and national politics. As the data in this study show, local elites of the state political parties can be more in touch with, and reflective of, the issue preferences of the party masses on whose votes federal officials in distant Washington depend. And where our data provide at best tentative support for this conclusion—among southern Republicans—we find an organization still under construction from the top down.

Obviously, local party elites are not, as Fenno's (1978) well-known case studies indicate, the only constituency elites upon whom federal elected officials may draw for insight into the popular mood. However, because of their grassroots location and their civic interestedness, local party elites frequently are well situated to provide intelligence about not only the voting public, but also about Fenno's other special constituencies, as well as transmitting political information and impulses in the opposite direction, from elected officials down to the electoral grassroots.

One source of the party organizations' potential and oft-realized political value to officeholders is their durability. The entrepreneurial candidate may have dislodged the political party as the focal point of American electoral politics in the late twentieth century, but is not and may never be as stable a political presence as the political party. Candidates are typically political entrepreneurs (Schlesinger 1966; Loomis 1990) who will depart a given political context for advantage, or because of disadvantage. They are also subject to human frailty. As a result, whatever political intimacy exists with the community they serve not only has its limits, but typically departs when they depart.

In contrast, political party organizations are institutions with fixed routines for replenishing the ranks of activists with new recruits and socializing them into the organizational tasks that are requisite to the party's roles in our political process—and to its survival in the political process. Admittedly, the parties typically are unable to recruit, socialize, and perform effectively in many locations. But then not even all McDonald's franchises are alike or work as well as customers would like. Indeed, that is precisely our point. To borrow from Samuel Johnson, criticizing American political parties for their many weaknesses is rather like criticizing how well a dog walks on its hind legs, when we should marvel that the dog can do so at all.

America's two major parties are living organisms that have succeeded in overcoming constitutional provisions meant to curb them—namely, federalism and the separation of powers—as well as political movements meant to displace or weaken them. With remarkable resilience and adaptability, the parties have survived not only Madisonianism, Jacksonianism, Progressivism, McGovernism, and campaign-finance reform, but also have adapted to the rise of rivals for electoral influence and political linkage, such as political action committees and mass media, and the rise of professional consultants and technological innovations that have supplanted a variety of campaign roles formerly filled by state and local party machines. Despite the loss of such roles, parties remain admirable training grounds and networking devices for politicians, as well as what Schlesinger (1991) terms efficient providers of economies for those needs that would be too costly for candidates to obtain individually. The Democrats and Republicans have been there for American politicians for nearly 150 years, despite the inroads of political development, and show no signs of departing from the scene anytime soon.

It is this survivability, this institutional quality of the major American parties that gives rise to their ability to effectively reflect the political values and aspirations of their grassroots followers. That capability enables them to be of some electoral value to office holding elites, and thereby of some democratic linkage value to the political system. Often as old as their states or communities, state and local political parties are expressions of the eccentricities of the political machinery, populations, and popular cultures specific to states and communities. Political party organizations have learned to adapt to and reflect their communities and regions in order to contest elections serially, over many election cycles for

many kinds of offices. In doing so, they become adept at political interpretation of their respective communities. They are repositories of local political folkways and lore. This is a valuable asset to individual candidates who are more narrowly engaged in the pursuit of specific offices, over a shorter span of time, and are thus on less intimate terms with the political pulse of the community or state for at least the initial portion of their political careers.

This view of the place and role of party organization elites in the democratic linkage process in American politics will be doubted by some. We must concede that state and local parties in numerous locales, especially in the South, cannot possibly link governors to the governed, or vice versa, because the party organizations are too weak, or do not even exist. They are thus no better positioned to "read" a community than any candidate-come-lately.

This lack of organizational development is a function of single-party electoral dominance. In such a setting, the minority party is not the only party underdeveloped organizationally because of its inability to compete electorally with the dominant party. For every voter, activist, contributor, and office seeker who asks "Why should I waste my political chips on a certain loser?" there are opposite numbers who ask "Why should I do more than the absolute minimum necessary to ensure victory for a certain victor?" The result has been that neither the minority party nor the dominant party ever obtains the political capital necessary to achieve the levels of institutionalization, durability, and mediation of popular political voice discussed above—or only the dominant party does.

But, as most readers will acknowledge, the one-party electoral dominance of the South is ending, or has ended. Electoral competition may mean the end of the underdevelopment of state and local party organizations, as well.

As the ebbing of the political role of state governments in American federalism—witness *Garcia v. San Antonio* (1985)—suggests, the political resilience of our political parties within such a hostile environment is a record to be envied by other political institutions. As the noted scholars of federalism cited above observed, increasingly, our resilient state political parties, expressing the diversity of their respective states, stand in for the abraded federal provisions of an aging, oft-interpreted social contract that contains more than a few dead letters along with its still operative passages. For that reason, we will suggest here that both Schattschneider (1942, 1), who claimed that political parties alone make democracy possible, and Epstein (1967, 8), who responded that the parties are less what they make of themselves than what their environment makes of them, have overlooked a subtle but critical distinction. Both appear to have underestimated the degree of reciprocity that exists between American political parties and their environment.

On the one hand, both federalism and American political culture have had a profoundly decentralizing, weakening effect upon the parties. As Epstein (1978, 4) has pointed out, subnationally based parties are a concomitant of federal systems: "Wherever there are substantial constitutionally-guaranteed powers at the regional level, parties organize to compete for power at that level." One of the powers guaranteed to the states is authority over the conduct of elections, which the states have taken to include the right to spawn diverse statutory regulations governing the structure and operation of the parties within their respective boundaries. Moreover, as subnational polities with their own elective offices to fill and governing functions to perform, the states rival the nation as a focus for the attentions of many voters and activists. Indeed, as mentioned above, both the present authors and Charles Hadley have found that startling percentages of southern state party elites and voters, respectively, do not identify with the same national party that they identify with in the context of state politics.

The result has been the development of distinct state institutional environments and political cultures which the respective parties must adapt to and reflect, if they wish to compete effectively in that state. In the aggregate, these numerous, distinct state settings sum to a national political culture that prefers parties weak and decentralized, not strong and disciplined (Devine 1972, 230; Dennis 1976). Consequently, national party organizations emerge as little more than a patchwork of idiosyncratic state parties.

On the other hand, these same decentralized political parties have assumed increasing responsibility for effective political expression in and of the states. Parties are becoming the fulcrum to balance and the stalwart to maintain the federal system. In other words, in postmodern American federalism, the weakened political voices of the states and those of their comparatively vibrant political parties have become virtually indistinguishable.

This suggests a codependence between the political parties and their environments that comes through in chapters 4 and 5 of this study. Our results provide ample evidence to support the causal views of both Epstein *and* Schattschneider, which can only mean that both at best have only reconnoitered the bull's-eye. In those chapters, we showed that controlling for exogenous, demographic and politocultural variables dramatically affected the measurement of intraparty issue cohesion, but no more so—in fact, frequently less so—than did controlling for variables endogenous to the parties themselves. Partisan context seemed to matter as much, if not more, than extrapartisan context in the clarification of how much elite-mass issue agreement exists, which turned out to be present in much greater amounts than could be seen when analysis was performed in the absence of context. Both of these simple, straightforward findings argue that there is a role for the political parties in the democratic linkage process. Party elites, especially those of the local variety, are indeed tribunes of the party masses.

As for the "functionalist" model of democratic linkage, in which geocentric constituencies are regarded as archaic and inferior to collective action organizations as expressions of the popular will, the new paradigm has yet to best the old as far as solving procedural democracy's longstanding fundamental flaw. Schlozman and Tierney (1986, 65–71) report that society's less advantaged citizens, whose lower rates of political attentiveness and voter turnout are widely known, also do not participate in organized collective action at the same rate as those who are better off. Given the skewed distribution of political resources found by Schlozman and Tierney (1986, chap. 5) and the skewed distribution of representation provided by what they refer to as "the Washington Pressure Community," it seems to us that dynamic, meaningful subnational polities that are physically proximate to the less advantaged are still essential for democratic linkage to exist in an imperfectly enlightened society. Federalism affords havenots more opportunities in which to grow the habit of conventional political participation, as well as affording them easier access for the exercise of unconventional forms of political participation (i.e., protests) when necessary.

Nor has the "functionalist" model of democratic linkage satisfactorily resolved the question: who are the constituents that officeholders are to represent? Substituting collective action organizations for geocentric constituencies as expressions of the popular will can create real problems, as was clearly evident during the presidential election of 1996. The influx of foreign contributions to both political parties, to the Clinton campaign, and to some congressional campaigns illustrates what can happen when the working definition of "constituency" gives priority to functional groups over the political subdivisions from which officeholders are elected to serve. The volume of illegal money given by foreign donors with business interests in the United States, that would have been legal if only the donors had written checks on the accounts of their American subsidiaries rather than on overseas accounts, underscores the danger inherent in the "functionalist" approach. Citizenship is a geocentric concept. Without the requirement that one have legal standing as a citizen in order to exercise full political rights, the functionalist notion of who is a "constituent" opens up the prospect of a geometric expansion of the "golden rule" of politics: "He who has the gold, rules." Most American voters would say there is already too much of this in our politics.

The American people have not indicated that they are ready to abandon the states as vehicles for the ex-

pression of the popular will, in favor of exclusive reliance upon organized collective action for such expression. Consider the reaction of Arkansans, for example, to the revelations and convictions collectively known as "Whitewater." Neither electoral nor elite support within the Arkansas Democratic party for Bill Clinton was significantly affected by Whitewater, whereas in Wisconsin a closed meeting of Democratic legislators serving on the Joint Finance Committee and a telephone credit card scandal involving a few legislators and a thousand dollars in personal calls precipitated electoral reprisals against the 1978 Democratic ticket. This is as the people of each state would have it. Wisconsinites would not abide a party whose elites had suffered so many convictions for misuse of office (in the 1990s alone, Arkansas has convicted a governor, an attorney general, a secretary of state, senior state legislators, and numerous local judges, prosecutors, and sheriffs) any more than Arkansans would tolerate the levels of taxation and regulation associated with Wisconsin Democratic elites. And voters in several mountain states would not tolerate either Wisconsin's or Arkansas' Democratic parties.

In a federal system in which not only the considerable domestic power of state government but also the political control of the U.S. Senate are subject to the voting choices of *statewide* electorates, political parties must focus their organizational energies at the state level. The Democratic party and Republican party are forced to disaggregate in order to mirror the political cultures of the fifty states sufficiently to compete for national *and* state power. In the vernacular of the doctrine of "people's war," which is not altogether an inappropriate metaphor here, political parties must be as "fish that swim in the waters of the people."

State political parties thus inevitably become expressions of the spectrum of popular values that distinguish the people of a state. Functional associations, in contrast, only give voice to specific, narrow interests. They lack the nuances provided by the juxtaposition of many such interests within the broader environmental context of which they are an important part, but *only* a part, nonetheless. To the extent that the state party elites of the eleven southern states examined here closely reflect the issue preferences and policy views of their respective electoral bases—and this issue integration is measurably stronger when state political context is controlled—they not only provide "voice" to the political aspirations of their respective electorates, but also contribute to the continuity of the topocratic rule explicit in the constitution in the face of the challenge of newer models of democratic linkage spun off by the political transformations of the twentieth century. To that degree, collective representation by southern parties works.

Party and Representation in the South

Historically, the South has been a region of weak party organizations, rent by candidate-centered, factional strife. Against this backdrop this study has uncovered considerable evidence that both the Democratic and Republican party organizations successfully reflect, at least broadly, the issue and ideological orientations of their respective mass partisans. This evidence remains constant regardless of which operationalization of party organizational activist or of mass partisan is employed.

Our findings show that there is considerable elasticity in the potential for political representation by parties in the South. As a practical matter, this suggests that both parties benefit when strong organizations confront one another. State party organizational strength and competitive elections create the atmosphere for vibrant representation. While parties cannot control the demographics of their context, they can control the vitality of their respective organizations. Empowering state party organizations (and later, perhaps, local organizations) can result in a closer connection between party policy and partisans' positions.

Republicans need to accept and internalize this lesson, if their march toward truly competitive status in the region is to continue. Top-down organizational commitments lose their effectiveness the farther from the top one migrates. Moreover, as established previously in other political settings (see Wekkin 1984), what animates activists focused on national concerns may prove alien to publics necessary for mobiliza-

tion at the local level. The relative dissension within Republican organizational ranks, despite their apparent allegiance to "conservatism," suggests that a meaningful integration of positions has eluded southern Republicans. Their Democratic brethren appear more conventionally attached to one another and to the cultural roots from which issue positions spring, despite their unwillingness to share ideological labels. Literally and figuratively, Republicans are the new children on the southern block. There is much they can learn from Democrats about building strength from diversity in the South.

To be sure, there is much that Democrats can learn from Republicans. The first and most obvious lesson is to wake up to the challenge Republicans pose. Southern Democrats have not stepped into the representational vacuum left by Republican elites' issue distance from their rank and file. Despite the proximity of both parties' ranks and file, as a rule, the asymmetry of the McClosky distribution does not obtain in the South. That is an opportunity lost by Democrats. If Republicans energize themselves organizationally at the state level and become more successful below constitutional offices in the states, the window of opportunity for southern Democrats may slam shut. The disjunction between Republican party activists and Republican party identifiers, supporters or voters in the South could catalyze a shift toward the Democrats, if southern Democrats quench the thirst for representation that our data suggest is present.

The answer to the straightforward question with which this book began ultimately rests on such tactical and strategic considerations. We have shown that the parties can represent the people and that the link that parties provide is vital to sustain the diversity and power of the states in a federal system. We feel that the dynamics of southern politics will provide opportunities for both parties to continue their evolutions as organizations. Consequently we answer our question with an emphatic "yes" for the present. What we cannot foretell is whether the parties will capitalize on the opportunities presented them.

For example, southern Republicans benefited from majority-minority redistricting following the

1990 census, but some of those districts were overturned by the Supreme Court (*Shaw v. Reno* [1993], *Johnson v. Mortham* [1995], *Miller v. Johnson* [1995], *United States v. Hays* [1995], *Bush v. Vera* [1996]). Which party will capitalize on the opportunity that court-mandated reconfigurations now present? Which party will succeed in laying the firmest foundation for a more inclusive stance as the 2000 census begins?

Data from state legislative races in the South indicate that, compared to 1990, Republicans after the 1998 elections held 74 more state senate seats and 188 more state house seats. Moreover, they controlled state senates in Florida, Texas, and Virginia and state houses in Florida and South Carolina, losing control in North Carolina following the 1998 election. In addition, Republicans controlled seven of eleven governorships in the South. These results should gladden the hearts of Republican strategists, especially as the presidential elections of 2000 loom nearer.

On the other hand, Republicans nationally were hurt by their hard-line stance that closed down the government more than once in 1995, by their close races in 1996—including that of House Speaker Newt Gingrich—and by their poor showing in the midterm elections of 1998, which resulted in Gingrich's resignation. Compounding this problem is the lurking aftermath of the impeachment controversy, including the resignation of Speaker-designate and Louisiana Republican Robert Livingston. Republican stalwarts continue to praise the "courage" displayed by House Republicans, especially their members on the Judiciary Committee, for their "principled" position on President Clinton's impeachment. At the same time, much of the rest of the political establishment and of the people—including Republicans—are distancing themselves from that act and trying to build a substantive record on which to run in 2000 and beyond. The question is what if any lasting changes will result from these calamities? While after the 1998 elections Republicans maintained their regional lead in seats in the U.S. Senate (fourteen to eight) and in the U.S. House of Representatives (sixty-eight to fifty-four), Republicans in the Senate and House must understand that governing requires compromise, which is the antithesis of ideological purity. The Republican rank and file in the South appears poised to accept more moderation from its leadership. Can the party communicate that, resonate that, and, in the end, represent that?

Who will benefit from the prosperity of the 1990s, especially when, at the same time, responsibility for welfare has devolved to the states? The South remains among the poorer regions of the country. Can it sustain its economic growth and incorporate those dispossessed of federal welfare dollars? How will the parties respond to the needy of the next decade? The back of southern populism is clearly not broken, nor is the bucket of southern need empty. Will southern Republicans rise above their concerns with issue litmus tests? Will southern Democrats join new-found fiscal prudence with old-time human compassion?

This list of scenarios is long. The list of questions is equally long. With each scenario and each question comes an opportunity. Linkage politics is not static, but neither is party politics. We share the optimistic view that, in the future, political parties will continue to serve as effective linkage mechanisms in the American South. And through them, collective representation in and of the region will prevail.

Appendix A

Question Wording

The core issue questions central to this study of elite-mass issue integration were worded exactly the same in both the elite and the mass samples. Only the Likert response categories varied slightly. The Southern Grassroots Party Activists Project questionnaire took a forced choice approach and offered elite respondents only four choices ("strongly agree," "agree," "disagree," and "strongly disagree") or no response. Mass respondents, by contrast, could choose a fifth response—"undecided"—as well as the above four standard Likert responses. In order to ensure consistency between the two samples, we have treated "undecided" responses given by mass respondents as "missing data" for the purpose of this study.

The core issue questions, then, in both samples are:

1. The government in Washington should make every effort to improve the social and economic situation for women.
2. By law a woman should be able to obtain an abortion as a matter of choice.
3. Defense spending should be increased.
4. The government in Washington should provide fewer services, even in areas such as health and education, in order to reduce government spending.
5. Prayer should be allowed in the public schools.
6. Government spending on improving and protecting the environment should be increased.
7. A constitutional amendment to balance the national budget should be passed.
8. If this state faces a financial crisis, the state legislature should raise taxes rather than reduce spending.
9. The government in Washington should make every effort to improve the social and economic position of blacks and other minority groups.
10. The government in Washington should see to it that every person has a job and a good standard of living.
11. Women should have an equal role with men in running business, industry, and government.
12. This country should pay more attention to problems at home and less attention to problems in other parts of the world.
13. The United States should continue to cooperate with Russia.
14. Because of past discrimination blacks should be given preference in hiring and promotion.
15. The government ought to help people get doctors and hospital care at low cost.

Other questions drawn from both the elite and the mass samples for purposes of comparison varied in wording, although not in conceptualization. For example, "party voters" were operationalized from the elite sample on the basis of the response given to the question:

16. In the 1988 election for president, when George Bush ran on the Republican ticket against Michael Dukakis for the Democrats, did you vote for a candidate for president?

(1) Yes, voted for Bush
(2) Yes, voted for Dukakis
(3) No, but favored Bush
(4) No, but favored Dukakis
(5) No, but favored other candidate
(6) No, didn't like anybody.

In contrast, respondents to the mass sample were asked:

17. For whom did you vote for president?

(1) George Bush–Republican
(2) Bill Clinton–Democrat
(3) H. Ross Perot–Independent
(4) Other
(5) Can't remember
(6) Refused.

The partisan identification questions used in the elite and mass samples also differed in wording, but not in concept. The partisan identification item in the elite sample reads:

18. How would you describe your own political party affiliation: In STATE politics? . . . In NATIONAL politics?

State Politics	National Politics
(1) Strong Democrat	(1) Strong Democrat
(2) Weak Democrat	(2) Weak Democrat
(3) Ind. but lean Democratic	(3) Ind.but lead Democratic
(4) Independent	(4) Independent
(5) Ind. but lean Republican	(5) Ind. but lean Republican
(6) Weak Republican	(6) Weak Republican
(7) Strong Republican	(7) Strong Republican

In contrast, respondents to the mass sample were asked two questions:

19. Thinking now only of national politics, do you usually consider yourself to be a Republican, a Democrat, an Independent, or what?

(1) Republican
(2) Democrat
(3) Independent
(4) Other
(5) Don't know.

20. Thinking now only of state politics, do you usually consider yourself to be a Republican, a Democrat, an Independent, or what?

(1) Republican
(2) Democrat
(3) Independent
(4) Other
(5) Don't know.

The standard NES probes for leaners and weak partisans followed.

Similarly, the ideological self-identification items asked of the two samples differed in form, although not conceptually. The ideological identification item in the elite sample reads:

21. What about your political beliefs? Do you consider yourself

(1) very liberal
(2) somewhat liberal
(3) middle of the road/moderate
(4) somewhat conservative
(5) very conservative?

In contrast, the mass sample respondents were asked:

22. Generally speaking, regardless of the political party you prefer, do you usually think of yourself as a conservative or a liberal or a moderate on most political matters?

(1) conservative
(2) liberal
(3) moderate
(4) other
(5) don't know.

These question-items and their response categories were carefully reconciled with one another with the help of Charles D. Hadley, who implemented the merging of the elite and mass data sets. Differences in the wording of sociodemographic questions and their response categories were reconciled in the same fashion, again with Hadley's help.

Appendix B

Bivariate Results

Testing for simple direct correlations between individual context variables and the distribution of responses to specific issue-items by each group of party elites and masses revealed very few significant relationships between facets of state political context and issue responses. Further, those Pearson coefficients that did meet the $p < .05$ test of significance all clustered near 0.0, indicating that even the few significant relationships obtained were very weak.

Republican Masses

For the sample of *Republican voters,* operationalized as those who cast ballots in November 1992 for President George Bush, only 7 Pearson coefficients out of 208 possible (16 issues $\times$ 13 control variables) were significant at $p < .05$ (see table B.1). No single issue showed a marked predilection to be influenced by political context variables ("This country should pay more attention to problems at home and less attention to problems in other parts of the world" came closest, correlating with three of thirteen context variables), and only one context variable influenced as

many as two issues. State political environmental factors seem to have had almost no impact on the distribution of Republican voters' issue opinions.

As tables B.2 and B.3 show, the opinion distributions of *national Republican identifiers* and *state Republican identifiers* are as unaffected by state political context variables as those of Republican voters were. Only 19 of 208 coefficients were significant for national Republicans, and only 7 of 208 coefficients were significant for those who deemed themselves state Republicans. Nor do any patterns emerge that suggest the susceptibility of a particular issue to direct environmental influence, or the potency of a particular context variable across several issues. Only the question-items about American cooperation with Russia, increasing defense spending, and equality for women in running business and government have as many as 4 or 5 significant correlates in table B.2, and of these only that dealing with Russia has as many as 3 significant correlates in table B.3. Moreover, neither these significant coefficients nor any others in these tables are as large as .16. Even assuming zero collinearity among the independent variables (for which we shall report multiple regression test results below), the percentage of variance explained for these three issues by significant environmental correlates in the sample of national Republican identifiers would be minimal at best. This goes double for the even weaker findings for the sample of state Republican identifiers reported in table B.3.

Republican Elites

Next we report the findings for the three kinds of Republican organization elites for which we have data—1992 national convention delegates, county party chairpersons, and county committee members.

Only 22 of the 208 Pearson coefficients obtained from correlation tests performed on the sample of almost 500 *Republican national convention delegates* were significant at .05. Further, no pattern of any kind emerges to suggest that a particular issue appears susceptible to direct environmental influence. The redistributive item "The government in Washington should make every effort to improve the social and economic position of blacks and other minorities groups" correlated significantly with only four of the thirteen context variables, and the largest coefficient of these was -.143 (see table B.4). No other issue correlated significantly with more than three context variables, and the largest coefficients remained in the teens.

For the sample of *Republican county chairs,* with almost 600 respondents, 23 of the 208 bivariate Pearson coefficients were significant at .05. Only two of the sixteen issue-items were affected significantly by more than three of the thirteen contextual variables. As table B.5 shows, the issues on which the distributions of Republican county chairs' issue responses were most sensitive to environmental influence had to do with higher taxes and increased government spending. Eight of the thirteen context variables correlated significantly with the item "If your state faces a financial crisis, the state legislature should raise taxes rather than reduce spending," and five of the thirteen correlated significantly with the item "Government spending on improving and protecting the environment should be increased." How-

ever, the largest coefficients for each, at .214 and -.193, respectively, are weak at best.

Turning to look at table B.5 from the perspective of which contextual independent variables stand out, the 1992 voter turnout rate significantly affected five of the sixteen issue-items, while college graduation rate and the Erikson, Wright, and McIver index of liberalism among state Republican identifiers each affected four issue-items. While affecting issues at a ratio of less than one out of three does not represent great influence on the part of these contextual variables, it is worth noting that two of the three variables are politocultural. This may suggest that the positions of Republican county chairs are more susceptible to the influence of politocultural factors than to that of structural and demographic considerations. This was not the case with Republican national convention delegates, whose opinions seemed very responsive to the primary election format variable, but not to any other contextual variables.

On the face of it, the sample of roughly 4,000 *Republican county committee members* provides results entirely at odds with those for the previous two groups of Republican elites. As table B.6 shows, 96 of the 208 bivariate Pearson coefficients generated for this group met or surpassed the $p < .05$ test of significance. Issue-items dealing with abortion, increased defense spending, increased taxes, government economic help for blacks, equality for women, health care, and government efforts to insure everyone has jobs all were affected significantly at $p < .05$ by more than half of the thirteen contextual control variables. As this list attests, both social and fiscal issues as well as issues that do not fit in either category evince significant responsiveness to a variety of environmental influences.

Overall for Republican county committee members, state demographic variables correlated significantly with an average of 7.8 issue-items, state structural variables did so with an average of 7.4 issue-items, and state politocultural variables did so with an average of 7.0 issue-items. Clearly, then, politocultural influences were neither as strong nor as exceptional for county Republican committee members as they were for the sample of county Republican chairs.

But the main significance of table B.6 is that although many of the coefficients therein achieved significance at $p < .05$, not one of these coefficients attained even .10 in weight. The thirteen state political context variables are even less associated with the issue distributions of Republican county committee members than they were for the Republican convention delegates and county chairs (or, for that matter, than was true for Republican voters and identifiers, respectively). That coefficients as weak as those in table B.6 are statistically significant is a function of sheer sample size. At $N > 4,000$, the sample of county Republican committee members is ten times as great as those for county Republican chairs and for Republican national convention delegates, and still greater compared to the Republican mass samples.

All in all, straightforward bivariate analysis clearly turns up very little systematic or otherwise compelling evidence that political environmental factors unique to the respective states may have directly affected distributions of opinions among southern Republican elites and masses during the 1992 elections.

Democratic Masses

The bivariate relationships that emerged for the samples of Democratic voters and Democratic identifiers very much mirror those obtained for their Republican counterparts. For *Democratic voters,* defined as the 270 or respondents in the mass sample who cast ballots for Bill Clinton in the 1992 presidential election, only 7 out of 208 bivariate Pearson coefficients met the $p < .05$ test of significance. Most issue-items had no significant correlates; of the seven that did, none correlated significantly with more than one state context variable (it goes without saying, then, that none of the latter affected more than one issue-item significantly), and the largest coefficient obtained was .155 (see table B.7).

Those in the mass sample who qualify as national and state *Democratic identifiers* register only a few more significant associations than were obtained for their Republican counterparts. For the 330 or so national Democratic identifiers, only 18 of 208 coefficients

proved significant, fully 8 of which were correlates of the above-mentioned abortion item (see table B.8). Similarly, only 14 out of 208 coefficients tested significant at $p < .05$ for the more than 300 mass sample respondents who were *state Democratic identifiers* (see table B.9), and 6 of those 14 coefficients were correlates of the abortion item. Clearly, for the approximately 330 mass respondents who fit under the respective definitions of Democratic identifiers, state political context variables may possibly influence the distribution of responses to this particular item, even if none of the coefficients reaches .20.

School prayer, another cleaving issue that frequently helps define social conservatives and liberals, is the only other issue-item that comes even close to indicating susceptibility to environmental factors in tables B.8 and B.9. Nor does any specific environmental variable show up in either table as a potent influence on more than three of the 16 issue-items.

Democratic Elites

For the sample of almost 490 *Democratic national convention delegates,* 59 of 208 coefficients were significant at $p < .05$ (see table B.10), but only 5 of them exceeded .20 in weight. The issue-items most heavily affected by state political context variables were those dealing with abortion rights (10 correlates), school prayer (8 correlates), and a federal balanced budget amendment (9 correlates), plus the overall personal ideological self-placement item (8 correlates). Other items showed some responsiveness to environmental influences, but not in a majority of correlates, and never with coefficients even as large as .150. Specifically, these items consisted of the affirmative-action hiring item, plus statements such as "The government in Washington should provide fewer services . . . in order to reduce spending," "This country should pay more attention to problems at home," and "The government in Washington should make every effort to improve the social and economic position of blacks and other minority groups."

This brings us to yet another contrast between the results for a Democratic elite sample and those obtained for its Republican counterpart. Unlike the results obtained for Republican county chairs, which were somewhat dissimilar from those obtained for Republican convention delegates, the results obtained for our sample of almost 600 *Democratic county chairs* are fairly similar to those obtained for Democratic national convention delegates. As many as 54 of the 208 bivariate Pearson coefficients are significant at $p < .05$, but this time no coefficients reach as high as .20 (see table B.11). Again the issue-items affected most often by environmental factors were abortion rights (12 of 13 contextual variables correlated significantly with it), school prayer (6 correlates), government efforts to improve the economic and social position of minorities (5 correlates), and the respondents' overall personal political philosophy (5 correlates).

Our findings for the sample of more than 4,500 *Democratic county committee members* parallel those for their Republican counterparts in essential theme, although somewhat larger in volume and weight of significant associations, as well as somewhat different in implied causal direction. Fully 155 of the 208 Pearson correlation coefficients obtained for this sample were significant at $p < .05$. However, once again the main finding is not the number of significant coefficients but the weakness of the coefficients themselves, which are stronger than those obtained for Republican county committee members, but pale in comparison to those obtained for all of the other elite and mass groups. Table B.12 shows that about 70 percent of the coefficients significant for the sample of Democratic county committee members were less than .10 in weight; only 45 reached .10 and another 2 reached .20. Once again a very large sample size has facilitated statistical confidence in extremely low coefficients.

Obviously, in such a situation significant variable associations are the rule, not the exception, which renders discussion either unnecessary or extremely tedious. Nevertheless, certain issue-items visibly stand apart from the others, but in this case because of the comparably higher weights of their correlation coefficients, rather than because of the number of such correlates. The abortion choice and school prayer

items not only are associated with all thirteen context variables, but in ten of thirteen cases for each the coefficients exceed .10, as well, resulting in average coefficients of around .15 for both issue items. Such coefficient weights do not add up to very much causal weight, but they do nevertheless stand apart from the norm in table B.12.

Summary

The simple bivariate analyses and means tests reported in this chapter have turned up very few significant associations, except in the case of the very large samples of county committee members provided by the Southern Grassroots Party Activists project. Moreover, even those findings that were significant were very weak at best, especially in the case of the large samples of county committee members. Clearly, then, direct and/or inverse relationships between context variables and the distribution of responses to election issue-items seem very unlikely to account for any of the findings reported in the previous chapters, or even to have affected any of those findings to any significant degree.

Multiple Regression Results
Republican Elites

For the sample of almost 500 *Republican national convention delegates,* the number of coefficients significant at $p < .05$ dropped from 22 out of 208 possible to 10 out of 208 possible when multiple regression analysis was substituted for bivariate analysis (see table B.13). Primary election format registered significant, but weak, inverse influence upon Republican delegates' attitudes toward national government efforts to help people with health care costs (Beta = -.244), assure employment and standard of living (Beta = -.187), and improve the socioeconomic situation of women (Beta = -.174) and of blacks and other minorities (Beta = -.188). The strength of the states' interest group systems exercised more potent inverse influence on Republican delegates' attitudes toward government help with health-care costs

(Beta = -.277) and on the item that said the national government should pay less attention to foreign affairs and more attention to problems at home (Beta = -.348). The state party identification index variable registered significant covariation (Beta = -.392) with the latter item ("America first"), as well, as did the local Republican organizational strength variable at -.334. Finally, state Republican organizational strength covaried inversely with the distribution of responses on the increased defense spending item (Beta = -.135), and positively with the responses to the item that said state governments should meet financial crises by raising taxes rather than by reducing spending (Beta = .191). All in all, however, the total explained variance in the distribution of responses across all issue-items that is explained by multiple regression against all context variables never exceeds an R^2 greater than .080, which is to say that despite a sizable standardized coefficient or two, state political context variables hardly affected the distribution of Republican delegates' responses at all.

For the sample of almost 600 *Republican county chairs*, the number of significant coefficients drops even further, from 23 out of 208 possible to only 4 out of 208, when multivariate analysis replaces bivariate analysis (table B.13). State per capita income covaries with the responses to the statements that America should continue to cooperate with Russia and that states should raise taxes rather than reducing their spending, at Beta weights of -.184 and .214, respectively. State party identification index scores also covary significantly and positively (Beta = .287) with the latter issue-item. Finally, percentage of blacks covaried in a weak fashion (Beta = -.171) with Republican chairs' attitudes on abortion. More tellingly, once again state political context accounted for less than 10 percent of the total explained variance for the distribution of responses to any issue-item.

The sample of roughly 4,000 *Republican county committee members* provides more fertile ground for the number of significant associations between context variables and issue distributions, but not for the size of the coefficients themselves. Once again, sheer sample size makes it possible for extremely small slope coefficients to be statistically significant. Even

so, the number of significant coefficients drops from 96 out of 208 possible during bivariate analysis to only 35 out of 208 possible when multivariate analysis is performed (table B.13). In most cases these 35 significant slopes are barely larger than zero. For example, state Republican organizational strength covaries with the spending for environmental protection item (Beta = .060) and with the school prayer item (Beta = -.066), local Republican organizational strength covaries with government assurance of jobs and standards of living (Beta = -.069), and primary election format and percentage of blacks are inversely related to four and three items, respectively, at Beta weights of less than 0.1.

There are also several issue-items for which several contextual variables achieve statistical significance: voter participation rate; state party identification index; percentage of college graduates; and Erikson, Wright, and McIver's liberalism index score for states' Republican masses all covary significantly with the distribution of responses to the item about increasing defense spending, but explain less than 2 percent of the total explained variance. As many as six contextual variables (voter turnout, interest group strength, per capita income, percentage of college graduates, percentage of blacks, and liberalism index for states' Republican masses) covary significantly with the "America first" issue-item but explain less than even 1 percent of the total explained variance for this item. Indeed, in no case does the explained total variance for any issue distribution exceed $R^2 = 0.033$.

Republican Masses

For *Republican voters*, the number of significant coefficients out of 208 possible dropped from 7 to 3 when multivariate analysis was used (table B.13). Erikson, Wright, and McIver's liberalism index score for states' Republican masses covaried (Beta = -.335) with responses to the statement that defense spending should be increased, and both state party organizational strength (Beta = .206) and Erikson, Wright, and McIver's state party identification index (Beta = .726) covaried with responses to the statement that the national government should attempt to improve the socioeconomic position of blacks and other minorities. However, the adjusted R^2 for the latter distribution is only .049, and that for the former is only .018.

The number of significant coefficients produced by multivariate analysis of context variables and the issue distributions for respondents in the mass sample who were *national Republican identifiers* is similarly small, at 4 out of 208 possible. Here, too, state party organizational strength (Beta = .219) and state party identification index (.631) covaried significantly (with slope coefficients very comparable to those for the voter sample) with the item about government efforts to improve the socioeconomic position of minorities. Despite the presence of a third significant regressor, the percentage of blacks (Beta = -.265), the adjusted R^2 for the distribution of responses to this item explained by these variables is only .038. Finally, state party organizational strength also covaries (Beta = .240) with responses to the item concerning affirmative action hiring and promotion, which, however, has a total explained variance of only .022.

Finally, only 4 out of 208 possible coefficients proved significant for respondents in the sample who were *state Republican identifiers* (table B.13). Percentage of blacks again covaries significantly, but inversely at Beta = -.322 with attitudes toward government efforts to improve the socioeconomic position of minorities. State party identification index (Beta = .524) covaries impressively with the same item. State per capita income (Beta = .541) covaries similarly strongly with responses to the item about whether fiscally strapped states should raise taxes or cut spending, and the Erikson, Wright, and McIver index score for the liberalism of state Republican masses covaries healthily (Beta = -.363) with attitudes toward defense spending increases.

Democratic Elites

Although 59 of 208 coefficients were significant at $p < .05$ when the sample of about 490 *Democratic national convention delegates* was subjected to bivariate analysis, only 5 of 208 coefficients remained sig-

nificant during multivariate analysis (see table B.14). Local Democratic organization strength covaried significantly and very strongly with responses to the items about government efforts to improve the socioeconomic position of women (Beta = .542) and of blacks and other minorities (Beta = .505), respectively. Primary election format covaried inversely with the same two items (Beta = -.337 and -.324, respectively). Black population percentage covaried inversely, as expected, but not very strongly (Beta = -.283) with responses to the statement that the national government should provide fewer services in order to reduce spending (see table B.14). Total explained variance for each issue item was extremely weak at adjusted $R^2 = .032$ for efforts to improve the position of women, .049 for efforts to improve the status of blacks, and .038 for the item about reduction of government services.

Similarly, the number of significant coefficients for the sample of almost 600 *Democratic county chairs* drops from 54 to 14 out of 208 possible when multivariate analysis is performed. Two issue-items—abortion and helping Russia—account for 9 of these significant coefficients. State Democratic organizational strength (Beta = .437) covaries strongly with responses to the abortion item, with percentage black (.277), voter turnout rate (.565), and mass party identification index (-.393) also making substantial contributions to a nevertheless weak total explained variance of .059 (see table B.14). State Democratic organizational strength (Beta = .448) also covaries impressively with attitudes toward U.S. cooperation with Russia, and is joined by significant contributions from mass party identification index (Beta = -.320) and percentage of fundamentalist Christians (Beta = .497). Nevertheless, here too the adjusted R^2 of .055 indicates that very little of the total variance is explained.

Other issue-items influenced significantly, but very weakly, by context variables for the sample of Democratic chairs included spending on environmental protection (Beta = -.401 for percentage urban and .261 for Erikson et al.'s measure of Democratic mass liberalism), the balanced-budget amendment (Beta = -.276 for the measure of Democratic mass liberalism), equality for women in business, industry, and government (Beta = -.127 for primary election format), affirmative action (Beta = .299 for state party identification index), and state tax increases rather than budget cuts (Beta = .354 for state party identification index and .218 for interest group strength). But in none of these cases did the total explained variance even approach 0.1.

For the sample of nearly 4,500 *Democratic county committee members,* the number of correlations that proved significant dropped from 155 to only 39 of 208 possible when multivariate analysis was performed. Every issue-item except that dealing with U.S. cooperation with Russia covaried significantly with at least one context variable, and those dealing with the socioeconomic betterment of blacks, equality for women in business and government, affirmative action hiring and promotion policies, increased environmental protection spending, and more attention to problems here at home ("America first") covaried significantly with four or more context variables. However, most of the slope coefficients that registered "significant" for this very large sample weighed in thousandths, and the largest Beta weight recorded for this sample was .197, for state party identification index with the item on increasing state taxes rather than state spending cuts. Moreover, the largest adjusted R^2 compiled by contextual variables for any issue-item was .045, for the abortion issue. Thus, once again, the comparatively frequent occurrence of significant associations misleads us: it is an artifact of the very large sample size. The distribution of opinions among Democratic county committee members is in fact affected negligibly by political context variables.

Democratic Masses

Multivariate analysis for the subsample of 270 or so *Democratic voters* in the mass sample turned up no cases, out of 208 possible, in which a context variable covaried significantly at $p < .05$ with the distribution of responses for any of the 15 issue-items (table B.14).

Multivariate analysis for the 270 or so *national Democratic identifiers* in the mass sample turned up only 4 cases out of 208, compared to the 18 turned up during bivariate analysis, in which a context variable covaried significantly with the distribution of responses. State Democratic organizational strength covaried significantly and positively (Beta = .471) with the item that asked whether fiscally strapped states should raise taxes instead of cutting spending. Percentage of blacks covaried significantly and solidly (Beta = .484) with the position that the national government should do more to raise the socioeconomic status of women, and percentage urban covaried similarly solidly (Beta = .520) with the position that the national government should assure everyone employment and a decent standard of living. Finally, primary election format covaried significantly but inversely (Beta = -.434) with the position that a federal balanced-budget amendment to the Constitution should be enacted. Since the adjusted R-squares for these four issue-items, in the order they are discussed here, are .015, .049, -.011, and .040, respectively, it is fair to conclude that statistical significance is no guarantor of causal significance, even given the presence of so healthy a coefficient as that for state Democratic organizational strength.

When one turns to apply multivariate analysis to those in the mass sample who were *state Democratic identifiers,* the number of significant covariations turned up drops from 14 of 208 to 5 of 208 (table B.14). State Democratic organizational strength covaries strongly and directly with the position that the national government should do more to improve the socioeconomic position of women (Beta = .461) as well as with the position that fiscally strapped states should increase taxes, rather than reduce spending, and yet also with the idea of a federal balanced-budget amendment (Beta = .455). Also covarying significantly, but inversely (no surprise here), with the balanced-budget amendment item is the state interest group strength variable (Beta = -.370). Finally, also covarying with the sentiment that the government should do more for women is the percentage of blacks, which at Beta = .408 is comparable in size but slightly less than it was for the sample of national Democratic identifiers. Again, despite the weight of the coefficients associated with the balanced-budget item, the total explained variance is only .064, and the adjusted R-squares for the other two items are smaller still at .029 (improving the position of women) and .013 (raising state taxes).

Summary

The central findings produced by multivariate testing are fourfold. First, multiple regression confirms the bivariate findings that contextual variables in most cases are not significantly related to the distributions of responses obtained for the various 1992 election issue-items. Second, as suspected, many of the significant covariations that were turned up during bivariate analysis were multicollinear or otherwise spurious, and fell out of significance during multivariate analysis. Third, those few contextual variables that continued to covary significantly with opinion distributions even during multivariate analysis did so infrequently at best, and almost always produced very marginal gains in the slope coefficients (not shown in the tables because the different kinds of data called for reportage of standardized coefficients). The lone exception to these generalizations would be state party organizational strength, which related significantly to a handful of issues within both parties and within every operationalization of party elite and mass except one, and which nearly always registered sizable slope coefficients in doing so, although these did not translate into sizable standardized coefficients for the Republican samples reported in table B.13. However, even this exception falls within the norm of the fourth finding produced by multivariate analysis: even significant political context variables contribute very little to the total explained variance of the issue distributions. This is as true for state party organizational strength as it is for the weaker significant covariates, and it is as true when state party organizational strength clusters with other significant covariates as it is when it stands alone.

Thus, we conclude that the distributions of issue responses that are the dependent variables in the chapters above are not subject to frequent or strong direct effects from the environmental variables.

TABLE B.1

CORRELATION COEFFICIENTS ($P < .05$) FOR STATE CONTEXT VARIABLES AND ISSUE PREFERENCES OF SOUTHERN REPUBLICAN VOTERS

	State Party Organization	Local Party Organization	Inter-party Competition Index	State Party Identification Index	Liberalism of Party Identifiers Index	Precentage Black	Percentage fundamentalist	State Party Competition Index	Percentage Urban	Percentage College Graduates	Percentage Voter Turnout	Interest Group Strength	Primary Election Format
More for women's SES													
Abortion by choice													
More defense spending													
Cut services and spending													
Allow school prayer													
More spending to protect environment													
Pass balanced budget amendment													
More state taxes, not cuts													
More SES for minorities	.141												
Guarantee jobs and good living													-.143
Equal power for both sexes													
America first, overseas second						.161	.169		.199				
Continue cooperation with Russia							.170						
Keep affirmative action													
Help people get health care													
Ideological self-placement		.149											

TABLE B.2

CORRELATION COEFFICIENTS ($P < .05$) FOR STATE CONTEXT VARIABLES AND ISSUE PREFERENCES OF SOUTHERN NATIONAL REPUBLICAN IDENTIFIERS

	State Party Organization	Local Party Organization	Inter-party Competition Index	State Party Identification Index	Liberalism of Party Identifiers Index	Percentage Black	Percentage fundamentalist	State Party Competition Index	Percentage Urban	Percentage College Graduates	Percentage Voter Turnout	Interest Group Strength	Primary Election Format
More for women's SES													
Abortion by choice													
More defense spending					-.133	-.123	.143			.142			
Cut services and spending													
Allow school prayer													
More spending to protect environment													
Pass balanced budget amendment					.114								
More state taxes, not cuts													
More SES for minorities													
Guarantee jobs and good living													
Equal power for both sexes				.119	.134	.112				.113	.127		
America first, overseas second													
Continue cooperation with Russia				.143			.126	.133					.116
Keep affirmative action													
Help people get health care	.120					-.112							
Ideological self-placement						.159	.117						.042

TABLE B.3

CORRELATION COEFFICIENTS ($P < .05$) FOR STATE CONTEXT VARIABLES AND ISSUE PREFERENCES OF SOUTHERN STATE REPUBLICAN IDENTIFIERS

	State Party Organization	Local Party Organization	Inter-party Competition Index	State Party Identification Index	Liberalism of Party Identifiers Index	Precentage Black	Percentage funda-mentalist	State Party Comp-etition Index	Percentage Urban	Percentage College Graduates	Percentage Voter Turnout	Interest Group Strength	Primary Election Format
More for women's SES													
Abortion by choice													
More defense spending													
Cut services and spending													
Allow school prayer													
More spending to protect environment													
Pass balanced budget amendment													
More state taxes, not cuts													
More SES for minorities													
Guarantee jobs and good living													
Equal power for both sexes				.153	.153								.122
America first, overseas second												.119	
Continue cooperation with Russia							.119	-1.59					
Keep affirmative action													
Help people get health care													
Ideological self-placement						.141							

TABLE B.4

CORRELATION COEFFICIENTS ($P < .05$) FOR STATE CONTEXT VARIABLES AND ISSUE PREFERENCES OF SOUTHERN REPUBLICAN NATIONAL CONVENTION DELEGATES

	State Party Organization	Local Party Organization	Interparty Competition Index	State Party Identification Index	Liberalism of Party Identifiers Index	Percentage Black	Percentage fundamentalist	State Party Competition Index	Percentage Urban	Percentage College Graduates	Percentage Voter Turnout	Interest Group Strength	Primary Election Format
More for women's SES													-.122
Abortion by choice					-.190								-.192
More defense spending											-.111		
Cut services and spending													
Allow school prayer					.177			.103					-.113
More spending to protect environment													
Pass balanced budget amendment													
More state taxes, not cuts	.155		.124			.104							
More SES for minorities				.102			.096	-.096					-.143
Guarantee jobs and good living													-.152
Equal power for both sexes													
America first, overseas second		.104							.106				
Continue cooperation with Russia													
Keep affirmative action						.102			-.097				-.110
Help people get health care					-.098								-.182
Ideological self-placement													

TABLE B.5
CORRELATION COEFFICIENTS ($P < .05$) FOR STATE CONTEXT VARIABLES AND ISSUE PREFERENCES OF SOUTHERN REPUBLICAN COUNTY PARTY CHAIRS

	State Party Organization	Local Party Organization	Inter-party Competition Index	State Party Identification Index	Liberalism of Party Identifiers Index	Precentage Black	Percentage fundamentalist	State Party Competition Index	Percentage Urban	Percentage College Graduates	Percentage Voter Turnout	Interest Group Strength	Primary Election Format
More for women's SES					-.100					.123	-.089		
Abortion by choice											-.083		
More defense spending													
Cut services and spending													
Allow school prayer													
More spending to protect environment					-.193	-.127				.172	-.152	-.138	
Pass balanced budget amendment						.087	.083			-.097			
More state taxes, not cuts					-.126	-.165	-.059	.214	.170	.207	-.165	-.146	
More SES for minorities													
Guarantee jobs and good living													
Equal power for both sexes													
America first, overseas second													
Continue cooperation with Russia													
Keep affirmative action													
Help people get health care											-.100		
Ideological self-placement-		.091			-.090								

TABLE B.6

CORRELATION COEFFICIENTS ($P < .05$) FOR STATE CONTEXT VARIABLES AND ISSUE PREFERENCES OF SOUTHERN REPUBLICAN COUNTY COMMITTEE MEMBERS

	State Party Organization	Local Party Organization	Inter-party Competition Index	State Party Identification Index	Liberalism of Party Identifiers Index	Precentage Black	Percentage funda-mentalist	State Party Competition Index	Percentage Urban	Percentage College Graduates	Percentage Voter Turnout	Interest Group Strength	Primary Election Format
More for women's SES					.040								-.044
Abortion by choice		-.031	.045	.063		.065	.075	-.069	-.070	-.071			-.040
More defense spending	-.031	.045	.059		.040		-.049	.090	.043	.098	-.064	-.073	
Cut services and spending			-.039	-.043	.035	-.032							
Allow school prayer	-.052					-.078	-.006	.034	.033	.052		-.054	
More spending to protect environment	.038				-.051					.048	-.040	-.034	-.042
Pass balanced budget amendment	.036			-.059				.036					.030
More state taxes, not cuts	-.035	-.039		.053	-.051	-.060	-.053	-.061	.059	.072	-.053	-.080	
More SES for minorities	.045		.064	.035		.076	.033					.038	-.061
Guarantee jobs and good living	.054	-.067	.064		-.041	.047		-.046			-.039		
Equal power for both sexes			.032	.045		.073	.074	-.064	-.059	-.080		.038	-.039
America first, overseas second						.033							
Continue cooperation with Russia		.038			-.049								
Keep affirmative action	.039	-.041	.058	.038		.054						-.043	
Help people get health care			.043	.030	-.031	.049	.055		-.033			-.083	
Ideological self-placement				.041		.032	.055			-.046			

TABLE B.7

CORRELATION COEFFICIENTS ($P < .05$) FOR STATE CONTEXT VARIABLES AND ISSUE PREFERENCES OF SOUTHERN DEMOCRATIC VOTERS

	State Party Organization	Local Party Organization	Inter-party Competition Index	State Party Identification Index	Liberalism of Party Identifiers Index	Precentage Black	Percentage funda-mentalist	State Party Competition Index	Percentage Urban	Percentage College Graduates	Percentage Voter Turnout	Interest Group Strength	Primary Election Format
More for women's SES													
Abortion by choice					-.122								
More defense spending													
Cut services and spending													
Allow school prayer	.155												
More spending to protect environment													
Pass balanced budget amendment													
More state taxes, not cuts									-.132				
More SES for minorities													
Guarantee jobs and good living					.139								
Equal power for both sexes													
America first, overseas second			.127										
Continue cooperation with Russia													
Keep affirmative action												.121	
Help people get health care													.123
Ideological self-placement													

TABLE B.8

CORRELATION COEFFICIENTS ($P < .05$) FOR STATE CONTEXT VARIABLES AND ISSUE PREFERENCES OF SOUTHERN NATIONAL DEMOCRATIC IDENTIFIERS

	State Party Organization	Local Party Organization	Inter-party Competition Index	State Party Identification Index	Liberalism of Party Identifiers Index	Precentage Black	Percentage fundamentalist	State Party Competition Index	Percentage Urban	Percentage College Graduates	Percentage Voter Turnout	Interest Group Strength	Primary Election Format
More for women's SES								-.113					
Abortion by choice	-.126	-.123	.114	.162	-.159	.113		-.152			.114		
More defense spending													
Cut services and spending													
Allow school prayer	.212					-.117		.123		.134	-.113		
More spending to protect environment													
Pass balanced budget amendment													
More state taxes, not cuts													
More SES for minorities													
Guarantee jobs and good living													
Equal power for both sexes													-.121
America first, overseas second													
Continue cooperation with Russia													
Keep affirmative action													
Help people get health care													
Ideological self-placement	-.119	-.118											-.121

TABLE B.9

CORRELATION COEFFICIENTS (P < .05) FOR STATE CONTEXT VARIABLES AND ISSUE PREFERENCES OF SOUTHERN STATE DEMOCRATIC IDENTIFIERS

	State Party Organization	Local Party Organization	Interparty Competition Index	State Party Identification Index	Liberalism of Party Identifiers Index	Precentage Black	Percentage fundamentalist	State Party Competition Index	Percentage Urban	Percentage College Graduates	Percentage Voter Turnout	Interest Group Strength	Primary Election Format
More for women's SES													
Abortion by choice		-.159	.143	.176	-.156			-.130			.111		
More defense spending													
Cut services and spending													
Allow school prayer	.183									.122	-.136		
More spending to protect environment													
Pass balanced budget amendment													
More state taxes, not cuts													
More SES for minorities													
Guarantee jobs and good living													
Equal power for both sexes													
America first, overseas second													
Continue cooperation with Russia					.124								
Keep affirmative action												.112	
Help people get health care											-.147		
Ideological self-placement	-.132												-.131

TABLE B.10

CORRELATION COEFFICIENTS ($P < .05$) FOR STATE CONTEXT VARIABLES AND ISSUE PREFERENCES OF SOUTHERN NATIONAL DEMOCRATIC CONVENTION DELEGATES

	State Party Organization	Local Party Organization	Inter-party Competition Index	State Party Identification Index	Liberalism of Party Identifiers Index	Precentage Black	Percentage fundamentalist	State Party Competition Index	Percentage Urban	Percentage College Graduates	Percentage Voter Turnout	Interest Group Strength	Primary Election Format
More for women's SES							.099		-.099				
Abortion by choice	-.207		.124	.176	-.213	.173		-.220	-.120	-.179	.198	.098	
More defense spending													
Cut services and spending				-.107	.108	-.144			.106	.103			
Allow school prayer	.120			-.157	.202	-.134	-.127	.204	.171	.146			
More spending to protect environment			.115										
Pass balanced budget amendment	.106		-.092	-.133	.153	-.162		.133	.102	.148			
More state taxes, not cuts	.109										-.111		
More SES for minorities				.093			.127	-.108	-.130	-.137		-.120	
Guarantee jobs and good living													
Equal power for both sexes							.092						
America first, overseas second	.090			-.106	.126			.121					
Continue cooperation with Russia													
Keep affirmative action				.122			.103		-.090	-.106			
Help people get health care													
Ideological self-placement	-.121			.102	-.103	.111	.171	-.154	-.167	-.140			

TABLE B.11

CORRELATION COEFFICIENTS ($P < .05$) FOR STATE CONTEXT VARIABLES AND ISSUE PREFERENCES OF SOUTHERN DEMOCRATIC COUNTY PARTY CHAIRS

	State Party Organization	Local Party Organization	Inter-party Competition Index	State Party Identification Index	Liberalism of Party Identifiers Index	Precentage Black	Percentage fundamentalist	State Party Competition Index	Percentage Urban	Percentage College Graduates	Percentage Voter Turnout	Interest Group Strength	Primary Election Format
More for women's SES	-.122		.093			.103	.116			-.129			
Abortion by choice	-.091	-.099	.153	.094	-.109	.139		-.165	-.112	-.090	.108	.111	-.095
More defense spending		.086		-.084	.101						-.111	-.098	
Cut services and spending			-.121	-.117		-.108							
Allow school prayer			-.145	-.124		-.145		.112	.128	.087			
More spending to protect environment													
Pass balanced budget amendment			-.150	-.102		-.136				.104			
More state taxes, not cuts	.085		.120										
More SES for minorities	-.106			.137			.105			-.121			-.103
Guarantee jobs and good living													
Equal power for both sexes	-.081			.088			.091						-.103
America first, overseas second													
Continue cooperation with Russia													
Keep affirmative action				.112						-.087			
Help people get health care							.085						
Ideological self-placement			.110	.140			.092	-.088		-.103			

TABLE B.12

CORRELATION COEFFICIENTS ($P < .05$) FOR STATE CONTEXT VARIABLES AND ISSUE PREFERENCES OF SOUTHERN DEMOCRATIC COUNTY COMMITTEE MEMBERS

	State Party Organization	Local Party Organization	Inter-party Competition Index	State Party Identification Index	Liberalism of Party Identifiers Index	Precentage Black	Percentage funda-mentalist	State Party Competition Index	Percentage Urban	Percentage College Graduates	Percentage Voter Turnout	Interest Group Strength	Primary Election Format
More for women's SES	-.085	-.051		.060	-.062	.038	.073	-.080	-.050	-.086	.049	.049	-.059
Abortion by choice	-.160	-.133	.057	.113	-.166	.091	.140	-.187	-.137	-.170	.089	.112	-.122
More defense spending	.158	.091		-.089	.155	-.036	-.105	.153	.081	.151	-.080	-.054	-.054
Cut services and spending	.055	.039		-.072	.051		-.052	.054	.045	.058	-.037		
Allow school prayer	.188	.143	-.066	-.155	.191	-.138	-.199	.213	.162	.207	-.063	-.081	.105
More spending to protect environment	-.029	-.062			-.030		.057	-.058	-.044	-.038			-.060
Pass balanced budget amendment	.097	.068	-.043	-.134	.125	-.069	-.099	.130	.092	.135	-.045		
More state taxes, not cuts		.090	.045	.114	-.072	.035	.057	-.065	-.041	-.072			-.066
More SES for minorities	-.124	-.078		.124	-.111		.106	-.146	-.087	-.147	.084		-.057
Guarantee jobs and good living				.030									
Equal power for both sexes	-.122	-.066	.033	.095	-.100	.070	.134	-.126	-.107	-.144	.046	.061	-.071
America first, overseas second								.030					
Continue cooperation with Russia	-.084	-.056		.054	-.083	.052	.083	-.099	-.074	-.092	.036	.050	-.047
Keep affirmative action	-.055		-.089	.078	-.042	-.100	.050	-.077		-.090	.046		
Help people get health care	-.037	-.053		.043			.047	-.046	-.030	-.038			-.044
Ideological self-placement	-.101	-.096	.038	.125	-.099	.043	.108	-.121	-.081	-.129	.048	.040	-.081

TABLE B.13

STANDARDIZED REGRESSION COEFFICIENTS FOR ISSUES WITH CONTEXT VARIABLES, ALL REPUBLICAN SAMPLES

	State Party Organization	Local Party Organization	Inter-party Competition Index	State Party Identification Index	Liberalism of Party Identifiers Index	Precentage Black	Percentage fundamentalist	State Party Competition Index	Percentage Urban	Percentage College Graduates	Percentage Voter Turnout	Interest Group Strength	Primary Election Format
More for women's SES					-.100m			.154m					-.049m -.174m
Abortion by choice					-.116m	-.177c		.099m		-.178m			
More defense spending	-.135d			.092m	.202m -.355v -.363s								
Cut services and spending									-.320m	-.096m			
Allow school prayer	-.066m												
More spending to protect environment	.060m												-.071m
Pass balanced budget amendment				-.124m									
More state taxes, not cuts	.191d			.209m .287c		.073m -.265n -.322s		.214c .541s			-.090m		
More SES for minorities	.206v .219n			.726v .631n .524s									-.188d
Guarantee jobs and good living		-.069m				.070m							-.187d
Equal power for both sexes					-.130m	.069m		.094m		-.209m			
America first, overseas second	-.344d			-.392d	-.104m	.103m		.140m		-.145m	.123m	-.111m -.348d	
Continue cooperation with Russia					-.148m			-.184c		-.117m			.053m
Keep affirmative action	.240n												
Help people get health care												-.277d	-.086m
Ideological self-placement					-.087m					-.148m			

Note: Type of sample is indicated by letter following beta coefficient: c = party chairs, d = convention delegates, m = committee members, n = national identifiers, s = state identifiers, and v = party voters.

TABLE B.14
STANDARDIZED REGRESSION COEFFICIENTS FOR ISSUES WITH CONTEXT VARIABLES, ALL DEMOCRAT SAMPLES

	State Party Organization	Local Party Organization	Interparty Competition Index	State Party Identification Index	Liberalism of Party Identifiers Index	Precentage Black	Percentage fundamentalist	State Party Competition Index	Percentage Urban	Percentage College Graduates	Percentage Voter Turnout	Interest Group Strength	Primary Election Format
More for women's SES	.461s	.542d				.484n .408s			-.069m			.068m	-.337d
Abortion by choice	.437c			-.343c		.277c			-.091m		.555c	.084m	-.072m
More defense spending	.132m			-.101m	.189m							-.075m	
Cut services and spending						-.283d							
Allow school prayer			.104m						.054m				.063m
More spending to protect environment				-.104m	.261c				-.059m -.401c				-.072m
Pass balanced budget amendment	.455s			-.134m	-.276c							-.063m -.330s	-.434n -.058m
More state taxes, not cuts	.471n .505s			.197m .354c								.218c	-.051m
More SES for minorities	-.095m	.505d		.128m					-.113m			.071m	-.324d
Guarantee jobs and good living								.520n					
Equal power for both sexes	-.125m			.094m					-.073m			.070m	-.127c
America first, overseas second					-.154m						-.164m		
Continue cooperation with Russia	.448c			-.320c			.497c						
Keep affirmative action			-.124m	.118m .299c	.097m				-.102m				
Help people get health care													-.052m
Ideological self-placement				.127m					-.058m				

Note: Type of sample is indicated by letter following beta coefficient: c = party chairs, d = convention delegates, m = committee members, n = national identifiers, s = state identifiers, and v = party voters.

Appendix C

Analysis of Variance of Additional Variables

As mentioned in note 1 to chapter 4, we have a concern that additional environmental variables of an institutional character—specifically, *primary election format* and *interest-group strength*—conceivably could affect intraparty issue cohesion. Since these variables have not been converted into index scores that can be used as interval-level covariate variables, we did not use them as such in chapters 4 or 5. However, we did test them to see if they had any direct effect upon the dependent variable (distributions of issue responses), as can be seen in the tables reporting bivariate correlations and multiple regression results in Appendix B. Even though both of these really are ordinal variables, we report analysis of variance (ANOVA) results to see if the mean distributions of issue responses suggest variation from state to state according to interest group strength or openness of nominating process. Our reasoning for conducting such additional analyses follows.

Open primaries encourage the participation of nonidentifiers in addition to that by partisans. Indeed, according to some political practitioners in the minority parties of states such as Wisconsin, the open-primary format encourages nonidentifiers to become, first, voters, and then partisan supporters. Thus in states where primary formats are progressively more open, one should expect to witness greater centrism among the partisan masses, and thus greater issue distance between them and the party organization elites than in closed-primary states. In the latter states, a type of party politics that emphasizes less democracy *within* the parties and their internal decision processes should result in more democracy (that is, more choice) *between* the parties (see Wekkin 1984), in keeping with Schattschneider's famous observation. Choices between meaningful alternative programs, however, are not wanted by American voters as much as the security of having two competent, attractive, safely middle-of-the-road candidates between whom to choose. Therefore, one might expect to see at least some issue distance between party organization elites and the party masses occur in those states that use closed primaries, of which there are two (Florida and North Carolina) in the South. The rest of the southern states, however, are de facto (although not usually de jure) open-primary states in which voters of any political persuasion can gain access to the primary contest of their choice, subject to challenge (rarely if ever used) by party workers assigned to election precincts as "election sheriffs." Given the preference for the closed-primary format in states where strong party organizations exist in a context of stiff two-party competition, it seems probable that the dearth of closed primaries in the South is connected to the weakness of two-party competition and of party organizations in that region (until recently).

Turning to a justification for including interest-group strength in the analysis, many have hypothesized (Zeigler 1983; Morehouse 1981; Petracca 1992) that in states where not only the political parties but also the economy and governmental institutionalization (especially legislative professionalization) are underdeveloped, interest groups will be strong political role-players. Absent incentives for investment in organizational development, party organizations in the southern states historically were weak. Moreover, for a long time the agrarian-based economies of the southern states were sufficiently undiversified that statehouses had little revenue with which to professionalize their activities. Both of these tendencies resulted in an inordinate amount of influence for the select few interests that had established footholds in the South.

As greater economic diversification, fiscal capacity, and two-party competition have blossomed in the developing South, one should expect to witness a correspondent decline in the influence of interest groups in state capitols, if established theory is correct. However, as the newest study of interest groups in southern politics points out, with political and economic growth the South has not witnessed a decline in the role of interest groups—especially economic ones. In six southern states (Alabama, Florida, Louisiana, Mississippi, South Carolina, and Tennessee), interest groups are "dominant" relative to other common political institutions. In four states (Arkansas, Georgia, Texas, and Virginia), interest groups have a "dominant/complementary" role in relation

to other political institutions. Only in one state (North Carolina) is the role of interest groups strictly "complementary" (that is, not in any sense dominant), and nowhere in the South are interest groups either "subordinate" or "subordinate/complementary" (Thomas and Hrebenar 1991; Hrebenar and Thomas 1992).

Moreover, another new study by Baer and Dolan (1994), using state party data, indicates that many convention delegates and county activists see themselves as representatives of various interest groups or special constituencies within the party organizations. This finding suggests significant party-group linkage, although it should be noted that such linkages frequently involved special issue constituencies interested in descriptive representation, rather than the more potent economic forces that Hrebenar and Thomas (1992) found to be still preeminent in southern politics today.

Thus, whereas traditional wisdom about the party–interest group nexus might have suggested greater elite-mass issue distance in those states where interest groups were stronger (and party organizations weaker), the most recent research about the party-group nexus could lead one to reject that expectation. It now seems possible that the relationship between interest-group strength and elite-mass issue distance may prove to be positive, albeit likely closer to null than to strongly positive.

Although the method of testing is different, the overall results achieved when our two categorical variables, interest-group strength and primary-election format, are subjected to analysis of variance (ANOVA) resemble those of the simple tests of correlation reported in the preceding section. Only 35 of the 192 cells in table C.1 contained F scores significant at $p < .05$ or less, indicating that the distribution of responses for that particular sample to that specific issue-statement varied significantly depending upon whether the respondent was from a state in which partisan primaries were accessible to enrolled or sworn partisans, or to all voters regardless of enrollment or identification. Similarly, only 23 of the 192 cells in table C.2 contained significant F scores, indicating that the distribution of responses for that particular sample and item varied significantly as one moved from states in which interest groups are considered politically "dominant" to those in which interest groups are considered either "complementary" to or "subordinate" to other political institutions at the state level.

In addition to emphasizing the overall weak performance of these two variables across the various samples and issues, it should be pointed out that it is mostly within the county committee member samples, both of which are extremely large, that one finds instances in which primary format or interest-group strength accounted for significantly different means. Only two or three cases of significantly different means turned up in the six mass samples that comprised half of each table, and only five cases of significantly different means turned up across the samples of party chairs within the two tables. Only the delegate samples defy easy categorization. In table C.1, the Democratic delegates do not divide significantly over any of the issues, while the Republican delegates do so over seven issues; whereas in table C.2, the Republican delegates divide over only half as many issues (two) as do the Republican delegates (four), and neither party's delegates can be said to be consistently affected by the factor of interest-group strength.

TABLE C.1

SIGNIFICANT ($P < .05$) ANOVA RESULTS FOR STATES USING DIFFERENT (OPEN-CLOSED) PRIMARY ELECTION FORMATS

F RATIO

	DEMOCRATS						REPUBLICANS					
	Convention Delegates	Party Chairs	Committee Members	Party Voters	National Identifiers	State Identifiers	Convention Delegates	Party Chairs	Committee Members	Party Voters	National Identifiers	State Identifiers
More for women's SES			16.3				7.2		7.9			
Abortion by choice		5.4	70.5				18.3		6.7			
More defense spending			13.5									
Cut services and spending									4.8			
Allow school prayer			52.6				6.2					
More spending to protect environment			16.8						7.3			
Pass balanced budget amendment									3.8			
More state taxes, not cuts			20.5									
More SES for minorities		6.6	15.2				9.9		15.5			
Guarantee jobs and good living						11.4		8.8				
Equal power for both sexes			23.8						6.2			
America first, overseas second												
Continue cooperation with Russia			10.8									
Keep affirmative action	5.9								8.0		4.1	
Help people get health care	16.4		9.4	4.2					28.5		4.2	
Ideological self-placement			32.3		4.5	5.4						

TABLE C.2
SIGNIFICANT ($P < .05$) ANOVA RESULTS FOR STATES USING DIFFERENT LEVELS OF INTEREST-GROUP STRENGTH

| | F RATIO | | | | | | | | | | | |
| | DEMOCRATS | | | | | | REPUBLICANS | | | | | |
	Convention Delegates	Party Chairs	Committee Members	Party Voters	National Identifiers	State Identifiers	Convention Delegates	Party Chairs	Committee Members	Party Voters	National Identifiers	State Identifiers
More for women's SES			5.7						3.4			
Abortion by choice	6.4	3.7	29.8						3.7			
More defense spending			12.9						15.5			
Cut services and spending	4.3											
Allow school prayer			20.3						14.2			
More spending to protect environment			5.8					16.0	4.4			
Pass balanced budget amendment	8.7		5.1									
More state taxes, not cuts	4.7							13.6				
More SES for minorities												
Guarantee jobs and good living							5.8					
Equal power for both sexes			9.6									
America first, overseas second												
Continue cooperation with Russia			6.8									
Keep affirmative action												
Help people get health care							6.9					
Ideological self-placement			4.5									

Notes

Introduction: Parties, Linkage, and Southern Politics

1. The Southern Grassroots Party Activists Project is a collaborative effort funded by the National Science Foundation under grant SES-9009846 and administered through the University of New Orleans. The government has certain rights to the data. Any opinions, research findings, conclusions, or recommendations reported from this project are those of the authors and do not necessarily reflect the views of the National Science Foundation. We are deeply indebted to Professor Charles D. Hadley, principal investigator of this project, for his work in preparing these data and making them available to us.

2. Though not in the original research design, the national Democratic party inadvertently included its "Super Delegates" (members of Congress, governors, big-city mayors, and the like who were delegates by position rather than having to stand for election) in its computer disk file. A decision was made to include them in mailing waves two and three, since a number had responded initially. The final number of observations from this group was forty-three, or 25 percent of the total surveyed. Super Delegates are included in this analysis.

Also, to be clear, the 1,230 county party chairs in our sample are separate from the 10,458 county committee members interviewed. We deal with these two groups of local elites separately because we feel that the position of county chair describes a leadership position of qualitatively different value, symbolically and empirically. Generally, the commitment of chairs to, and the responsibility of chairs for, the organizational vitality of the local party organization exceeds that of any individual committee member. Chairs are the conduits for information up and down the party organizational structure, from and to the local area. Given the asymmetry of their responsibilities and the differences in the contact with the party's organizational structure, chairs and committee members may represent different perspectives on other than organizational issues. To ensure that we do not submerge those differences of ideology or issue position—which are the principal focuses of this book—we have chosen to analyze these groups separately.

3. As noted in the preface, funding for this project was generously provided by the National Science Foundation under grant SES-9212646, by our home universities, and by the Ray Bliss Institute. The project is jointly administered by Bowling Green State University and the University of Central Arkansas. The government has certain rights to the data. Any opinions, research findings, conclusions, or recommendations reported from this project are those of the authors and do not necessarily reflect the views of the National Science Foundation or the Bliss Institute.

Chapter 1. Rank-and-File Partisans in the South

1. The questions underlying the party-identification measurement can be found in Appendix A. You will note that they yield a standard seven-point scale. For the purposes of this analysis, however, this scale was collapsed into a five-point scale, with independent leaners summed together with weak identifiers (see Keith et al. 1992). The "best candidate" and presidential vote questions can also be found in Appendix A. They are represented in categories exactly as coded.

2. The table of Goodman and Kruskal Taus that relates the results of successive 2×2 tables is symmetrical above and below the diagonal. Of the ten off-diagonal elements, only one, between best candidate for governor and best candidate for president is below .5, at .47. With one exception, national and state partisanship at .82, the remainder fall within the range of .54 to .66.

Chapter 3. Collective Representation by Southern Party Organizations

1. For the purposes of our analyses in this and subsequent chapters, differences will be deemed statistically significant if the null hypothesis can be rejected at $p \leq .05$.

2. The web sites referred to in the text are at http://www.democrats.org and http://www.rnc.org.

3. See Appendix A for the wording of the ideology question and for the wording of the issue questions to which we refer in the remainder of the chapter.

4. The exception is county party committee members and Democrats defined by their 1992 presidential vote. There was no significant difference in the agreement pattern of these two groups.

5. County party members agree with Bush voters on this issue.

6. The data for this statement are not shown in the tables for this chapter but are clearly seen in the ANOVAs, whose paired comparisons are the principal data for this chapter.

Chapter 4. Political Context and Intraparty Cohesion

1. Although indexes like the interparty competition index and the politocultural indexes constructed by Erikson, Wright, McIver (1993) are not available for the measurement of interest-group strength and of primary format openness, good arguments can be made as to why such variables are possible, albeit not very likely, influences on intraparty elite-mass issue cohesion. Consequently, although the ordinal nature of such data prevents their use as covariates and interaction terms in multiple analysis of variance, interest-group strength and primary format can be and have been analyzed for this study using regular analysis of variance technique in order to eliminate the possibility that they may have some significant direct influence on the distribution of issue responses obtained from respondents gathered from across the eleven various southern states. See those results in Appendix B and the related discussion in Appendix C.

2. Cotter et al. (1984) lacked data on two of the twenty-two southern state party organizations—the Alabama Democrats and the Arkansas Republicans—and thus present no index scores for these two. Using our professional familiarity with Cotter at al.'s central organizing concept (POS, or Party Organizational Strength) and its indicators (1984, chap. 2 and Appendix B; see also Gibson et al. 1983), and our special familiarity with the Arkansas Republicans (Wekkin is a fifteen-year resident observer of party organization in that state) and with the Alabama Democrats (Wekkin has twice been a consultant in federal litigation targeting the Alabama Democratic state central committee), we have made an informed but admittedly imperfect estimate of where these two organizations would fit on the Cotter et al. scale.

3. In the personal experience of one of the authors, a dynamic county chair with strong local roots can personally recruit as many as two hundred new dues-paying members in less than twelve months, even in a small (711 square miles), underpopulated (less than fifteen thousand) rural county. And a state party organization can go from $40,000 in debt and four state headquarters employees to black ink and three additional employees within ninety days by virtue of recruiting a wealthy businessman to serve as state chair, yet within two years of his resignation can revert to $180,000 in debt and a single part-time employee as a result of mismanagement by a "reformist" chair who was a well-intentioned mathematics professor.

4. There is even less variation in southern voter-turnout rates, which is why that measure of civic virtue is not included as a contextual control variable in this chapter, although one can examine its direct covariation with issue distributions in the tables in Appendix B.

5. Davison and Krassa's data on this are at best only suggestive, not convincing, due to their use of an ecological fallacy pointed out by Bullock's comment (1991a) published in an exchange with Davison and Krassa (1991a, 1991b).

6. These neofundamentalist denominations in-

clude United Missionary, Church of God, Church of God in Christ, Church of Christ, Nazarene, Plymouth Brethren, Pentecostal, Salvation Army, Seventh-day Adventist, and Missouri Synod Lutheran (Erikson, Wright, and McIver 1993, 65).

7. In so doing, Erikson, Wright, and McIver (and, indirectly, ourselves) follow closely the division used by Wald (1987, 1992).

8. Although the theoretical stance of our explanation of the political rise of the Christian Right is different from Wald's (1987) in that we incorporate the well-known political theories of Truman and Salisbury, the structure of the discussion that follows owes much to his summary of the literature on evangelical mobilization on pages 206–10.

9. The substantially different sizes of the various elite and mass samples that are compared to each other here are not a problem for the unique sum of squares approach that is employed in SPSS for Windows 6.1's MANOVA procedure. Consult the SPSS web site at http://www.spss.com for technical papers about this and other aspects of the unique sum of squares approach used here.

10. When analyses of variance were performed controlling only for the presence of environmental covariates, disregarding any possible interaction between them and the factors, four quite distinct patterns recurred throughout the data. First of all, environmental alteration of the base intraparty cohesion results reported in chapter 3 did not occur often. Slightly more than 10 percent—11.01, to be exact—of the base results were altered when environmental covariates were introduced. Hardly affected at all were issues of political economy, as well as those propositions that suggest that the government give maximum priority to improving the social and economic situation of women and of blacks and other minority groups.

Second, environmental covariates were more likely to alter rates of cohesion between Democratic elites and masses, rather than between Republican elites and masses, unless the issue concerned had to do with foreign policy or national security. Environmental alterations of intra-Democratic cohesion outnumbered environmental alterations of intra-Republican cohesion for ten of sixteen issues. The reverse was true on the three foreign/external issues. On three other issues (reducing services in order to reduce spending, and government efforts to improve the social and economic status of minorities and women, respectively) there were so very few environmental alterations of the base results in either party panel that the result is a "wash."

Third, and most important, environmental effects, when they occurred, were almost always conducive to issue distance rather than to issue cohesion. Of the 349 cases (out of 3,168 cases) in which intraparty cohesion changed from the base results when environmental covariates were introduced, 340 converted from intraparty cohesion to dissensus, versus 9 in which cohesion replaced dissensus.

Fourth, the three classes of environmental variables did not differ significantly from one another in terms of their respective likelihoods of affecting intraparty cohesion. Leaving the cross-party cells out of the analysis and taking into account the different shares of the remaining cells for which each class of variable accounts, we found that the two politocultural variables have a 12.33 percent likelihood of altering the base finding for a given dyad in chapter 3, compared to a 12.15 percent likelihood of same for the five demographic variables, and, at 9.38 percent, a somewhat smaller likelihood that the three institutional variables would alter the base finding for a given dyad.

Thus, overall, environmental variables, when included strictly by themselves as covariate controls in MANOVA procedures, did not massively alter the base findings presented in chapter 3, although it is noteworthy that when they do so, the effect is almost always inimical to intraparty cohesion.

11. For presentational purposes, the ideological self-placement item is simply included here as the "sixteenth issue."

12. Readers interested in other, specific context variables lacking sufficient statistical impact to merit discussion in these pages may do so by examining the tables in this chapter closely.

13. Anthony Lake, national security advisor to President Clinton, had to demand that the president meet with him for more than thirty minutes a week at one point in 1993.

Chapter 5. Partisan Linkage and Party Environments

1. For two additional independent variables of an ordinal nature (primary election format and interest group strength) that conceivably could have an impact upon intraparty issue cohesion (see chapter 4, note 1), analysis of variance of means tests instead of Pearson's correlation tests were conducted across the categories of the independent variables. See the discussion and report of results in Appendix C.

Works Cited

Abramson, Paul R., John H. Aldrich, and David W. Rohde. 1994. *Change and Continuity in the 1992 Elections.* Washington, D.C.: CQ Press.

———. 1998. *Change and Continuity in the 1996 Elections.* Washington, D.C.: CQ Press.

Almond, Gabriel, and Sidney Verba. 1963. *The Civic Culture: Political Attitudes and Democracy in Five Nations.* Princeton, N.J.: Princeton Univ. Press.

Anderson, Charles W. 1979. "Political Design and the Representation of Interests." In *Trends Toward Corporatist Intermediation,* ed. Philippe Schmitter and G. Lehmbruck, 271–98. Beverly Hills, Calif.: Sage.

Baer, Denise L., and David A. Bositis. 1988. *Elite Cadres and Party Coalitions: Representing the Public in Party Politics.* New York: Greenwood Press.

———. 1993. *Politics and Linkage in a Democratic Society.* Englewood Cliffs, N.J.: Prentice-Hall.

Baer, Denise L., and Julie A. Dolan. 1994. "Intimate Connections: Political Interests and Group Activity in State and Local Parties." *American Review of Politics* 15:257–89.

Baker, Tod A. 1990. "The Emergence of the Religious Right and the Development of the Two-party System in the South." In Baker, Hadley, Steed, and Moreland, *Political Parties in the Southern States: Party Activists in Partisan Coalitions,* 135–47.

Baker, Tod A., Charles D. Hadley, Robert P. Steed, and Laurence W. Moreland, eds. 1990. *Political Parties in the Southern States: Party Activists in Partisan Coalitions.* Westport, Conn.: Praeger.

Banfield, Edward C. 1961. *Political Influence.* New York: Free Press.

Banfield, Edward C., and James Q. Wilson. 1963. *City Politics.* Cambridge: Harvard Univ.

Barnes, Samuel H., and Max Kaase, eds. 1979. *Political Action: Mass Participation in Five Western Democracies.* Beverly Hills, Calif.: Sage Publications.

Barone, Michael, and Grant Ujifusa. 1993. *The Almanac of American Politics 1994.* Washington, D.C.: National Journal.

Bartels, Larry M. 1988. *Presidential Primaries and the Dynamics of Public Choice.* Princeton, N.J.: Princeton Univ. Press.

Bartley, Numan V., and Hugh D. Graham. 1975. *Southern Politics and the Second Reconstruction.* Baltimore: Johns Hopkins Univ. Press.

Bass, Jack, and Walter DeVries. 1976. *The Transformation of Southern Politics: Social Change and Political Consequence Since 1945.* New York: Basic Books.

Beck, Paul Allen. 1977. "Partisan Dealignment in the Postwar South." *American Political Science Review* 71 (June): 477–96.

Beer, Samuel H. 1978. "Federalism, Nationalism, and Democracy in America." *American Political Science Review* 72: 9–21.

Bentley, Arthur F. 1908. *The Process of Government.* Chicago: Univ. of Chicago Press.

Berelson, Bernard R., Paul F. Lazarsfeld, and William N. McPhee. 1954. *Voting: A Study of Opinion Formation in a Presidential Campaign.* Chicago: Univ. of Chicago Press.

Berry, Jeffrey M. 1997. *The Interest Group Society.* New York: Longman.

Bibby, John F., Cornelius P. Cotter, James L. Gibson, and Robert J. Huckshorn. 1990. "Parties in State Politics." In *Politics in the American States,* ed. Virginia Gray, Herbert Jacob, and Robert B. Albritton, 85–122. 5th ed. Glenview, Ill.: Scott, Foresman/Little, Brown.

Black, Earl. 1998. "The Newest Southern Politics." *Journal of Politics* 60 (Aug.): 591–612.

Black, Earl, and Merle Black. 1987. *Politics and Society in the South.* Cambridge: Harvard Univ. Press.

———. 1992. *The Vital South: How Presidents Are Elected.* Cambridge: Harvard Univ. Press.

Bledsoe, Timothy, Susan Welch, Lee Sigelman, and Michael Combs. 1995. "Residential Context and Racial Solidarity Among African Americans." *American Journal of Political Science* 39 (May): 434–58.

Brace, Kimberly, Bernard Grofman, and Lisa Handley. 1987. "Does Redistricting Aimed to Help Blacks Necessarily Help Republicans?" *Journal of Politics* 49 (Feb.): 169–85.

Brace, Kimberly, Lisa Handley, Richard G. Niemi, and Harold Stanley. 1995. "Minority Turnout and the Creation of Majority-Minority Districts." *American Politics Quarterly* 23 (Apr.): 190–203.

Brady, Henry E., Sidney Verba, and Kay Lehman Schlozman. 1995. "Beyond SES: A Resource Model of Political Participation." *American Political Science Review* 89 (June): 271–94.

Breaux, William, Steven Shaffer, and Patrick Cotter. 1998. "Mass-Elite Linkage." In Steed, Clark, Bowman, and Hadley, *Party Organization and Activism in the American South,* 162–83.

Browning, Rufus P., Dale Rogers Marshall, and David H. Tabb. 1984. *Protest Is Not Enough: The Struggle of Blacks and Hispanics for Equality in Urban Politics.* Berkeley: Univ. of California Press.

Bullock, Charles S., III. 1990. "Creeping Realignment in the South." In *The South's New Politics: Realignment and Dealignment,* ed. Robert H. Swansbrough and David M. Brodsky, 220–37. Columbia: Univ. of South Carolina Press.

———. 1991a. "Southern Partisan Changes: When and How." *Midsouth Political Science Journal* 12 (Summer): 23–32.

———. 1991b. "Republican Strength at the Grass Roots: An Analysis at the County Level." *Midsouth Political Science Journal* 12 (Autumn): 80–99.

———. 1995a. "The Impact of Changing the Racial Composition of Congressional Districts on Legislators' Roll Call Behavior." *American Politics Quarterly* 23 (Apr.): 141–58.

———. 1995b. "Winners and Losers in the Latest Round of Redistricting." *Emory Law Journal* 44 (Summer): 943–77.

———. 1995c. "Comment: The Gift that Keeps On Giving? Consequences of Affirmative Action Gerrymandering." *American Review of Politics* 16 (Spring/Summer): 33–40.

Bullock, Charles S., III, and Mark J. Rozell. 1998. *The New Politics of the Old South: An Introduction to Southern Politics.* Lanham, Md.: Rowman and Littlefield.

Bush v. Vera. 116 S. Ct. 1941 (1996).

Cain, Bruce, John Ferejohn, and Morris P. Fiorina. 1987. *The Personal Vote: Constituency Service and Electoral Independence.* Cambridge, Mass.: Harvard Univ. Press.

Cameron, Charles, David Epstein, and Sharyn O'Halloran. 1996. "Do Majority-Minority Districts Maximize Black Representation in Congress?" *American Political Science Review* 90 (Dec.): 794–812.

Campbell, Angus, Philip E. Converse, Warren E. Miller, and Donald E. Stokes. 1960. *The American Voter.* New York: John Wiley & Sons.

Carmines, Edward G., and James A. Stimson. 1989. *Issue Evolution: Race and the Transformation of American Politics.* Princeton, N.J.: Princeton Univ. Press.

Center for Gender Equality. 1999. "The Impact of Religious Organizations on Gender Equality: A Report of Findings from a National Survey Conducted for the Center for Gender Equality." News release, Jan. 27, 1999.

Chambers, William Nisbet, and Walter Dean Burnham, eds. 1975. *The American Party System: Stages of Political Development.* New York: Oxford Univ. Press.

Clark, Peter B., and James Q. Wilson. 1962. "Incentive

Systems: A Theory of Organization." *Administrative Science Quarterly* 6 (Sept.): 129–66.

Conway, M. Margaret. 1991. *Political Participation in the United States.* Washington, D.C.: CQ Press.

Cook, Rhodes. 1997. "Suburbia: Land of Varied Faces and a Growing Political Force." *Congressional Quarterly Weekly Report,* May 24, 1997, 1209–17.

Cotter, Cornelius P., James L. Gibson, John F. Bibby, and Robert J. Huckshorn. 1984. *Party Organizations in American Politics.* New York: Praeger.

Cotter, Patrick R., and James G. Stovall. 1992. "Party Identification and Level of Government: The Validity of Mixed Party Identifications." *Midsouth Political Science Journal* 13 (Winter): 515–34.

Cox, Gary W., and Samuel Kernell, eds. 1991. *The Politics of Divided Government.* Boulder, Colo.: Westview.

Crotty, William, ed. 1986. *Political Parties in Local Areas.* Knoxville: Univ. of Tennessee Press.

Crotty, William, and John S. Jackson, III. 1985. *Presidential Primaries and Nominations.* Washington, D.C.: CQ Press.

Crotty, William, and Gary C. Jacobson. 1984. *American Parties in Decline.* Boston: Little, Brown.

Dahl, Robert A.1956. *A Preface to Democratic Theory.* Chicago: Univ. of Chicago Press.

———. 1961. *Who Governs?* New Haven, Conn.: Yale Univ. Press.

———. 1971. *Polyarchy-Participation and Opposition.* New Haven, Conn.: Yale Univ. Press.

———. 1989. *Democracy and Its Critics.* New Haven, Conn.: Yale Univ. Press.

Dalton, Russell, J. 1996. *Citizen Politics: Public Opinion and Political Parties in Advanced Western Democracies.* Chatham, N.J.: Chatham House.

Davidson, Roger H. 1969. *The Role of the Congressman.* New York: Pegasus.

Davison, Donald L., and Michael Krassa. 1991a. "Blacks, Whites and the Voting Rights Act: The Politics of Contextual Change." *Midsouth Political Science Journal* 12 (Summer): 3–22.

———. 1991b. "Rejoinder to Bullock." *Midsouth Political Science Journal* 12 (Summer): 33–40.

Dennis, Jack. 1976. "Trends in Support for the American Party System." *British Journal of Political Science* 5:187–230.

De Tocqueville, Alexis. 1961. *Democracy in America.* New York: Schocken.

Devine, Donald. 1972. *The Political Culture of the United States.* Boston: Little, Brown.

Downs, Anthony. 1957. *An Economic Theory of Democracy.* New York: Harper and Row.

Elazar, Daniel. 1972. *American Federalism: A View from the States.* 2d ed. New York: Crowell.

Eldersveld, Samuel J. 1964. *Political Parties: A Behavioral Analysis.* Chicago: Rand McNally.

———. 1982. *Political Parties in American Society.* New York: Basic Books.

Epstein, Leon D. 1958. *Politics in Wisconsin.* Madison: Univ. of Wisconsin Press.

———. 1967. *Political Parties in Western Democracies.* New York: Praeger.

———. 1978. "The Old States in a New System." In *The New American Political System,* ed. Anthony King, 325–69.

———. 1986. *Political Parties in the American Mold.* Madison: Univ. of Wisconsin Press.

Erikson, Robert S., Gerald C. Wright, and John P. McIver. 1993. *Statehouse Democracy: Public Opinion and Policy in the American States.* New York: Cambridge Univ. Press.

Fenno, Richard F., Jr. 1978. *Homestyle: House Members in Their Districts.* Boston: Little, Brown.

Fiorina, Morris P. 1981. *Retrospective Voting in American National Elections.* New Haven, Conn.: Yale Univ. Press.

———. 1992. *Divided Government.* New York: Macmillan.

Fishbein, Martin. 1967. "Attitude and the Prediction of Behavior." In *Readings in Attitude Theory and Measurement,* ed. Martin Fishbein, 477–92. New York: John Wiley & Sons.

Fleischer, Richard. 1993. "Explaining the Change in Roll-Call Voting Behavior of Southern Democrats." *Journal of Politics* 55 (May): 327–41.

Fleury, Christopher J. 1992. "Explaining Voter Registration Levels in the American States." *Midsouth Political Science Journal* 13:253–65.

Franklin, Charles H., and John E. Jackson. 1983. "The Dynamics of Party Identification." *American Political Science Review* 77 (Dec.): 957–73.

Garand, James C. 1988a. "The Socialization of Partisan Legislative Behavior: An Extension of Sinclair's Task Force Socialization Thesis." *Western Political Quarterly* 41:391–400.

———. 1988b. "Membership in Speaker's Task Forces: A Multivariate Model." Paper presented at the annual meeting of the American Political Science Association, Washington, D.C.

Gibson, James P., Cornelius P. Cotter, John F. Bibby, and Robert J. Huckshorn. 1983. "Assessing Party Organizational Strength." *American Journal of Political Science* 27 (May): 193–222.

Gilens, Martin. 1996. "'Race Coding' and White Opposition to Welfare." *American Political Science Review* 90 (Sept.): 593–604.

Graham, Cole Blease, Jr., William V. Moore, and Frank T. Petrusak. 1995. "Republicans and Democrats, Christian Coalition Members and African-Americans: Comparing Party Activists in South Carolina." Paper delivered at the annual meeting of the Southern Political Science Association, Tampa, Fla.

Green, John C., James L. Guth, Corwin E. Smidt, and Lyman A. Kellstedt. 1996. *Religion and the Culture Wars.* Lanham, Md.: Rowman and Littlefield.

Grodzins, Morton. 1966. *The American System,* ed. Daniel J. Elazar. Chicago: Rand McNally.

Hadley, Charles D. 1985. "Dual Partisan Identification in the South." *Journal of Politics* 47 (Feb.): 254–68.

———. 1993. "Southern Politics After the Election of President Clinton: Continued Transformation Toward the Republican Party." *American Review of Politics* 14 (Summer): 197–212.

Hadley, Charles D., and Lewis Bowman, eds. 1995. *Southern Sate Party Organizations and Activists.* Westport, Conn.: Praeger.

———. 1998. *Party Activists in Southern Politics.* Knoxville: Univ. of Tennessee Press.

Hadley, Charles D., and Susan E. Howell. 1980. "The Southern Split Ticket Voter, 1956–1976: Republican Conversion or Democratic Decline." In *Party Politics in the South,* ed. Robert P. Steed, Laurence W. Moreland, and Tod A. Baker, 127–51. New York: Praeger.

Haeberle, Steven H. 1985. "Closed Primaries and Party Support in Congress." *American Politics Quarterly* 13 (July): 341–52.

Hamilton, Alexander, James Madison, and John Jay. 1938. *The Federalist Papers.* New York: New American Library.

Handley, Lisa, and Bernard Grofman. 1994. "The Impact of the Voting Rights Act on Minority Representation: Black Officeholding in Southern State Legislatures and Congressional Delegations." In *Quiet Revolution in the South,* ed. Chandler Davidson and Bernard Grofman, 335–50. Princeton, N.J.: Princeton Univ. Press.

Havard, William C., ed. 1972. *The Changing Politics of the South.* Baton Rouge: Louisiana State Univ. Press.

Herrnson, Paul S., and John C. Green, eds. 1997. *Multiparty Politics in America.* Lanham, Md.: Rowman and Littlefield.

Hershey, Marjory Randon. 1984. *Running for Office.* Chatham, N.J.: Chatham House.

Hill, Kevin A. 1995. "Does the Creation of Majority Black Districts Aid Republicans? An Analysis of the 1992 Congressional Elections in Eight Southern States." *Journal of Politics* 57 (May): 384–401.

Hill, Kim Quaile, and Angela Hinton-Andersson. 1995. "Pathways of Representation: A Causal Analysis of Public Opinion–Public Policy Linkages." *American Journal of Political Science* 39 (Nov.): 924–35.

Hirschman, Albert O. 1970. *Exit, Voice and Loyalty: Responses to Decline in Firms, Organizations and States.* Cambridge, Mass.: Harvard Univ. Press.

Hosansky, David. 1996. "Christian Right's Electoral Clout Bore Limited Fruit in the 104th." *Congressional Quarterly Weekly Report,* Nov. 2, 1996, 3160–62.

Hrebenar, Ronald J., and Clive S. Thomas. 1992. *Interest Group Politics in the Southern States.* Tuscaloosa: Univ. of Alabama Press.

Huckfeldt, Robert. 1986. *Politics in Context: Assimilation and Conflict in Urban Neighborhoods.* New York: Agathon Press.

Huckfeldt, Robert, and John Sprague. 1995. *Citizens, Politics, and Social Communication.* New York: Cambridge Univ. Press.

Huntington, Samuel P. 1968. *Political Order in Changing Societies.* New Haven: Yale Univ. Press.

———. 1991. *The Third Wave: Democratization in the Late Twentieth Century.* Norman: Univ. of Oklahoma Press.

Hurwitz, Jon, and Mark Peffley. 1997. "Public Perceptions of Race and Crime: The Role of Racial Stereotypes." *American Journal of Political Science* 41 (Apr.): 375–401.

Inglehart, Ronald. 1990. *Cultural Shift in Advanced Industrial Society.* Princeton, N.J.: Princeton Univ. Press.

Jackson, John S. III, Barbara L. Brown, and David Bositis. 1982. "Herbert McCloskey and Friends Revisited: 1980 Democratic and Republican Elites Compared to the Mass Public." *American Politics Quarterly* 10 (Apr.): 158–80.

Jacobson, Gary C. 1987. *The Politics of Congressional Elections.* Boston: Little, Brown.

———. 1990. *The Electoral Origins of Divided Government.* Boulder, Colo.: Westview.

Jacobson, Gary C., and Samuel Kernell. 1983. *Strategy*

and Choice in Congressional Elections. New Haven, Conn.: Yale Univ. Press.

Jennings, M. Kent, and Richard G. Niemi. 1981. *Generations and Politics: A Panel Study of Young Adults and Their Parents.* Princeton, N.J.: Princeton Univ. Press.

Jewell, Malcolm E., and David M. Olson. 1988. *Political Parties and Elections in American States.* Chicago: Dorsey.

Johnson v. Mortham. 915 F.Supp 1529 (1995).

Joint Center for Political Research. 1994. *Black Elected Officials.* Washington, D.C.: Joint Center for Political Research.

Jones, Charles O. 1995. *Separate but Equal Branches: Congress and the Presidency.* Chatham, N.J.: Chatham House.

Kayden, Xandra, and Eddie Mahe Jr. 1985. *The Party Goes On: The Persistence of the Two-Party System in the United States.* New York: Basic Books.

Keefe, William J. 1991. *Parties, Politics and Public Policy.* 6th ed. Washington, D.C.: Congressional Quarterly Press.

Keith, Bruce E., David B. Magleby, Candice J. Nelson, Elizabeth Orr, Mark C. Westlye, and Raymond E. Wolfinger. 1992. *The Myth of the Independent Voter.* Berkeley: Univ. of California Press.

Key, V. O., Jr. 1949. *Southern Politics in State and Nation.* New York: Alfred A. Knopf.

———. 1955. "A Theory of Critical Elections." *Journal of Politics* 17 (Feb.): 3–18.

———. 1959. "Secular Realignment and the Party System." *Journal of Politics* 21 (May): 198–211.

———. 1961. *Public Opinion and American Democracy.* New York: Alfred Knopf.

———. 1964. *Politics, Parties and Pressure Groups.* New York: Thomas Y. Crowell.

———. 1966. *The Responsible Electorate: Rationality in Presidential Voting, 1936–1960.* Cambridge: Harvard Univ. Press.

Kinder, Donald R., and Tali Mendelberg. 1995. "Cracks in American Apartheid: The Political Impact of Prejudice among Desegregated Whites." *Journal of Politics* 57 (May): 402–24.

Kingdon, John W. 1981. *Congressmen's Voting Decisions.* New York: Harper and Row.

———. 1984. *Agendas, Alternatives, and Public Policies.* Boston: Little, Brown.

Kirkpatrick, Jeane Jordan. 1975. "Representation in the American National Conventions: The Case of 1972." *British Journal of Political Science* 5 (July): 265–322.

———. 1978. *Dismantling the Parties: Reflections on*

Party Reform and Party Decomposition. Washington, D.C.: American Enterprise Institute.

Knoke, David. 1976. *Change and Continuity in American Politics: The Social Bases of Political Parties.* Baltimore: Johns Hopkins Univ. Press.

Kuklinski, James H., Michael D. Cobb, and Martin Gilens. 1997. "Racial Attitudes in the New South." *Journal of Politics* 59 (May): 323–49.

Ladd, Everett Carll, and Charles D. Hadley. 1975. *Transformations of the American Party System.* New York: Norton.

La Follette, Robert M., Sr. 1911. *La Follette's Autobiography.* Madison, Wis.: Robert M. La Follette.

Lamis, Alexander P. 1990. *The Two-Party South.* New York: Oxford Univ. Press.

Lawson, Kay, ed. 1980. *Political Parties and Linkage: A Comparative Perspective.* New Haven, Conn.: Yale Univ. Press.

Lawson, Kay, and Peter H. Merkl. 1988. *When Parties Fail: Emerging Alternative Organizations.* Princeton, N.J.: Princeton Univ. Press.

Layman, Geoffrey C., and Edward G. Carmines. 1997. "Culture Conflict in American Politics: Religious Traditionalism, Postmaterialism, and U.S. Political Behavior." *Journal of Politics* 59 (Aug.): 751–77.

Lazarsfeld, Paul, Bernard Berelson, and Hazel Gaudet. 1968. *The People's Choice: How the Voter Makes Up His Mind in a Presidential Campaign.* New York: Columbia Univ. Press.

Leege, David C., and Lyman A. Kellstedt. 1993. *Rediscovering the Religious Factor in American Politics.* Armonk, N.Y.: M. E. Sharpe.

Lijphart, Arend. 1977. *Democracy in Plural Societies: A Comparative Exploration.* New Haven, Conn.: Yale Univ. Press.

———. 1994. *Electoral Systems and Party Systems: A Study of Twenty-seven Democracies, 1945–1990.* New York: Oxford Univ. Press.

Lockerbie, Brad. 1992. "Prospective Voting in Presidential Elections: 1956–1988." *American Politics Quarterly* 20 (July): 308–25.

Lodge, Milton, and Kathleen M. McGraw. 1995. *Political Judgment: Structure and Process.* Ann Arbor: Univ. of Michigan Press.

Loomis, Burdette. 1990. *The New American Politician.* New York: Basic Books.

Lubell, Samuel. 1956. *Revolt of the Moderates.* New York: Harper.

Lublin, David. 1997a. "The Election of African Americans and Latinos to the U.S. House of Representatives,

1972–1994." *American Politics Quarterly* 25 (July) 269–86.

———. 1997b. *The Paradox of Representation: Racial Gerrymandering and Minority Interests in Congress.* Princeton, N.J.: Princeton Univ. Press.

Luttbeg, Norman R. 1981. *Public Opinion and Public Policy.* Itasca, Ill.: F. E. Peacock Publishers.

Mackey, Eric M. 1991. "Industrialization and Two-Party Democracy." *Midsouth Political Science Journal* 12: 100–12.

MacKuen, Michael B., Robert S. Erikson, and James A. Stimson. 1989. "Macropartisanship." *American Political Science Review* 83 (Dec.): 1125–42.

Maggiotto, Michael A. 1983. "Ideological Self-Definitions and Evaluative Consistency: An Exploratory Look at 1978." Paper presented at the annual meeting of the Southern Political Science Association, Nov., Birmingham, Ala.

———. 1984a. "Ideological Awareness and Presidential Campaigning: Inferences from 1980." Paper presented at the annual meeting of the Southwestern Political Science Association, Mar., Fort Worth, Tex.

———. 1984b. "Ideological Self-Definitions and Group Membership." Paper presented at the annual meeting of the Midwest Political Science Association, Apr., Chicago.

Maggiotto, Michael A., and James Piereson. 1977. "Partisan Identification and Electoral Choice: The Hostility Hypothesis." *American Journal of Political Science* 21 (Nov.): 745–67.

Maggiotto, Michael A., and Ronald E. Weber. 1986. "The Impact of Organizational Incentives on County Party Chairpersons." *American Politics Quarterly* 14 (July): 201–18.

Maggiotto, Michael A., and Gary D. Wekkin. 1992. "Segmented Partisanship in a Federal System." *Midsouth Political Science Journal* 13 (Winter): 425–43.

———. 1993. "His to Lose: The Failure of George Herbert Walker Bush, 1992." *American Review of Politics* 14 (Summer): 163–82.

———. 1998a. "Segmented Partisanship: The Impact of Federalism on Party Identification in the United States." Paper delivered at the annual meeting of the American Political Science Association, Sept., Boston, Mass.

———. 1998b. "Independent Leaners and the Party Identification Scale: Open-Ended Evidence of Political Independence." Paper delivered at the annual meeting of the Southern Political Science Association, Oct., Atlanta, Ga.

Marcus, Gregory B., and Philip E. Converse. 1979. "A Dynamic Simultaneous Equation Model of Electoral Choice." *American Political Science Review* 73 (Dec.): 1055–70.

Mayhew, David R. 1986. *Placing Parties in American Politics.* Princeton, N.J.: Princeton Univ. Press.

———. 1991. *Divided We Govern: Party Control, Lawmaking, and Investigations, 1946–1990.* New Haven, Conn.: Yale Univ. Press.

Mazmanian, Daniel A. 1974. *Third Parties in Presidential Elections.* Washington, D.C.: Brookings Institution.

McClosky, Herbert, Paul J. Hoffman, and Rosemary O'Hara. 1960. "Issue Conflict and Consensus Among Party Leaders and Followers." *American Political Science Review* 54 (June): 406–27.

McGlen, Nancy E., and Karen O'Connor. 1983. *Women's Rights: The Struggle for Equality in the 19th and 20th Centuries.* New York: Praeger.

Miller v. Johnson. 1995 WL 382020 (U.S.)

Miller, Warren E. 1991. "Party Identification, Realignment, and Party Voting: Back to the Basics." *American Political Science Review* 85 (June): 557–68.

Miller, Warren E., and M. Kent Jennings. 1986. *Parties in Transition: A Longitudinal Study of Party Elites and Party Supporters.* New York: Russell Sage Foundation.

Miller, Warren E., and J. Merrill Shanks. 1996. *The New American Voter.* Cambridge: Harvard Univ. Press.

Montjoy, Robert S., William R. Shaffer, and Ronald E. Weber. 1980. "Policy Preferences of Party Elites and Masses." *American Politics Quarterly* 8 (July): 319–44.

Morehouse, Sarah McCally. 1981. *State Politics, Parties, and Policy.* New York: Holt, Rinehart & Winston.

Moreland, Laurence W., Robert P. Steed, and Tod A. Baker, eds. 1987. *Blacks in Southern Politics.* Westport, Conn.: Praeger.

———. 1991. *The 1988 Presidential Election in the South: Continuity Amidst Change in Southern Party Politics.* Westport, Conn.: Praeger.

Muller, Edward N., and Mitchell A. Seligson. 1994. "Civic Culture and Democracy: The Question of Causal Relationships." *American Political Science Review* 88 (Sept.): 635–52.

Nesbit, Robert C. 1973. *Wisconsin: A History.* Madison: Univ. of Wisconsin Press.

Nexon, David. 1971. "Asymmetry in the Political System: Occasional Activists in the Republican and Democratic Parties, 1956–1964." *American Political Science Review* 65 (Sept.): 716–30.

Nie, Norman, Sidney Verba, and John R. Petrocik. 1976.

The Changing American Voter. Cambridge: Harvard Univ. Press.

Norrander, Barbara. 1992. *Super Tuesday: Regional Politics and Presidential Primaries.* Lexington: Univ. of Kentucky Press.

Overby, L. Marvin, and Kenneth M. Cosgrove. 1996. "Unintended Consequences? Racial Redistricting and the Representation of Minority Interests." *Journal of Politics* 58 (May) 540–50.

Page, Benjamin I., and Calvin C. Jones. 1979. "Reciprocal Effects of Policy Preferences, Party Loyalties and the Vote." *American Political Science Review* 73 (Dec.): 1071–89.

Peffley, Mark, Jon Hurwitz, and Paul Sniderman. 1997. "Racial Stereotypes and Whites' Political Views in the Context of Welfare and Crime." *American Journal of Political Science* 41 (Jan.): 30–59.

Petracca, Mark P., ed. 1992. *The Politics of Interests: Interest Groups Transformed.* Boulder, Colo.: Westview.

Petrocik, John R. 1981. *Party Coalitions: Realignments and the Decline of the New Deal Party System.* Chicago: Univ. of Chicago Press.

Petrocik, John R., and Scott W. Desposanto. 1998. "The Partisan Consequences of Majority-Minority Redistricting in the South, 1992 and 1994." *Journal of Politics* 60 (Aug.): 613–33.

Phillips, Kevin B. 1970. *The Emerging Republican Majority.* New York: Doubleday.

Piltes, Richard H., and Richard G. Niemi. 1993. "Expressive Harms, 'Bizarre Districts,' and Voting Rights: Evaluating Election-District Appearances after *Shaw v. Reno.*" *Michigan Law Review* 92:483–587.

Pitkin, Hannah. 1967. *The Concept of Democracy.* Berkeley: Univ. of California Press.

Polsby, Nelson W. 1983. *Consequences of Party Reform.* New York: Oxford Univ. Press.

Pomper, Gerald M. 1992. *Passions and Interests: Political Party Concepts of American Democracy.* Lawrence: Univ. of Kansas Press.

Pomper, Gerald M., and Susan S. Lederman. 1971. *Elections in America.* New York: Longman.

Pomper, Gerald M., F. Christopher Arterton, Ross K. Baker, Walter Dean Burnham, Kathleen A. Frankovic, Marjory Randon Hershey, and Wilson Carey McWilliams. 1993. *The Election of 1992.* Chatham, N.J.: Chatham House.

Powell, G. Bingham. 1982. *Contemporary Democracies: Participating, Stability and Violence.* Cambridge: Harvard Univ. Press.

Prewitt, Kenneth. 1970. *The Recruitment of Political Leaders: A Study of Citizen-Politicians.* Indianapolis: Bobbs-Merrill.

Ranney, Austin. 1965. "Parties in State Politics." In *Politics in the American States,* ed. Herbert Jacob and Kenneth N. Vines, 61–99. 1st ed. Boston: Little, Brown.

———. 1975. *Curing the Mischiefs of Faction: Party Reform in America.* Berkeley: Univ. of California Press.

Rapoport, Ronald B., Alan I. Abramowitz, and John McGlennon. 1986. *The Life of the Parties: Activists in Presidential Politics.* Lexington: Univ. Press of Kentucky.

Ricci, David M. 1970. "Democracy Attenuated: Schumpeter, the Process Theory and American Democratic Thought." *Journal of Politics* 32 (May): 239–67.

Rice, Tom W., and Meredith L. Pepper. 1997. "Region, Migration and Attitudes in the United States." *Social Science Quarterly* 78 (Mar.): 83–95.

Riker, William F. 1964. *Federalism: Origin, Operation, Significance.* Boston: Little, Brown.

Rosenstone, Steven J., Roy T. Behr, and Edward H. Lazarus. 1984. *Third Parties in America.* Princeton, N.J.: Princeton Univ. Press.

Rosenstone, Steven J., and John Mark Hansen. 1993. *Mobilization, Participation and Democracy in America.* New York: Macmillan.

Rozell, Mark J., and Clyde Wilcox. 1995. *God at the Grassroots: The Christian Right in the 1994 Elections.* Lanham, Md.: Rowman and Littlefield.

———. 1996. *Second Coming: The New Christian Right in Virginia Politics.* Lanham, Md.: Rowman and Littlefield.

Sale, Kirkpatrick. 1975. *Powershift.* New York: Vintage Books.

Salisbury, Robert H. 1969. "An Exchange Theory of Interest Groups." *Midwest Journal of Political Science* 13:1–32.

Sartori, Giovanni. 1967. *Democratic Theory.* New York: Praeger.

Schattschneider, E. E. 1942. *Party Government.* New York: Holt, Rinehart & Winston.

Schlesinger, Joseph A. 1966. *Ambition and Politics: Political Careers in the United States.* Chicago: Rand McNally.

———. 1991. *Political Parties and the Winning of Office.* Ann Arbor: Univ. of Michigan Press.

Schlozman, Kay Lehman, and John T. Tierney. 1986. *Organized Interests and American Democracy.* New York: Harper & Row.

Schmitter, Philippe C. 1974. "Still the Century of Corporatism?" *Review of Politics* 36 (Jan.): 85–131.

Schumpeter, Joseph. 1942. *Capitalism, Socialism and Democracy.* New York: Harper and Brothers.

Seligman, Lester G., Michael R. King, Chong Lim Kim, and Roland E. Smith. 1974. *Patterns of Recruitment: A State Chooses Its Lawmakers.* Chicago: Rand McNally.

Shafer, Byron E. 1983. *Quiet Revolution: The Struggle for the Democratic Party and the Shaping of Post-Reform Politics.* New York: Russell Sage Foundation.

Shaw v. Reno. 113 S. Ct. 2816 (1993).

Shea, David M., and John C. Green, eds. 1994. *The State of the Parties: The Changing Role of Contemporary American Parties.* Lanham, Md.: Rowman and Littlefield.

Sinclair, Barbara Deckard. 1981. "The Speaker's Task Force in the Post-Reform House of Representatives." *American Political Science Review* 75:397–410.

———. 1989. "Leadership Strategies in the Modern Congress." In *Congressional Politics,* ed. Christopher J. Deering, 135–54. Washington D.C.: Congressional Quarterly Press.

Stanley, Harold W. 1987. *Voter Mobilization and the Politics of Race: The South and Universal Suffrage, 1952–1984.* Westport, Conn.: Praeger.

———. 1994. "The South and the 1992 Presidential Election." In *The 1992 Presidential Election in the South: Current Patterns of Southern Party and Electoral Politics,* ed. Robert P. Steed, Laurence W. Moreland, and Tod A. Baker, 197–210. Westport, Conn.: Praeger.

Stanley, Harold W., and David S. Castle. 1990. "Partisan Changes in the South: Making Sense of Scholarly Dissonance." In *The South's New Politics: Realignment and Dealignment,* ed. Robert H. Swansbrough and David Brodsky, 238–52. Columbia: Univ. of South Carolina Press.

Stanley, Harold W., and Richard G. Niemi. 1995. "The Demise of the New Deal Coalition: Partisanship and Group Support, 1952–92." In *Democracy's Feast: Elections in America,* ed. Herbert F. Weisberg, 220–40. Chatham, N.J.: Chatham House.

Steed, Robert P., John Clark, Lewis Bowman, and Charles D. Hadley, eds. 1998. *Party Organization and Activism in the American South.* Tuscaloosa: Univ. of Alabama Press.

Strong, Donald S. 1955. "The Presidential Election in the South, 1952." *Journal of Politics* 17 (Aug.): 343–89.

Sullivan, John L., and Robert E. O'Connor. 1972. "Electoral Choice and Popular Control of Public Policy." *American Political Science Review* 66 (Dec.): 1256–68.

Sundquist, James L. 1973. *Dynamics of the Party System.* Washington, D.C.: Brookings Institution.

Swain, Carol M. 1993. *Black Faces, Black Interests: The Representation of African-Americans in Congress.* Cambridge: Harvard Univ. Press.

Tate, Katherine. 1993. *From Protest to Politics: The New Black Voters in American Elections.* Cambridge: Harvard Univ. Press.

Thibaut, J. W., and H. H. Kelley. 1959. *The Social Psychology of Groups.* New York: John Wiley & Sons.

Thomas, Clive S., and Ronald J. Hrebenar. 1991. "Interest Group Politics in the New South." *Midsouth Political Science Journal* 12:80–113.

Trish, Barbara. 1994. "Party Integration in Indiana and Ohio: The 1988 and 1992 Presidential Contests." *American Review of Politics* 15:235–56.

Truman, David B. 1971. *The Governmental Process: Political Interests and Public Opinion.* New York: Alfred A. Knopf.

———. 1967. "Federalism and the Party System." In *American Federalism in Perspective,* ed. Aaron Wildavsky, 81–109. Boston: Little, Brown.

United States v. Hays. 115 S. Ct. 2431 (1995).

Valentine, David C., and John R. van Wingen. 1980. "Partisanship, Independence, and the Partisan Identification Question." *American Politics Quarterly* 8 (Apr.): 165–86.

Verba, Sidney, and Norman H. Nie. 1972. *Participation in America: Political Democracy and Social Equality.* New York: Harper and Row.

Verba, Sidney, Norman H. Nie, and Jae-on Kim. 1978. *Participation and Political Equality: A Seven-Nation Comparison.* New York: Cambridge Univ. Press.

Verba, Sidney, Kay Lehman Schlozman, Henry Brady, and Norman H. Nie. 1993. "Citizen Activity: Who Participates? What Do They Say?" *American Political Science Review* 87 (June): 303–18.

Verba, Sidney, Kay Lehman Schlozman, and Henry Brady. 1995. *Voice and Equality: Civic Voluntarism in American Politics.* Cambridge: Harvard Univ. Press.

Vertanin, Simo V., and Leonie Huddy. 1998. "Old Fashioned Racism and New Forms of Racial Prejudice." *Journal of Politics* 60 (May): 311–32.

Wahlke, John C., Heinz Eulau, William Buchanan, and Leroy C. Ferguson. 1962. *The Legislative System:*

Explorations in Legislative Behavior. New York: John Wiley & Sons.

Wald, Kenneth D. 1987. *Religion and Politics in the United States.* New York: St. Martin's Press.

———. 1992. *Religion and Politics in the United States.* 2d ed. Washington, D.C.: Congressional Quarterly.

Ware, Alan. 1987. *Citizens, Parties, and the State: A Reappraisal.* Princeton, N.J.: Princeton Univ. Press.

Wattenberg, Martin P. 1990. *The Decline of American Political Parties, 1952–1988.* Cambridge: Harvard Univ. Press.

———. 1991. *The Rise of Candidate-Centered Politics: Presidential Elections of the 1980s.* Cambridge: Harvard Univ. Press.

Weisberg, Herbert F. 1980. "A Multidimensional Conceptualization of Party Identification." *Political Behavior* 2 (1): 33–60.

———. 1983. "A New Scale of Partisanship." *Political Behavior* 5 (4): 363–76.

Weisberg, Robert. 1978. "Collective vs. Dyadic Representation." *American Political Science Review* 72 (June): 535–47.

Wekkin, Gary. D. 1984. *Democrat versus Democrat.* Columbia: Univ. of Missouri Press.

———. 1988. "The Conceptualization and Measurement of Crossover Voting." *Western Political Quarterly* 41:105–14.

———. 1991. "Why Crossover Voters Are Not `Mischievous Voters.'" *American Politics Quarterly* 19 (Apr.): 229–47.

Wekkin, Gary D., Shannon Davis, and Michael A. Maggiotto. 1988. "Party Identification and Partisan Realignment in Arkansas." *Comparative State Politics* 8 (Oct.): 8–11.

Wekkin, Gary D., Donald E. Whistler, Michael A. Kelley, and Michael A. Maggiotto, eds. 1993. *Building Democracy in One-Party Systems.* Westport, Conn.: Praeger.

Whitby, Kenny J., and Franklin D. Gilliam Jr. 1989. "Changing Times and Changing Attitudes Among Southern Congressmen." Paper delivered at the annual meeting of the Midwestern Political Science Association, Chicago.

———. 1991. "A Longitudinal Analysis of Competing Explanations of the Transformation of Southern Congressional Politics." *Journal of Politics* 53 (May): 504–18.

Wiarda, Howard J. 1977. *Corporatism and Development: The Portuguese Experience.* Amherst: Univ. of Massachusetts Press.

Wilson, James Q., and John J. DiIulio Jr. 1995. *American Government: The Essentials.* Lexington, Mass.: D. C. Heath.

Wolfinger, Raymond E., and Steven J. Rosenstone. 1980. *Who Votes?* New Haven, Conn.: Yale Univ. Press.

Zeigler, L. Harmon. 1983. "Interest Groups in the States." In *Politics in the American States,* ed. Virginia Gray, Herbert Jacob, and Kenneth Vines, 97–131. 4th ed. Boston: Little, Brown.

Index

Partisan Linkages in Southern Politics was designed and typeset on a Macintosh computer system using PageMaker software. The text and the chapter openings are set in Minion. This book was designed by Ellen Beeler, typeset by Kimberly Scarbrough, and manufactured by Thomson-Shore, Inc. The paper used in this book is designed for an effective life of at least three hundred years.